Missionary Responses
to Tribal Religions
at Edinburgh, 1910

Studies in Church History

William Fox
General Editor

Vol. 1

PETER LANG
New York • Washington, D.C./Baltimore
Bern • Frankfurt am Main • Berlin • Vienna • Paris

J. Stanley Friesen

Missionary Responses to Tribal Religions at Edinburgh, 1910

PETER LANG
New York • Washington, D.C./Baltimore
Bern • Frankfurt am Main • Berlin • Vienna • Paris

Library of Congress Cataloging-in-Publication Data

Friesen, J. Stanley (John Stanley).
Missionary responses to tribal religions at Edinburgh, 1910/
J. Stanley Friesen.
p. cm. — (Studies in church history; vol. 1)
Includes bibliographical references and index.
1. Christianity and other religions—Animism—History. 2. Animism—
Relations—Christianity. 3. World Missionary Conference (1st: 1910:
Edinburgh, Scotland). 4. Missions—Theory. 5. Missions—Africa,
Sub-Saharan—History—20th century. I. Title. II. Series: Studies in church
history (New York, N.Y.); vol. 1.
BR128.A26F75   261.2'09'041—dc20   94-17919
ISBN 0-8204-2552-4
ISSN 1074-6749

Die Deutsche Bibliothek-CIP-Einheitsaufnahme

Friesen, John Stanley:
Missionary responses to tribal religions at Edinburgh, 1910/
J. Stanley Friesen. - New York; Washington, D.C./Baltimore; San Francisco;
Bern; Frankfurt am Main; Berlin; Vienna; Paris: Lang.
(Studies in church history; Vol. 1)
ISBN 0-8204-2552-4
NE: GT

Cover design by James F. Brisson.

The paper in this book meets the guidelines for permanence and durability
of the Committee on Production Guidelines for Book Longevity
of the Council of Library Resources.

Printed in the United States of America.

"I have come not to destroy but to fulfill."

–Matthew 5:17

"God is ever working and never tired,
so His working is his rest
His rest and work are both eternal.
He works and rests in the 'eternal now.'
'My Father worketh hitherto and I work...'"

–Henry Callaway, 1871

Table of Contents

Foreword

In his study of missionary theory and practice in the late nineteenth and early twentieth century, J. Stanley Friesen challenges some of the current attitudes concerning the work of missionaries among tribal peoples at that time in history. Friesen disabuses us of the notion that missionaries then had little or no regard for the positive values of tribal beliefs and practices and that they saw tribal religions simply as something to oppose and to replace with missionaries' presumably higher religion.

The papers of the missionary scholars at the Edinburgh Missionary Conference in 1910, show a level of ethnographical sophistication and of respect toward the tribal cultures in which they lived and worked. Those who presented papers were competent field anthropologists in their sensitivity and understanding of tribal peoples. They have been misjudged by those who today rightly affirm self expression in religion and who advocate control of religious institutions by those whose recent ancestral roots are in tribal cultures.

Friesen has been able to delineate significant philosophical differences in mission approaches to tribal cultures. These differences are related to the particular national cultures from which the missionaries have come. With their differing approaches they were united in seeking to build upon and to fulfill tribal values.

The evolutionary ideas of E. B. Tylor, the founder of the science of cultural anthropology, were so dominant that this section of the Edinburgh Mission Conference was entitled by Tylor's key term, "animism." Tylor's own direct field experience was six months in Mexico where he was simply an observant traveler with a competent guide. The field work of these missionary anthropologists brought evidence that did not fit in with either Tylor's concept of animism or with his evolutionary approach.

Friesen's research has given us a linkage with the past that has significance for contemporary missiology.

Professor James C. Spalding
School of Religion, University of Iowa

Preface

Missionaries of the imperialist era (1880–1920) have frequently been stereotyped and inadequately heard or represented with respect to their understanding and evaluation of religion in tribal societies. In the imperialist era, the philanthropy of the "white man's burden," the economics of colonialism, and the philosophic ideas of progress and evolution which permeated social theory and science, combined to place tribal societies on the bottom of the human scale of technological and moral development, and western societies at the pinnacle. The dominant impression given by historians and missiologists is that missionaries of the imperialist era similarly condemned the traditional religious systems of tribal societies.

The research of this book is based upon the records of the First World Missionary Conference at Edinburgh 1910, which was held in the very midst of the imperialist era. This conference attempted to be representative of the Protestant Christian missionary movement, and to chart the direction and goals for the movement. The findings of this book indicate that the participants at Edinburgh 1910 had a more independent and prophetic stance, distinct from the mainstream of nineteenth-century western society, than they have been given credit for.

The paternalistic mood, and the structure and design of Edinburgh 1910 did not encourage dialogue with the younger churches of Asia and Africa in order to contextualize the Christian Gospel. However, missionaries with anthropological interests contributed to the report on "Animistic Religions." Their studies of African mythology and social structure made a significant contribution to the study of African religions. Today, their works are regarded among the early anthropological classics. They conceived of the relationship of Christianity to African religions in complimentary ways using the concepts of fulfillment and transformation.

This book develops five models of how missionaries surveyed for the "Animistic Religions" report conceived of the relationship of Christianity to tribal religions based upon their theological and ethical positions: (1) the "two level displacement" model of Johannes Warneck and German Lutheran pietists, which held in tension the corporate ideals of religions in tribal societies with their own personal and individual understanding of Christianity, (2) the "radical displacement" model of W. D. Armstrong of the interdenominational Regions Beyond Missionary Union, (3) the "moral reconstruction" model of Donald Fraser and others from the British and American mainline Protestant denominations, (4) Robert Nassau's "affiliation/bridging" model and (5) the "fulfillment/affirmation" model of Godfrey Callaway and other missionaries predominantly from the Anglo-Catholic branch of the Anglican Church.

All of the models, except that of W. D. Armstrong, have the capacity to discriminate between those elements of tribal religion that can be accepted, incorporated, transformed, or fulfilled and those that are clearly incompatible with the Christian faith. The characterization that missionaries at Edinburgh regarded African religions as demonic and to be uprooted is therefore a judgment that is unsupported by the research of the Edinburgh 1910 materials.

This review of Edinburgh 1910 is an attempt to set forth a variety of missionary points of view. It awakens us to the tremendous vision, energy, creativity, and compassion of people who were committed to communicating the Gospel in spite of their limitations.

The pilgrimage back to Edinburgh 1910 has only been possible because it was encouraged and enabled by many who have provided essentials for the journey, direction when the road was uncertain, and companionship when the miles seemed impossibly long. I want to acknowledge those gifts and express heart felt thanks:

To the missionaries of Edinburgh 1910 whose vision, lifework, and writings continue to inspire and inform Christian mission.

To Dr. Wilbert Shenk and the Mennonite Board of Missions who encouraged and provided resources for the study.

To Professor Andrew Walls at the University of Edinburgh, who first suggested the topic and directed me to the Edinburgh 1910 records in the John R. Mott collection of the Day Missions Library at Yale Divinity School.

To my Advisor, Professor James C. Spalding at the University of Iowa, for the freedom and encouragement to pursue this study.

To Anne Guenther, Librarian at Fresno Pacific College, who searched from Interlibrary loan my obscure requests.

To my readers, Dr. T. Dwight Bozeman, Dr. Dennis Bricker, Dr. Jacob Loewen, and Dr. John Voth whose comments and suggestions have clarified the study.

To Dr. Heidi Burns, Phyllis Martens, Grant Jones-Wiebe, and David Richert whose gracious editorial skills and computer know-how transformed manuscript into text.

To Rachel, Ingrid and Jonathan, who have all matured and left home in the duration of my study.

To my wife, Delores, who has been companion, fellow scholar, pilgrim and disciple before the pilgrimage to Edinburgh 1910 began, but is even more so, now that the journey has been completed.

I. Edinburgh 1910: A Retrospective View

In the summer of 1910, 1200 delegates converged for ten days on the gray stone city of Edinburgh for the First World Missionary Conference. It could hardly have met at a more strategic time in history. It was held, interestingly enough, just a century after the proposed date of a similar one suggested by William Carey, the venerable pioneer of the modern Protestant missionary movement. It stood at the crest of the nineteenth-century's foreign mission expansion and thrust. It convened in the middle of what has been designated the "high imperialist era," between 1880 and 1920. This era was bounded on one side by the scramble for African colonies by European powers, which resulted in the partitioning of Africa at the Berlin Conference in 1884; and on the other by the post-World War I period, which witnessed the resurgence of nationalist movements within the colonial empires of the European powers, especially in India under Gandhi, and on the African continent in the African National Congress, which was coming to life in South Africa.[1] Edinburgh 1910 marked, more than most of those present realized, the beginning of the end of the colonial missionary era.

Western missionaries who worked in Africa in the imperialist era (1880–1920) have been inadequately interpreted by late twentieth-century historians and Christians. On the one hand, theologians in younger African churches, who are working toward a more indigenous theology integrating their traditional religious past with the Christian faith, have predominantly heard from the missionaries of the Edinburgh 1910 era the condemnation of indigenous religions. On the other hand, Western church leaders who are wrestling with the questions of dialogue with non-western religious traditions have focused on the theme of fulfillment which was prominent at Edinburgh 1910. Fulfillment places the emphasis on continuity with the pre-Christian past and the affirmation of indigenous religious traditions. These two radically opposite evaluations of Edinburgh 1910 would indicate that a more careful analysis is required if we seek to understand these early missionaries. The way they held continuity with the culture and traditional religious heritage in tension, with a simultaneous call for radical changes, demanded by the Gospel, is worthy of patient examination. A careful search will yield creative insight and will make the missionaries of this era worthy conversational partners in the development of a more indigenous theology and faith growing out of the soil of tribal societies in Asia and Africa.

A goal of this pilgrimage back to Edinburgh 1910 is to present some of the richness, variety, and creativity of that generation of missionaries and to recognize their contributions to the missionary vocation in terms of relating to persons of other religious traditions. Their contributions and viewpoints are remarkable, considering that they had far fewer resources in terms of the anthropological and linguistic tools now available for crosscultural understanding.

In order to get a clearer concept of the ways missionaries of the imperialist era wrestled with the question of the relationship of Christianity to other religious traditions, we will focus in this book on the World Missionary Conference at Edinburgh in 1910, particularly the report of Commission IV. This report addressed the question of the missionary message in relation to non-Christian religions and especially the missionary responses entitled "Animistic Religions." The missionaries' contributions to that conference and the reports and documents from that conference constitute the primary resources for this book.

To understand more adequately the ways in which imperialist era missionaries worked at the relationship of Christianity to tribal religious traditions, we will explore the following questions: (1) What kind of representation was at Edinburgh 1910? What was the role and function of representatives from Africa? (2) What theories and insights from the emerging science of anthropology and comparative religion contributed to the formulation of the report entitled "Animistic Religions"? (3) What understandings or definitions of religion shaped and informed the missionary respondents' attitudes toward tribal religions? An additional dimension that will be noted is the colonial history and policy which influenced missionary attitudes toward tribal religions.

Since there is little primary research based on the actual writings of missionaries of this time, exploration of the questionnaires and other documents written by the missionaries surveyed for Edinburgh 1910 will be employed to clarify missionary thinking during the imperialist era. Missionary ideology at the beginning of the twentieth-century offers valuable reference points for understanding theology, comparative religions, and anthropology.

The Christian missionary enterprise of the nineteenth and early twentieth centuries occupied a large place in the drama of the expansion of Western societies from Europe and North America into Asia, Africa, and Latin America. The missionary, however, is the "invisible person" in the histories of most Western and non-Western societies. Missionaries of the "high imperialist era" 1880–1920, are rarely listened to now, because their voices are almost a century in the past; and yet they are still near enough to the present that it is possible to think one knows what they were saying. Furthermore, there is an expectation that much of what they said would be embarrassing to present day ears since one tends to assume that it would sound "paternalistic" and "colonial."

Edinburgh 1910 was a landmark event by its design and purpose. The Edinburgh Conference was planned from the first by John R. Mott and the early organizing committee as a conference to strategize a plan of action and priorities for the missionary enterprise. Its purpose was to bring together the most talented missionary historians, strategists and executives on the home front, along with the most creative forward looking missionaries on the field, with the most influential western politicians, philanthropists, and educators sympathetic to the missionary cause. This conference contrasted with its predecessors in that it included only delegates appointed by mission boards and societies. It was not an open convention. By design the conference was selective and represented the thinking of the leadership of the missionary enterprise at the turn of the century. It was an "elitist" meeting. It reflected articulate intention and self-critique of the mission of the Western church. The Report of Commission IV, "The Missionary Message in Relation to Non-Christian Religions, Edinburgh 1910," reflected a remarkably extensive Protestant survey of missionary attitudes and thinking about non-Christian religions.

Interpretations of Edinburgh 1910

Kwame Bediako argues in his article, "The Roots of African Theology," that the chief religious question with which African Christian theologians must struggle concerns the non-Christian religious traditions of their own people.[2]

Since the development in the late 1950s of African scholarship regarding African theology, there has been a heightened interest in the African pre-Christian religious tradition, both among Westerners concerned with Africa and among African Christians.

Archbishop Desmond Tutu, for example, addressing the conference on Christianity in Independent Africa in Jos, Nigeria, in 1975, articulated the significance and import of this reevaluation of the African religious heritage and experience. Tutu, an Anglican Archbishop from South Africa, claimed that the African religious heritage should have formed the vehicle for conveying the Gospel verities to Africa. The rehabilitation of the African religious heritage was vital for the Africans' self-respect. This new honesty has helped to expose the tacit assumptions that religion and history in Africa dated from the arrival on the continent of the white man. For example, the Rhodes Monument by Victoria Falls on the Zambezi carries the inscription "Cecil Rhodes: Discoverer of Victoria Falls," disregarding the fact that African people had known about "the water that thunders" for millennia. Recognition of the value of their beliefs and world view has assured Africans that they can speak authentically for themselves, in the realm of religious experience and reflection, and not as a pale imitation of others. Finally, this reevaluation is a recognition that Africans have a great store from which to fashion new ways of speaking to and about God, and can contribute new styles of worship consistent with their faith.[3] For example, they have a much more profound understanding of the Old Testament than do Westerners because of the similarity of their culture with ancient Semitic cultures.

African writers and scholars, even those sympathetic with the Christian Church, have consistently expressed their pain and anger regarding the negative and devaluing attitudes expressed by Westerners, particularly missionaries, toward the African religious traditions.[4] This pain can be seen in the writings of Harry Sawyerr, an African theologian who served as principal of Fourah Bay College and as Vice Chancellor of the University of Sierra Leone, and who was himself a member of the World Council of Churches Commission on Faith and Order after 1962. In a retrospective assessment seventy years after the first World Missionary Conference at Edinburgh in 1910, he was convinced that

> we can show some advance on the missionary outlook of the conference. In particular, we no longer think of the non-Christian religions as perfect specimens of absolute error and masterful pieces of hell's inventions which Christianity was simply called upon to oppose, uproot and destroy.[5]

This negative evaluation of Edinburgh 1910's assessment of non-Christian religions is supported by Ghanaian Kwame Bediako, who is the Director of Akrofi-Christaller Memorial Centre for Mission Research and Applied Theology. Bediako, citing the Report of Commission IV, *The Missionary Message in Relation to Non-Christian Religions,* claims that, "the Edinburgh World Missionary Conference of 1910 had concluded that the traditional religions of Africa, roundly described as 'Animism,' contained 'no preparation for Christianity.'"[6]

Sawyerr and Bediako concur that the Edinburgh Missionary Conference of 1910 took a harsh and exclusivist attitude toward the African religious heritage. Examining the historical records of Edinburgh 1910 is one way to test this interpretation.

It is possible that contemporary scholars and historians have come to this material with anti-colonial biases. In fact, it is one of the findings of this study that both Sawyerr and Bediako may have overstated and somewhat caricatured the position of missionaries at the 1910 Edinburgh Conference. When one examines the contexts of their quotations, one does not sense the radically abrasive and totally rejecting tone that Sawyerr and Bediako report. Sawyerr excerpts from W. H. T. Gairdner's *Edinburgh 1910: An Account and Interpretations of the World Missionary Conference* the lines that state the non-Christian religions are "perfect specimens of absolute error and masterpieces of hell's invention which Christianity was simply called to oppose, uproot and destroy,"[7] but he neglects to view this statement in its context. Gairdner was a Church Missionary Society (CMS)

missionary in Cairo, working among Muslims. He was therefore aware
that the above position, which Sawyerr quotes, was "the exaggeration of
one extreme aspect of a wide question," and he goes on to say that ". . .
they (the non-Christian religions) must be approached with very real
sympathy and respect. . . ."[8] The quotation used by Sawyerr was not
typical of the sentiment of the mission leaders at the conference.

On the contrary, the editors of the Edinburgh 1910 "Animistic
Religions" conference report point out:

> Some deny the existence of any point of contact or preparation for Christianity
> in any of the beliefs and rites of Animism . . . (but) over against that opinion
> must be set the view of the majority of the contributors, who allow at least
> points of contact, though some hesitate to apply the term 'preparation for
> Christianity.'[9]

Commission IV, after analyzing almost two hundred questionnaires
received from missionaries all over the world, reported in its general
conclusions that there were two practically universal themes in the attitude
of Christian missionaries to the non-Christian religions. The respondents
agreed on, first, the need for true understanding and sympathy, and second,
the recognition that the Spirit of God is working in all these religions, but
is ultimately fulfilled in Christianity. Both of these themes are reflected in
the conclusions of Commission IV's report:

> the true method is that of knowledge and charity, that the missionary should
> seek for the nobler elements in the non-Christian religions and use them as steps
> to higher things, that in fact all these religions without exception disclose
> elemental needs of the human soul which Christianity alone can satisfy, and that
> in the higher forms they plainly manifest the working of the Spirit of God. On
> the other hand the merely iconoclastic attitude is condemned as radically unwise
> and unjust.[10]

The Commission found that these two points, true understanding and
the exclusive claims of Christianity, which appear to be opposed to each
other, were in fact held in tension by the missionaries in the following
manner: "They know that in Christ they have what meets the whole range

of human need, and therefore they value all that reveals that need, however imperfect the revelation may be."[11]

These statements from Commission IV seem to stand in contrast to current interpretations of early twentieth-century missionary thought and intentions. It would seem appropriate, therefore, to examine the original responses of missionaries to the questionnaire distributed by Commission IV, and interpret these against the other written reports and correspondence of these respondents.

The present seems to be a particularly appropriate time to investigate the interactions of the imperialist era and the Christian missionary enterprise, for it is both far enough away for some perspective, yet near enough to test our analysis with those who personally knew that generation of missionaries to be composed of creative individuals, and the missionary movement to be a dynamic social force. One of our objectives will be to articulate the variety and range in missionaries' thought regarding the relationship of the Christian Gospel to the African religions in 1910.

A comprehensive view of the religious and cultural ideas by which the missionary forces of various Western countries justified their activities is difficult to attain. This book contributes to that more comprehensive picture by focusing on the participants of the first World Missionary Conference held at Edinburgh in 1910. Special attention is paid to the relationship between Christianity and tribal religious traditions, referred to at Edinburgh 1910 as "Animistic Religions," with a particular focus on Africa.

This first World Missionary Conference gives us a significant point from which to test the scholarly and popular ideas that have been accumulating regarding missions. Edinburgh 1910 comes at the climax of the 19th-century missionary expansion, but is also the first of a series of International Missionary Councils, followed by Jerusalem in 1928 and Madras in 1938. The last and eighth conference occurred at Legon, Ghana, in 1958. The International Missionary Council merged with the World Council of Churches at their next meeting in New Delhi in 1961.

There are several reasons why Edinburgh 1910 is an appropriate testing point: (1) Edinburgh 1910 consciously addressed the question of the missionary message to the non-Christian world, (2) Among the two hundred missionary reports, at least twenty-five focused on religions in tribal societies, which were identified in Commission IV's Report as animistic religions, (3) Edinburgh 1910 was the first of a series of councils, beginning with the International Missionary Councils up until 1961, followed by the Assemblies of the World Council of Churches, that wrestled with the questions of Christian witness and mission.

Edinburgh 1910 was a significant event at the turn of the century and thus offers a reference point for developments in the theology of religions, particularly within the Protestant churches associated with the World Council of Churches. A closer examination of Edinburgh 1910 can contribute to a clearer understanding of missionary thinking during the imperialist era.

Primary Sources and Conference Records

The primary sources for the problem identified are located in the records of the first World Missionary Conference at Edinburgh. Especially relevant is the report of Commission IV, published in 1910, under the title *The Missionary Message in Relation to the Non-Christian Religions.* It has sections on Hinduism, Islam, Japanese religion, Chinese religion, and animism. The African traditional religions are discussed under the category of animistic religions.

The Edinburgh missionary conference represents an articulate and representative sample of Protestant missionary thought. Commission IV was composed of twenty members; nine members were directors of mission boards, and five were university and seminary professors. The chairman was Rev. Professor D.S. Cairns, D.D., of the United Free Church College in Aberdeen, Scotland. The vice-chairman was Robert E. Speer, D.D., Secretary of the Board of Foreign Missions of the Presbyterian Church, USA, in New York.[12]

In preparation for its report to the conference, Commission IV circulated a questionnaire[13] to a selection of mission board staff members and missionaries throughout the world. The commission received 185 responses: 65 on Hinduism, 29 on Islam, 28 on Japanese religion, 38 on Chinese religion, and 25 on animism.[14] Of the 185 respondents to the questionnaires, seven were women[15]; in addition one woman, Mrs. G.J. Romanes of Pitcalzean, served on Commission IV. It is interesting to note that two of the women respondents were from Asia: one from Burma, the other from India. Both of them represented women's missionary societies.[16] The inclusion of women and Asians, though few in number, makes it all the more striking that throughout the whole of the African continent no African pastors, churchmen or churchwomen were consulted regarding this questionnaire.

The report on animistic religions was based on fourteen replies from Africa, four from India and Burma, five from the Dutch Indies, and one each from Laos and Paraguay. Five of the African responses were from Southern Africa; the remaining nine were received from Central and West Africa. Elizabeth Chadwick, formerly from the Church Missionary Society in Uganda, was the only woman respondent to the "Animistic Religions" questionnaire.

The report on animistic religions was drafted by the following: Rev. Professor W. P. Paterson, Herr Johannes Warneck, and Dr. J. W. Gunning. Professor Paterson was on the faculty of the University of Edinburgh in Scotland. Dr. J. W. Gunning was Director of the Nederlandsche Zendeling Genootschap, Rotterdam, Holland. Johannes Warneck was Missions-Inspector of the Rheinische Missionsgesellschaft, in Barmen, Germany. Warneck had earlier been a missionary in Sumatra. His book *The Living Forces of Gospel: Experiences of a Missionary in Animistic Heathendom,* which is a study of the missionary work among the Batak of Sumatra, had been published in Edinburgh in 1909, a year before the Edinburgh conference.

The missionary responses received from the questionnaires of Commission IV were uniformly typed and are on file at the Day Missions Library of Yale Divinity School.[17]

Many of the missionaries contacted for the survey of "Animistic Religions" were leaders and writers for their respective missionary organizations. In addition to the primary sources, i.e., the missionary responses to the questionnaire, a substantial body of periodical literature and monographs written by several of the persons who responded to the questionnaire are available. These written materials from the period around Edinburgh 1910 provide considerable background information and are a valuable research resource.

There are therefore two sources of primary material for the Edinburgh 1910 report on "Animistic Religions" in *The Missionary Message*. First, there are the individual questionnaire responses on "Animistic Religions" from twenty-five individual missionaries, the majority of whom worked in Africa. Second, there is a considerable body of materials (books, articles, monographs, and mission reports) written by the individual missionaries themselves. This material will be cited here when it is relevant to the topics and missionaries under discussion.

Research Materials and Study Approach

Since the World Missionary Conference of Edinburgh took place, much has been written about its origins and background, its findings and its impact, particularly on the development of the International Missionary Council and the Ecumenical Movement.[18] While mission historians of the stature of Kenneth Scott Latourette, Wilhelm Andersen, and Ruth Rouse regard the achievement of Edinburgh as one of the great landmarks in the history of the church, most historians, including Latourette, Andersen, and Rouse themselves, have been content to treat the documents of the conference in a summary fashion. There are very few histories which examine the primary documents in detail.

W. Richey Hogg's research on the history of the International Missionary Council is one of the most thorough examinations of the World Missionary Conference. Hogg, however, has been mainly concerned with its origins and background. He has examined a great deal of the manuscript material, particularly the printed and unbound minutes of Edinburgh's preparatory committees.[19] The manuscript material sent in by missionary correspondents seems to have been peripheral to his concern and therefore he has given it very little consideration. He does not discuss the survey materials prepared for the various commissions, other than to acknowledge that they exist. The work of the commissions is either omitted or not taken seriously. Therefore his treatment of the conference does not place it in its theological or missiological context with respect to the question of the relationship of Christianity to other religious traditions.

The scholar who has most rigorously and carefully examined the questionnaire data of Commission IV is Eric Sharpe.[20] Sharpe, however, limited himself to the section on missionary attitudes toward Hinduism. There is no indication that Sharpe has looked at the data from Japanese, Chinese, or animistic religions. Sharpe's study was doctoral research in missiology done under the Swedish missionary scholar and Bishop, Bengt Sundkler in Uppsala. His dissertation on J. N. Farquhar (1861–1929), *Not to Destroy But to Fulfill*, was published in 1965.[21] It gives background to the larger debate in missionary circles on the question of the relationship of Christianity to other religious traditions.

Farquhar had gone to Calcutta in 1890 as a teacher with the London Missionary Society, at the invitation of John R. Mott. From 1902–1923, he served as Literature Secretary of the Indian YMCA. He was Professor of Comparative Religion at Manchester until his death in 1929.[22]

Subsequently Sharpe has written on Farquhar's contemporary, A. G. Hogg (1875–1954). Hogg served under the United Free Church of Scotland from 1903–1928 as professor and from 1928–1938 as principal of Madras Christian College in South India.[23]

Both Hogg and Farquhar made extensive replies to the Commission IV questionnaire regarding Hinduism. They had been in vigorous debate with one another before Edinburgh 1910.[24]

Farquhar argued that Hinduism could prepare the way for Christianity, but Christianity remained the "crown." Christianity was best viewed as the fulfillment of the highest Hindu traditions, even as it had fulfilled the Jewish expectations in the Old Testament. Farquhar's best known study was published after Edinburgh 1910, under the title, *The Crown of Hinduism*.[25] His article, "The Relation of Christianity to Hinduism," summarized his position.[26]

Hogg was far from being unsympathetically inclined toward Hinduism. In fact, he states that one of his objectives in writing *Karma and Redemption: An Essay Toward the Interpretation of Hinduism and the Restatement of Christianity* (1909) was to gain a greater appreciation of the Hindu point of view. But Hogg's approach to Hindu-Christian relations and understanding was the method of selective contrast. This differed radically from Farquhar's fulfillment idea. One root difference for Hogg between Hindu and Christian views of life had to do with the nature of the universe. The concept of Karma led to a judicial view: while redemption led to a moral view. Hogg's view was that the doctrine of Karma fits into a system which recognizes no purpose in life other than expiation; Christianity is a religion of mercy and grace, not a judicial system.[27]   Hogg rejected the "fulfillment" concept that there was a continuous line of development from the higher concepts of Hinduism to Christianity.   Hogg held that Christianity was the "solution to a religious problem which the typical Hindu does not feel, the answer to questions he has never asked."[28] He regarded the idea that "Christianity fulfills Hinduism" as a liberal point of view that was somewhat naive.[29]   He felt that Christianity fulfilled Hinduism only in the sense that the religious ideas of Hinduism are fulfilled by being reoriented and reframed in relationship to Christ, who is Christianity. Farquhar regarded the method of "contrast" as part of the older missionary point of view of discontinuity.

Among the respondents on the Hinduism questionnaire, Farquhar was the most notable. T. E. Yates, in his study of the responses to the questionnaires, observes that the majority of the respondents belonged to the fulfillment school, rather than to A. G. Hogg's position of contrast.[30]

Sharpe reports a "rich intellectual friendship" between A. G. Hogg and David Cairns of Aberdeen, the Chairman of Commission IV.   This friendship contributed to the particular influence that A. G. Hogg had on the final shaping of the General Conclusions of Commission IV.[31] Cairns had been impressed by the insight of Hogg's book, *Karma and Redemption* (1908) and ordered copies for all members of the subcommittee on Hinduism.[32] Cairns attested in his summation of Commission IV:

> The practically universal testimony that the true attitude of the Christian missionary to the non-Christian religions should be one of true understanding and, as far as possible, of sympathy. That there are elements in all these religions which lie outside the possibility of sympathy is, of course, recognised, and that in some forms of religion the evil is appalling is also clear. But nothing is more remarkable than the agreement that the true method is that of knowledge and charity, that the missionary should seek for the nobler

> elements in the non-Christian religions and use them as steps to higher things, that in fact all these religions without exception disclose elemental needs of the human soul which Christianity alone can satisfy, and that in their higher forms they plainly manifest the working of the Spirit of God. On all hands the merely iconoclastic attitude has been universally rejected as both unwise and unjust.[33]

Cairns, drawing upon Hogg, attempted to hold in tension the themes of "fulfillment" and "contrast" and clearly rejected an outright condemnation of other religions by Christians.

Sharpe's work has limited significance for this study since Sharpe has only examined the manuscript material that pertains to Hinduism in the questionnaires of Commission IV. However, since India was the dominant mission field at the conference, the debate between Hogg and Farquhar provides the context of the larger missiological debate going on at Edinburgh 1910. It also helps to explain the background and the atmosphere in which the report "Animistic Religions" was written.

The periodical literature which directly relates to the research of the present study is limited. T. E. Yates, Anglican Rector,[34] and Kenneth Cracknell of Cambridge University have recently examined the questionnaires of Commission IV. Yates examined the returns from missionaries for Commission IV in an article in preparation for the WCC Commission on World Mission and Evangelism in Melbourne in 1980.[35] Yates compares and contrasts Edinburgh 1910 and Melbourne, particularly on the issues of religious pluralism, the appeal to Jesus Christ, the doctrine of the Trinity, and the approach to other religions. Yates notes that the "aggressive" language in mission strategy at Edinburgh owed more to the language of world-wide assault in the home-based strategists than to the responses sent in by missionaries on the field. It is interesting to note that Yates confined his study to the resources from missionaries working in either Islamic or Hindu contexts. He dismisses the others with the sentence, "Confucianism, the other great tradition represented, is no longer a live option since the advent of communism in China, and animism is less pressing for today's pluralist setting. Melbourne 1980 can be expected to give little attention to either."[36] So once again the "Animistic Religions" documents pertinent to animistic relitions remain unexamined.

Kenneth Cracknell's recent article, "The Theology of Religion in the International Missionary Council and the World Council of Churches 1910–1989," is an ambitious project for a single article. Cracknell looks back to the "fulfillment" motifs in Edinburgh 1910 as being more in tune with the current theme of dialogue with peoples of other faiths than either the International Missionary Council conferences at Jerusalem in 1958 or Tambaram in 1938. "In the Edinburgh findings," Cracknell claims, "we see much that we would call today interfaith dialogue, though the term was not yet known."[37] Cracknell finds support for this opinion from Wesley Ariarajah, a Methodist minister from Sri Lanka, who was Director of the Dialogue Sub-Unit of the World Council of Churches. Dr. Ariarajah suggests that we pick up the discussion on the issues of relating to people of other faiths from where it left off in 1910.[38]

Cracknell quotes one missionary from each of the five religious traditions surveyed that make up the Report of Commission IV. It appears that Cracknell's small sample and selectivity implies a more unified consensus at Edinburgh 1910 regarding the "fulfillment" model than actually existed. Cracknell's excerpts from the surveys are limited to the quotations in *The Missionary Message,* since he did not examine the original questionnaires themselves. His generalizations regarding Edinburgh 1910 cannot be justified on the basis of his cursory survey and excerpted materials. Furthermore, his study does not adequately represent the great variety in the missionaries' responses in the questionnaires.

T. E. Yates in his article, "Christian Approaches to Other Religious Traditions," emphasizes the wide differences in points of view among missionaries surveyed for Edinburgh 1910. Their estimates of other religious traditions range from a broad acceptance of the authenticity of their experience of God to outright rejection; from the emphasis on fulfillment to an outright rejection of fulfillment as an appropriate missionary stance.[39] Yates observes that national Christians generally appear to be more accepting and affirming of other religious traditions than do western missionaries.[40]

Yates only cites the questionnaires in order to introduce his main purpose, which is to trace the development of the theology of religions between 1912 and 1939 as presented in articles published in *The*

International Review of Missions, the missionary journal to which Edinburgh 1910 gave birth. The basic thrust of Yates' article is to point out that the general direction of the International Missionary Council (as it is represented by Hendrik Kraemer's monumental study, *The Christian Message in a Non-Christian World* for the Tambaram meeting of 1938) shares more in common with David Cairns and A. G. Hogg's concept of contrast than with the fulfillment ideas of Farquhar.

In surveying the literature, we find one more category of materials related to the present study. Three dissertations written on two missionaries are within the scope of this study, since these missionaries completed questionnaires for Commission IV. Two of these dissertations have been written on Robert Hamill Nassau (1835–1921), a Presbyterian missionary, who served in Gabon, Equatorial West Africa. David Mandeng's dissertation, "The Philosophy of Mission of Robert Hamill Nassau in the Contemporary World,"[41] is written from an African perspective. Mandeng is a Christian from the Bassa people of Cameroun, where Nassau spent the last two years of his missionary service. Mandeng's thesis is that Nassau pioneered in the "rapproachment mode" of relating to African peoples. Mandeng feels that Nassau was among a minority of missionaries who have "transmitted Christianity in its most essential form, and in conjunction with the best of that which is African."[42]

Mandeng examines Nassau's approach to African culture and religious traditions and compares and contrasts it with four other contemporary approaches: the Muslim approach to Africa traditional religions, Bassa understanding of religion, the work of a contemporary African Christian theologian John Mbiti, and finally the writings of British missiologist David Barrett. Mandeng finds Nassau a gifted missionary who exhibited the "right attitude" towards another culture: adapt and adopt.[43] Raymond W. Teeuwissen's dissertation, "Robert Hamill Nassau 1835–1921 Presbyterian Pioneer Missionary to Equatorial West Africa,"[44] is more historical in design and intent. Teeuwissen corroborates Mandeng's evaluation of Nassau as missionary with an unusual ability to relate to African culture, beliefs, religious forms, and language with a "complete lack of contempt, on the one hand, and the appreciation, on the other . . . his love, concern, and respect for persons, caused him to seek what he could appreciate."[45] Teeuwissen's historical concern gives details on how Nassau came to record his lifetime observations on the religious traditions in Africa in his book, *Fetishism in West Africa.*[46]

However, Teeuwissen makes no attempt to present Nassau's theology of religions or the principles that guided his understanding of African religious traditions as a Christian missionary. Since Nassau is one of the missionaries included in the Commission IV survey, and one of the few missionaries who has made the effort to record his experiences and observations on religion, the present study will survey Nassau's book with the intent of drawing out his theology of religions and its implications for his understanding of African traditional religions. One of the limiting factors in Teeuwissen's research on Nassau is that while he has carefully examined the archival materials in the United States, there is no indication that he has consulted any African resources—interviews, oral history, or church records. This same critique would also apply to Mandeng's study of Nassau. One can sympathize with the scholar facing the limitations of financial resources for research, but these studies must be read with the awareness that they were written from the perspective of the missionary's sending church and not from the African context of Nassau's lifetime work.

The third dissertation, by Thomas J. Thompson, has researched Donald Fraser, a well known missionary of the United Free Church of Scotland who worked in Central Africa at the turn of the century.[47] Thompson's research has covered not only archival sources in Great Britain, but is also based on personal interviews and the examination of records of the Presbyterian Church in Malawi (formerly known as Nyasaland).

Thompson claims that Fraser had a more sympathetic attitude toward Ngoni culture than that displayed by missionaries to other Ngoni groups elsewhere in Malawi.[48] The distinctive hallmarks of Fraser's policy were the use of large conventions, the encouragement of African music, the use of sub-sessions and the encouragement of African leadership, and the use of women elders. Thompson regards the key to Fraser's more enlightened policy to be his ability to respond to African initiatives and feels that Fraser's policies succeeded to the extent to which they were in tune with

Ngoni thinking.[49] Thompson's purposes are to examine Fraser's policies in respect to the larger cultural issues, rather than to focus on Fraser's understanding of African traditional religion.

Thompson's study is valuable in giving both an historical and a cultural context for Fraser's writing on African traditional religion. With the increasing research on individual missionaries, such as that of Thompson on Fraser, a more composite picture of early twentieth-century missionary thought becomes more accurate and feasible.

A central purpose of this present study is to uncover some of the major models and varieties of approach to animistic religions among the twenty-five missionaries who responded to the Commission IV questionnaire on animism. A careful reading of the manuscripts written by the missionaries makes it clear that the committee drafting the Edinburgh 1910 report on animism—W. P. Paterson, J. Warneck, and J. W. Gunning—have written a fair summary of the opinions of the correspondents, frequently quoting at length from the questionnaires of nearly all the correspondents. The response of Johannes Warneck is the most extensive and articulate and receives the greatest coverage in the report. W. P. Paterson identifies on several occasions a minority opinion particularly associated with W. D. Armstrong.

The individual questionnaire responses generally are so brief that it is difficult to differentiate, except for the broadest variations, the nuances and shades of differences between their various missionary approaches to tribal religions.

The approach in this book therefore is to use the list of missionaries contacted to set the parameters for the sample of missionaries to be studied and to identify within these parameters the major missionary perspectives on the relationship of Christianity to tribal religions. Our approach will be to elaborate the positions identifiable in the report, and to expand upon those ideas from the larger body of writings of the missionaries who contributed to the survey and the report "Animistic Religions". Inasmuch as the majority of missionary respondents were from Africa, the focus will be in that direction.

There are three objectives in this book. First, Commission IV's Report on Animistic Religions will be set in its wider context, within the structure of Edinburgh 1910. Second, the book will examine the resources which the report on "animistic religions" cites from anthropology and comparative religion in order to explore some of the movement, vision, and directions of missionary thought at Edinburgh 1910. The two primary resources for this section are the writings of Henry Callaway and Henri Junod, two missionaries with anthropological interests. Third, the study will seek to delineate several missionary models of the relationship of Christianity to tribal religions that lie behind Commission IV's "Animistic Religions" report, using the resources in the questionnaires and the other writings of individual missionaries.

An attempt is made to articulate five distinct yet overlapping models: (1) The "two level displacement" model of Johannes Warneck and German Lutheran pietists, (2) the "radical displacement" model of W. D. Armstrong of the interdenominational Regions Beyond Missionary Union, (3) the "moral reconstruction" model of Donald Fraser, a Scottish Presbyterian, (4) the "bridging/affiliation" model of Robert Nassau, an American Presbyterian, and finally (5) the "fulfillment/affirmation" model of Godfrey Callaway from the Anglo-Catholic branch of the Anglican Church.

This study provides a clearer point of reference at the beginning of the twentieth century from which the study of interrelationships of Christianity and African traditional religions by both national Christians and missionaries can proceed. It contributes to a clearer understanding of the theology of religion as it has developed within the International Missionary Council and World Council of Churches, particularly since there appears to be a renewed interest in Edinburgh 1910 by persons in the ecumenical tradition, such as W. Ariarajah, T. E. Yates, and K. Cracknell.

As has been noted, there are two very contrasting opinions regarding Edinburgh 1910. Harry Sawyerr and Kwame Bediako tend to portray the view of African traditional religions as "perfect specimens of absolute error and masterpieces of hell's inventions which Christianity was simply called upon to oppose, uproot and destroy,"[50] as the predominant view of missionaries of Edinburgh 1910; whereas Gairdner saw this "uprooting" as only one of many approaches that were articulated at Edinburgh 1910.[51] Ariarajah, Yates, and Cracknell, in contrast to Sawyerr and Bediako, seem to suggest that missionaries at Edinburgh 1910 made a good beginning and found appropriate places and ways to begin dialogue with people of other religious faiths. They see Edinburgh 1910 as having a theology of religions that opened the possibilities of rapproachment and understanding, whereas Sawyerr and Bediako see primarily a negative disregard for the African traditional beliefs and religions. Delineating some of the historical influences and facts surrounding Edinburgh 1910 and examining the historical records of the conference can bring some clarity to this seeming divergence.

Religion is a human activity and experience that is often interwoven with other aspects of human life, and therefore it has been the subject of study by many academic disciplines. Inasmuch as the two disciplines of anthropology and comparative religions were emerging sciences in the late 19th and early 20th centuries, already influential at the time of Edinburgh 1910, it is important to take a more interdisciplinary approach, drawing upon resources from anthropology, history, and the comparative study of religion and theology. Missionaries of this era were well aware of these disciplines and were active participants in the ferment and development of all of these disciplines.

The attitudes and approaches of missionaries towards tribal religions were integrally related to their definitions of religion. One task will be to determine from the missionaries' work and writings some of the explicit and/or implicit definitions from which they approached the missionary task. These definitions should provide a more accurate tool with which to assess the missionaries' attitudes and the stance they took toward tribal religions. This should also provide a more appropriate way to interpret the diverse evaluations made by their twentieth-century critics.

II. The Setting and Background of Edinburgh 1910

Historical Setting

In order to understand the missionary ethos surrounding Edinburgh 1910, it is necessary to sense the imperialist mood that was pervasive in the early twentieth century. This chapter considers the general optimism of the missionary enterprise, the elitist nature of the conference, the role of the delegates from younger churches, and the lack of representation from Africa.

The significance of the First World Missionary Conference held in Edinburgh in the summer of 1910 resides in its having occurred at a critical, transitional moment of history, between the 19th and 20th centuries. The nineteenth century has been called by Kenneth Scott Latourette "the great century of mission."[1] The missionary movement of the 19th century was an integral part of the expansion of the Western world. The 19th century witnessed the development of a cosmopolitan culture created by science and inventions of the machine age, especially in Europe and America. It also saw some development and nurturing of overseas empires by Great Britain, France, Russia, Germany, Belgium, Spain, Portugal, and The Netherlands. Even the United States was establishing an empire in the territories which were called "areas of influence." There was an emerging globalization of culture based on the civilization of Europe.

The 19th century had been marked by a spirit of "abounding optimism"[2] and belief in evolutionary progress. The confidence in science, the democratic political system, and the buoyant economic advances tended to make Westerners confident that they had a mission to civilize and educate the world. For example, Lord Lugard's book, *Dual Mandate* (1922), stressed the task of protecting the integrity of local institutions and cultures, yet on the other hand advocated introducing the scientific advances which the West was producing.[3]

Four years after the Edinburgh Conference, the first of the great 20th-century wars broke over Europe; because of the existence of colonial empires it soon involved the entire world. That war was a source of disenchantment with the virtues of European culture and western civilization. Yet during the preparation for the conference and throughout the meetings, to all but a few far-sighted spirits, the world appeared relatively peaceful. In the conference's addresses one finds almost no hint of the possibility of the wars that were soon to convulse the world.

Philip Potter, General Secretary of the World Council of Churches in the 1970s, has interpreted the Edinburgh conference's "abounding optimism" as a result of the age of Western imperialism and its belief in the so-called "white man's burden."[4] This phrase, which captured the mood of the times, was popularized by Rudyard Kipling, who urged the United States to take up its "civilizing" responsibilities in the imperialist era at the end of the 19th century. The churches and missionary agencies saw it as their duty to bring the best they had, namely the Gospel, to all peoples as the most effective civilizing influence. The first speaker at the Edinburgh Conference, Lord Balfour of Burleigh, described the great opportunity before the Christians of the West in these terms:

> Nations in the East are awakening. They are looking for two things: they are looking for enlightenment and for liberty. Christianity alone of all religions meets these demands in the highest degree. There cannot be Christianity without liberty, and liberty without at least the restraint of Christian ideals is full of danger. There is a power unique in Christianity of all religions to uplift and to ennoble, and for this reason, that it has its roots and its foundations in self-sacrifice and in love.[5]

Lord Balfour went on to add that the hope of the conference is "to increase in the minds of professing Christians their deep responsibility to the whole world."[6]

The dominant mood of abounding optimism was criticized by a few prophetic spirits who dared to point to the crisis looming on the horizon. W. H. T. Gairdner, who was asked to write an interpretative account of the conference, was one of these prophetic voices. He had been a CMS missionary in Cairo since 1899. At the close of the century, Gairdner shared the excitement of one world more closely and organically knit by the nerves of electric cable, and telegraph wire, more richly fed by the arteries and veins of the railway line, and steamships ocean-way . . . so that its inhabitants for all the differences of tribe and race became daily more convinced of the unity of their humanity.[7]

But Gairdner was also aware of the crisis facing the missionary enterprise and the coming radical changes in the situation which demanded the church do some fundamental rethinking. This change in vision would profoundly affect mission in the days to come.

The Boxer Uprising in China of 1900, which protested the carving up of the country by foreign powers, including Japan, was evidence of the awakening of the East. The event which might almost be said to have ushered in the 20th century was Japan's defeat of Russia in 1904–1905, where the tide of Western advance and domination was checked and rolled back. Japan, a small island kingdom, emerged victorious from a struggle with a great Western power. It was more than a mere coincidence that the defeat of Russia at the hands of an Asian power saw the rapid development of nationalism in Egypt, Muslim North Africa, Persia and Turkey. In subsaharan Africa, political and religious nationalism was associated with the rise of "Ethiopianism"[8]: in Ethiopia there existed an independent Christianity which predated the European conquest of Africa. Ethiopianism idealized the independence of the earliest planting of Christianity in subsaharan Africa. For Gairdner, the Christian missionary enterprise faced a new and changed situation. In every country there was an awakening to self-consciousness, which was not unconditionally enthusiastic about things European. Nevertheless, the entire world was beginning to realize that it was a unity. The big question at Edinburgh 1910 was whether that unity would be centered in "One Lord and One Faith."[9]

Representation at the Conference

Edinburgh 1910 stood in sharp contrast to the London Conference of 1888 and the New York Conference of 1900. These prior conferences were great missionary demonstrations, designed to inform, educate, and impress the public, and they were open to whomever might care to come. Edinburgh's primary aim, on the other hand, was to be a consultative assembly, and therefore attendance was limited to those who were delegated by their respective organizations and to the special nominations made by the Executive Committee. Representation was confined to missionary organizations having agents in the foreign field and expending on foreign missions not less than 2,000 pounds annually. Missionary societies were entitled to an additional delegate for every additional 4,000 pounds of foreign mission expenditure.[10]

Edinburgh 1910 was a missionary conference intended to set priorities and to articulate strategy. It was an action-oriented, "how to do it" conference rather than a time of reflective and analytic thinking about a viable theology of mission. This special character of the conference was underlined by the fact that the 1200 delegates represented mission boards and missionary societies, not churches. According to the Conference Report, the 1200 participants represented 46 British societies with over 500 delegates, 60 American societies with over 500 delegates, 41 Continental European societies with 170 delegates, with the remaining 26 delegates coming from South Africa and Australia.[11]

The conference brought together the most prominent Protestant missionary historians, theologians, and administrators. The official list of continental delegates included Dr. Gustav Warneck (who was unable to attend due to illness and age, though he did send a paper), Dr. Julius Richter; the foremost German and Dutch missionary historians; the Moravian bishops from Herrnhut; Count Von Moltke, sometime minister in Denmark; Dr. C. Mirbt of Marburg; Professor K. Meinhof of the Imperial Colonial Office of Germany; and Oberverwaltungsgerichtsrath Dr. Berner, the private counselor to the Berlin Foreign Office in all missionary matters.[12]

One cannot overlook the fact that the English-speaking world, represented by the British and American missionary movement dominated the conference, and could claim to represent a worldwide constituency.[13] With two exceptions, all addresses were delivered in English. Even the Japanese delegate, who occasionally used an interpreter, spoke good English. One of the prominent delegates was the former President of the United States, Theodore Roosevelt (who, while among the registered delegates, was unable to attend, but sent a letter). Present and representing his own Presbyterian Church was three-time presidential nominee, William Jennings Bryan. Another notable American delegate was the political activist for civic and political justice in New York, Seth Low. The British were also well represented by prominent social and political leaders: the Conference President, Lord Balfour of Burleigh, at one time a Cabinet Minister; Lord William Gascoyne-Cecil, philanthropist; Lord Kinnaird, Sir John Kennaway and Charles Harford; well-known Indian colonial administrators, who stood for English Christianity and English statesmanship: Lord Reay, ex-Governor of Bombay, Sir Andrew H. L. Fraser, ex-Lieutenant-Governor of Bengal, and Sir Mackworth Young, ex-Lieutenant-Governor of Punjab. Other delegates in high positions and with authority in educational science included Professor Michael E. Sadler and Dr. C. M. J. Parkin.[14]

The Role of Delegates From Younger Churches

Members of the younger churches played a far more important part at Edinburgh 1910 than at previous ecumenical missionary conferences,[15] but their numbers were still few, comprising less than 2% (17 out of 1200). Of the seventeen present, fourteen had been appointed by the missionary societies with which they were connected, and three had been specially chosen by the Executive Committees in Britain and America.[16] Latourette reports that there was opposition in some quarters even to the appointment of these few.[17] The seventeen members from the younger churches were accorded positions on the program quite out of proportion to their number: of the forty-seven public addresses given at noon and in the evenings, they presented six. Tasuku Harada, president of Doshisha University in Japan, spoke on "The Contribution of Non-Christian Races to the Body of Christ." President K. Ibuka of Meiji Gakuin in Japan and Rev. V. S. Azariah, who later became the first Indian Bishop of the Anglican Communion, both addressed "The Problem of Co-operation Between Foreign and Native Workers."

The word "native" was denounced by some delegates as patronizing and paternalistic. The conference delegates were aware of traces of condescension in the term "native," and a measure of peace and satisfaction was found in the term suggested by a Japanese delegate, that instead of "native churches" one might refer to "daughter churches."

V. S. Azariah[18] delivered what was to become one of Edinburgh's two best-remembered speeches. With an assurance from Mott that he should bare his heart, Azariah spoke with utter candor. He urged missionaries to acknowledge the patronizing attitudes that were so often felt by persons in India. "He asked not for 'condescending love' from missionaries, but for their 'friendship' and for the real 'love' that permits two Christians to shake hands and eat together."[19] Azariah concluded by affirming:

> Through all the ages to come the Indian Church will rise up in gratitude to attest the heroism and self-denying labour of the missionary body. You have given your goods to feed the poor. You have given your bodies to be burned. We also ask for *love*. Give us FRIENDS.[20]

The frankness of Azariah's words "roused some ire, but the address marked a high point of courageous, Christian honesty"[21] by a member of a daughter church.

Three members of the younger churches were appointed to the all-important Continuation Committee of the conference. These were Bishop Y. Honda of Japan, the Rev. Cheng Ching-yi, leader and moderator in the Church of Christ in China, and the Rev. Dr. K. C. Chatterji of India. This advance was prophetic of the growing place which the younger churches were to have in the ecumenical movement in the years ahead. Since the conference was attended primarily by representatives of mission societies, one of the major emphases was recruiting and training missionaries from the West. Many of the attenders seemed to feel that Western missionaries carried the main responsibility for fulfilling the Great Commission. The fallacy of this kind of thinking became apparent when, shortly after the conference, World War I gave a major impulse to the rising tide of revolt against white domination.[22]

When one turns to an analysis of the seventeen delegates representing the younger churches, there are several very significant observations to be made. The Continental mission boards and societies did not include even one non-Western Christian among their delegates, while the British missionary societies and boards sent four nationals, and the American

Boards sent thirteen.[23] The American Baptist Foreign Mission Society included among their 40 delegates five nationals representing Asian Churches.   One of these five, John Rangiah, was the first foreign missionary sent out by his Telegu Church in South India to the Indians working in Natal, South Africa.[24] The Presbyterians (Northern) sent four nationals, the Methodists and Congregationalists each sent one, and two were chosen by special invitation of the American Executive Committee of the conference.

There were eight delegates from India, one from Burma, three from China, one from Korea, and four from Japan, but none from Africa, or any of the regions such as Indonesia or the Islands of the Pacific, the homelands of peoples of animist or tribal religious traditions.[25]

The Absence of African Nationals

In his interpretation of Edinburgh 1910, Gairdner was impressed by

> . . .the Oriental and African delegates, yellow, brown, or black in race were scattered among the delegates in that World Conference. For not only by their presence, but by their frequent contributions to debates, they gave final proof that the Christian religion is now rooted in all those great countries of the Orient and South; and not only so, but that it possesses in those countries leaders who, for intellectual ability and all-around competence, were fully worthy of standing beside the men who have been mentioned, even without the traditions of two millenniums of Western Christianity at the back of them.[26]

Gairdner had earlier described the outstanding delegates from the West. After describing the delegates from the Orient he concluded, "and finally, men of African race, one a Negro of immense size, glorying in his African race, from Liberia, the only independent Negro organized state in Africa."[27] However, the "Negro...from Liberia" mentioned by Gairdner appears to be Rev. Alexander P. Camphor, D.D., an African American of the Methodist Episcopal Board of Foreign Missions.[28]   A further investigation of Camphor and his contributions to the conference will give us some insight into the underlying attitudes of the conference toward African cultures and society that permeated Western mission societies and the Edinburgh Conference itself.

Liberia, the small West African colony for emancipated American slaves, was founded in 1822 by the American Colonization Society. It became an independent country in 1847. The founders of the Society, many of whom were white clergymen, wanted not only to resettle African Americans, but to spread the Gospel in Africa. The Episcopal, Presbyterian, and Methodist Churches used African Americans as their representatives in their missionary enterprise. Alexander Crummell, an African American, educated at Queen's College of Cambridge University, was sent to Liberia by the British Anglican Church. It was there that Crummell began to articulate ideas of black nationalism.[29] But it was Edward Wilmot Blyden, an Americo-Liberian of the Presbyterian work in Liberia, who in the 1860s developed some of the more radical ideas of black nationalism. Blyden's greatest influence occurred after the 1887 publication of his book, *Christianity, Islam and the Negro Race*. Blyden had been influenced by the Islamic nations of the interior of West Africa, and after a visit to Egypt and Syria in 1866, he became increasingly respectful of Islam. Although he never became a convert to Islam, he moved toward a more universalistic deism. Blyden resigned from the Presbyterian ministry in 1866 to become a "minister of truth," and encouraged African Christians to secede from their white sponsors and set up their own independent churches, drawing as much from Islam as from Christianity.[30]

Into this atmosphere where the winds of black nationalism were blowing, the Northern Methodist Church sent Rev. and Mrs. Alexander Priestly Camphor. Camphor was a product of Freedmen's Air School in Louisiana. He graduated from New Orleans University and Gammon Theological Seminary in Atlanta and did postgraduate work at Columbia University and Union Theological Seminary in New York. Bishop Hartzell appointed him as principal of the denomination's struggling seminary in Monrovia in 1897. Under the inspiration of Edward Blyden, he changed the name to the College of West Africa, reflecting a more pan-African orientation. Within a year there were 140 students, thirty of whom were indigenous Africans. By the end of the century Blyden complimented them for making the college "one of the most important agencies for the regeneration and upbuilding of our people."[31]

Camphor frequently expressed his pleasure at being in Liberia and his hope for the future impact of his school. Bishop Hartzell was pleased with Camphor's progress and sent eight other African American missionaries there in 1898.[32] It is against this background that we must interpret Camphor's vigorous plea during the discussion at Edinburgh 1910 for the training and preparation of missionaries. "Africa has in the past greatly suffered from poorly prepared missionaries. . .The notion has been too prevalent that comparatively low students would do for Africa. But this idea must pass away as the continent becomes better known."[33]

When one searches the reports and discussions of Edinburgh 1910, there does not appear to be any awareness of the black nationalist movement and its concerns as a significant missiological issue. It is only in the recognition of the Ethiopian movements among the churches in South Africa that we notice an awareness of the racial and nationalist feelings that had been aroused in Africans by the Western belief that the evangelization and civilization of Africa was the "white man's burden."

It is disappointing that these issues were not in the missionary agenda, especially when one considers that the Church Missionary Society in Nigeria had experienced bitter racial feelings and schismatic movements since the 1880s. The mission-educated Africans, in particular African missionaries like Bishop Samuel Crowther, were gradually being discredited in the decade of 1880–1890. European missionaries were introduced into the Niger mission, and in January, 1891, Bishop Crowther was forced to resign.[34] He died, broken and bitterly disappointed, in December of that year.[35]

Racial and nationalist tensions were not confined to the CMS, but schismatic movements over these issues existed in all the missions, as is documented in James B. Webster's book *The African Churches Among the Yoruba 1888–1922*.[36]

It is significant that there were no truly African delegates to Edinburgh. This is particularly striking when practically every missionary society on the West Coast of Africa in the nineteenth century had engaged black missionaries from the Caribbean (as did the Scottish Presbyterians and the Basel Missions) or freed black slaves that had been educated in mission schools in Freetown, Sierra Leone (as did the CMS). There was a conscious missionary strategy to use black missionaries, and therefore it is all the more significant that they were not represented. It also is noteworthy that Camphor, an African American missionary, reflects at least in a small way the nationalist and social feelings that were to become the engines for the demise of the colonial and imperialist empires. He represented at Edinburgh 1910 the long search by African Christians for integrity and more profound respect for their own religious heritage rooted in the traditional tribal religions of Africa.

African Christians were not the only voices which were muted or excluded at the conference. As was noted earlier, there was only one woman respondent to the "Animistic Religions" questionnaire, and there was only one woman on Commission IV. The optimistic, confident mood that prevailed at Edinburgh 1910, arising from the notion that Westerners had an answer for the rest of the world, created an atmosphere that was less open to other viewpoints. The limitations of this perspective have become clearer with the demise of colonialism and the growing sensitivities in recent years to minority points of view.

We have observed the paternalistic attitude evidenced in the design of the conference, particularly in relation to Africa. Mission agencies were no more paternalistic than the rest of Western culture, they simply reflected the social attitudes of Western culture that were then current. It is important to note, however, that while the conference was not organized in a manner to encourage dialogue with younger churches, especially in Africa, missionaries on the field had been and were in the process of developing more appropriate and sensitive ways to understand and interpret the African religious traditions.

The initiatives and creative methodologies of Bishop Henry Callaway and Henri Junod, who were cited in Commission IV's report on "Animistic Religions," were significant attempts to represent African societies more faithfully. The value of their work is reflected in their contribution to the development of both the sciences of anthropology and comparative religions.

III. Anthropological Perspectives Informing the Report on "Animistic Religions"

The compilers of the report, "Animistic Religions" preferred the anthropological insights of those who had actual firsthand field experience to the evolutionary theories of religion developed in the academic communities. The reliance on missionaries with anthropological interests contributed to a more accurate and appreciative approach to African traditional religions.

Although missionaries in the imperialist era did not formally study anthropology, they came predominantly from the universities, mainly because of the influence of the Student Volunteer Movement, active on university campuses. Missionaries during this time were therefore more likely than those of earlier eras to be aware of the issues of anthropology and comparative religion being debated in academic circles. The consideration of Tylor's theories of the origins and evolutionary development of religion thus takes on partially added significance.

We will first look at the contributions of Henry Callaway and Henri Junod to the report entitled "Animistic Religions." A brief biographical and historical framework follows, intended to illustrate the interaction between missionaries with anthropological interests who had actual field experience and the academic theoreticians of anthropology at the turn of the century. The main focus will be on the two missionaries, Henry Callaway and Henri Junod, and the theoretician E. B. Tylor, all of whom are cited in the report. The latter part of the chapter looks further at the contributions of Callaway and Junod to the missionary understanding of African traditional religion. We will give more attention to the contribution of Callaway since Junod was still to make his major contribution after Edinburgh 1910, whereas Callaway's impact took place prior to Edinburgh 1910.

The Contributions of Callaway and Junod

The report entitled "Animistic Religions" contains a paucity of references to the sources used in what was then the emerging academic discipline of anthropology. The report focuses on firsthand accounts by missionaries on the field. The introduction to the report confidently states, "The missionaries in their ministry have come in contact with all classes of tribal society. Their knowledge of animism, therefore, is comprehensive, and their opinions are based on wide experience."[1] The emphasis of the report is more on firsthand experience and practical application than on identifying the kind of theoretical framework which undergirded the report.

The emerging discipline of anthropology at that time was directing much of its attention to the origins of religion in the evolution of human culture. Missionaries had their attention focused on the more practical hermeneutical questions related to the communication of the Christian message, such as the translation of the Scriptures and coming to terms with a different world view.

Missionaries in the nineteenth century were among the primary sources of data used by anthropological theorists in the academic communities of Britain and Europe. The tension and interplay between these two communities with their different agendas created part of the matrix in which missionaries formulated their attitudes toward the religious traditions of African and other tribal societies.

The article "Animistic Religions" utilized the ideas of three persons who, in the late nineteenth and early twentieth century, were recognized as authorities in the field of anthropology and ethnography. At the very outset of the report, Edward B. Tylor (1832–1917), a leader in British anthropology for thirty years before the First World Missionary Conference, is cited. It is his term, animism, that was used during the conference to describe the religious life of people who live in tribal societies.[2] Although Tylor had no field experience apart from a short trip to Mexico in 1856, he had been established at Oxford in 1883 as keeper of the university museum and lecturer on anthropology. In 1884 (before anthropology was established as an academic discipline) he was promoted to Reader in Anthropology. Twelve years later he became the first occupant of the new Chair of Anthropology established at Oxford. He held that chair from 1896 until 1909.

In addition to Tylor, two missionaries with anthropological interests who had served in southern Africa had gained the attention of both the missionary and the academic community for their anthropological reporting. These men were not only respected in their own day, but their anthropological studies are still regarded as early classics of anthropological reporting. The two men, Bishop Henry Callaway and Rev. Henri A. Junod, are cited in the Edinburgh report. Only Junod, however, attended the conference.[3] He contributed a paper on the tribes of Delagoa Bay, which was incorporated into the article "Animistic Religions," but his name does not appear on the list of missionaries answering questionnaires for the report, nor is his paper included with their questionnaires in the files.[4]

It is difficult to determine how the attitudes of missionaries toward the religious life of peoples in tribal societies at the turn of the century were guided and influenced by anthropological understandings of that time. We can, however, shed some light on this question if we compare descriptive styles of ethnographic missionary reporting of Henry Callaway and Henri Junod with E. B. Tylor's theoretical framework. While the three were contemporaries, in part Callaway preceded Tylor, and Junod followed in the wake of the wave that Tylor's theoretical anthropology created.

E. B. Tylor was cited only at the beginning of the 37-page article "Animistic Religions" for his definition of animism. However, the use of the term "animistic religions" for the religions of largely tribal peoples at the turn of the century is one indication of the prevailing familiarity and dominance of Tylor's theory of the evolutionary development of religion from its earliest form, animisim. Tylor's definition of animism as "the belief in spirits" opens the report.[5] Animism was seen as the first level in the evolutionary development of religion. This evolutionary scheme was prominent in British anthropology at the turn of the century.

Callaway and Junod likely reflected the direction in which missionary anthropology was moving at Edinburgh in relation to tribal societies. They both have a more substantive role to play in the report than does Tylor. Junod was first introduced into the report of missionary questionnaires as a counterpoint: W. P. Paterson cited Junod in order to challenge the missionary consensus. Junod stated "that the fears of animists are to be traced more to the superstitions about taboo than the ideas of the spirits of the dead."[6] His research on the Thonga had included a study of the taboo, particularly its relationship to morality.[7]

The second instance in which Paterson as the compiler of the report drew upon Junod's research was as a counterweight to Johannes Warneck. Warneck had the most experience on the mission field of anyone on the subcommittee drafting the report on animistic religions. In addition, he carried weight as an authority on animistic religions because of his book, *Living Forces of the Gospel* (1909). Paterson drew upon Junod to balance Warneck's assertion that the moral transformation of Christians coming out of animistic religions "must lag behind the religious change."[8] Junod, however, was more positive regarding the moral life of tribal societies and had recorded a rich folklore which illustrated the voice of conscience and ethical teaching.[9]

Junod's leadership as a missionary anthropologist was furthermore recognized by David Cairns in his "General Conclusions" of the Commission IV Report.[10] Cairns cites the need for monographs similar to Warneck's *Living Forces of the Gospel*, works that were of value not only to the student of comparative religion but also to the missionaries who worked in the "animistic field." Cairns noted that the commission was pleased to learn that Junod was in the process of publishing his research.

Bishop Henry Callaway's influence on the conference was more indirect than Junod's. While Junod was actually a delegate to Edinburgh 1910, Callaway had retired twenty-five years before the conference and had been dead twenty years prior to Edinburgh 1910. It is remarkable that even from that distance his careful study of Zulu folk tales was lifted up as an example to be emulated in the study of African religion. Henry Callaway's influence on the conference was largely through the missionaries who had served in his diocese of St. Johns Kaffraria, namely Bishop William M. Cameron and Godfrey Callaway. However, through his publications Callaway had a much wider influence on missionaries in Southern Africa. He is cited in the article "Animistic Religions" particularly for his methodology in the collection of Zulu folk tales.[11]

Early Accounts of African Traditional Religion

The study of African religions has passed through several phases, each involving different purposes and points of view. The early accounts, written in the eighteenth and nineteenth centuries by travelers, missionaries and colonial agents, were neither scholarly nor systematic studies but rather were collections of random observations, often based on anecdotes, joined with opinions designed to appeal to the popular European mind. The general unreliability of most of these early European accounts makes them of little use to the serious study of African social institutions, especially of religion. Their greatest significance instead is in the way they reveal the cultural bias of the authors and of the public for which they were written.

Special attention was often given to religion in these travelogues because it was regarded as one of the chief indices of the African mind, and observations about religion were used to justify strong judgments about African mental and moral character.[12] For example, the explorer Sir Samuel Baker wrote, in a presentation to the Ethnological Society of London, the following description of the Nilotes of the Southern Sudan in 1867:

> Without any exception, they are without a belief in a Supreme Being neither have they any form of worship or idolatry, nor is the darkness of their minds enlightened by even a ray of superstition. The mind is as stagnant as the morass which forms its puny world.[13]

By the mid-nineteenth century, however, there were missionaries who had become more knowledgeable and sympathetic observers of African societies. This can in part be attributed to the remarkable mastery of African languages which some of them had achieved. Missionary reports in the second half of the nineteenth century began to show more care and tolerance in the study of tribal societies and their beliefs. Particularly noteworthy was David Livingstone's *Missionary Travels in South Africa* (1857), which was an account of the first European exploration of the interior of Africa.[14] Livingstone also provided a sympathetic view of

African beliefs. In his argument with a rain doctor, Livingstone reported with a degree of fairness and objectivity the "rain doctor's" perspective:

> I use my medicines and you employ yours; we are both doctors, and doctors are not deceivers. You give a patient medicine. Sometimes God is pleased to heal him by means of your medicine: sometimes not--he dies. When he is cured, you take the credit of what God does. I do the same. Sometimes God grants us rain, sometimes not. When he does, we take the credit of the charm. When a patient dies, you don't give up trust in your medicine, neither do I when rain fails. If you wish me to leave off my medicines, why continue your own?[15]

Henry Callaway

Bishop Henry Callaway, who served the Anglican Church in Natal from 1854 to 1886, is among the foremost of missionaries in the second half of the nineteenth century who contributed to an understanding of Zulu religion by careful methods of linguistic research. Callaway collected Zulu folktales and traditions "in the same words as they (Zulus) had heard them around their hut fires."[16] He is best known for two volumes. *Nursery Tales, Traditions and Histories of the Zulus* (1868) contained parallel columns of Zulu and English texts, with many notes and observations on the text. His second volume, *The Religious System of the Amazulu* (1870) followed the same format. Callaway was concerned in his methodology to preserve as accurately as possible Zulu traditions, folklore and religious ideas in their own words, and to keep separate and distinguishable his interpretation regarding the Zulu way of life. The fact that Callaway's work was respected and recognized at Edinburgh, twenty-four years after he had retired and left Natal, reflects his stature as a pioneer among Protestant missionaries in the study of African religions.

Bishop Callaway was the first Anglican bishop of Kaffraria. He served the Anglican church in Natal from 1854 to 1886.[17] Callaway was first trained as a medical doctor and maintained his scientific orientation in all his work and observations. He was also sensitive and sympathetic in regard to religious and theological issues of faith. These two qualities aided him in becoming an astute observer of African society and religious life and an authority on the Zulu language.

Callaway was attracted to the teaching and religious outlook of the Society of Friends through a Quaker headmaster and eventually formally became a member of the Society. Callaway was principally attracted to the Society of Friends by its vital teaching about the immediacy of the presence and activity of the Holy Spirit, and in 1841 he wrote a religious pamphlet, *Immediate Revelation*.

That same year he began formal medical training. During the course of his training he developed tuberculosis, but twelve years later in 1853, he was graduated as an M.D. at Kings College Aberdeen. Medical school had been a time of illness and stress for him. In addition he was in some turmoil about questions of faith. A year before completing his studies he wrote in his journal: "I am no longer a Quaker."[18]

Callaway read F. D. Maurice's *Kingdom of Christ* (1838), the theme of which was that the church was a deliverance from all sects and parties. He was impressed by Maurice's theology and at this point read it as an answer to Quaker teaching. Callaway decided to seek ordination in the Church of England in 1853, the same year that he completed his medical training as an M. D. The following year, he wrote J. W. Colenso, who was also a disciple of Maurice and the newly appointed bishop of Natal, offering his services. He was accepted by the Society for the Propagation of the Gospel and arrived in Pietermaritzburg in 1854. After working with Colenso for three years, Callaway was ordained a priest and, in 1858 was sent by Colenso at the age of 41, to start a mission beyond the upper Umkomaas River on a former Boer farm at Insernguze, which he personally purchased and renamed Springvale. This station was to be the center of his life until 1873.

The Society for the Propagation of the Gospel and the Episcopal Church in Scotland joined in 1872 to establish a diocese in the Transkei. Callaway was called to be its first bishop, and was consecrated in Edinburgh in 1873. His new diocese came to be called St. John's Kaffraria. Callaway made Umtata his headquarters. When he became bishop in 1873, he was no longer a strong man, and some of his responsibilities devolved on Barnsby Lewis Key, a missionary sympathetically disposed toward the customs and culture of African people. Callaway resigned his bishopric in 1886.

Callaway achieved much as a translator of the Scriptures into Zulu. The first complete Zulu translation of the Bible, largely his contribution, appeared in 1883. His enthusiastic interest in anthropology and comparative religion grew largely out of his initial concerns to master the Zulu language. He started to learn Zulu in 1854 when few linguistic resources were available,[19] and when his fellow missionaries were not yet committed to mastering Zulu. Callaway was quick to observe that

> in common conversation the native naturally condescends to the ignorance of the foreigner, whom, judging from what he generally hears from the colonists, he thinks unable to speak the language of the Zulu; he is also pleased to parade his own little knowledge of broken English and Dutch; thus there is the danger of picking up a miserable gibberish, composed of anglicized Kafir . . .[20]

Callaway found this linguistic mixture "wholly insufficient to admit to any close communication of mind with mind, and quite inadequate to meet the requirements of scientific investigation."[21]

Callaway was able to acquire access to the way in which the Zulu language was spoken with an accurate knowledge of the meanings of words and idioms, but also with a knowledge of how the Zulu language was used in the conveyance of religious ideas and symbols. As a language learning technique, Callaway requested that a Zulu tell a folk tale exactly as he would to a child or friend. Callaway wanted to collect Zulu folk tales and traditions in the same words Zulus had heard around their hut fires. His journal of 1860 has an admirable passage on the particular care needed in investigations of this nature:

> It is very important whilst tracing out their traditions to be careful not to mingle with them suggestions of our own, or thoughts which they have already suggested to them by others.[22]

Not only was Callaway aware that extraneous ideas could be suggested and incorporated into these materials, he also was aware he could be selective and edit out materials he felt inappropriate, particularly the sexual references for his Victorian readers. He therefore states in the Preface:

There are some things retained in it which are not fit for the public generally; but which could not for the student (of the Zulu language, or of Comparative Folklore) be properly suppressed. The very value of such a work depends on the fidelity with which all is told. To be a trustworthy exposition of the native mind it must exhibit every side of it. . . I have had a trust committed to me and that I can only faithfully execute it by laying everything before others.[23]

Once he had a faithful verbatim record written down, he sought connections and explanations from others. These materials, which were originally for his own language instruction and mastery, gradually accumulated. Twelve years later he compiled and published in six parts an extensive collection: *Izinganekwana, nensumansumane, nezindaba Zabantu (Nursery Tales, Traditions, and Histories of the Zulus) in their own words, with a translation into English and notes* (1866–68). He originally published this collection at his own mission press at Springvale. This work is an impressive 374 pages of double columns of Zulu text with a parallel English translation and notes at the bottom of the page. It was received with enthusiasm by both his white contemporaries and by Zulu readers.

The great value of the collection was that Callaway had attempted to let Zulus speak for themselves as much as possible. Both Western missionaries and social scientists recognized Callaway's work as a primary resource in understanding and interpreting African society and one of a calibre that had not been available previously. Comparative mythology was an emerging field of study and research in the mid-nineteenth century. Sir William James had translated and worked on the *Zendavesta,* and Max Müller was working on translations of the *Vedas of India*. Max Müller was particularly attracted by the folklore that Callaway had collected.

The missionary periodicals *Mission Field* and *The Natal Witness* also saw Callaway's work as a rich resource. A review in the *Natal Witness* exclaims, "Some portions of the tale of *Ukcombekcansini* are as beautiful and graceful as a classic idyll."[24]

Two years later, Callaway issued a second work, comprising the first three parts of his projected four-part book, *The Religious System of the Amazulu* (Springvale, Pietermaritzburg and London, 1870). These first three parts deal with the traditions of creation, the veneration of the ancestors, and divination. The fourth section on medical magic and witchcraft (*abatakati*) was never completed, but a portion of the incomplete section was added to a London 1884 edition.[25] Callaway followed his earlier format: the verbatim Zulu text of his informant, a parallel English translation, and his own notes at the foot of the page.

Callaway's own estimate of his folklore collections was that it gave him a more subtle use of words and prepared him to "handle with a firmer and more assured grasp the graver task of translating the Bible and Prayer Book into the native tongue."[26] Callaway's reviewer in the *Natal Mercury* also points toward its linguistic usefulness: "It is undoubtedly a work that will teach the pure idiom of the Zulu language better than any other book yet published."[27]

Missionaries were not the only ones who recognized the value of the work. The publication of these primary source materials immediately caught the attention of Max Müller and E. B. Tylor, scholars in the emerging sciences of comparative religion and mythology at Oxford. The emerging science of comparative mythology was being led by Max Müller's philological approach. The most notable interests of the philologists were in the area of Indian mythology in the *Vedas* and the way in which religion was conceptualized in words and stories.

The field of anthropology was still at a formative stage. E. B. Tylor was just in the process of writing his most definitive work, *Primitive Culture*, which appeared in 1871. Tylor's respect for and dependence upon Callaway is evidenced by the fact that Callaway is cited more than twice as often as any other single source. This is not surprising since Callaway's data were the most current, objective and reliable by standards at that time.

In an appeal Tylor wrote for government funds to complete the final unfinished section of *The Religious System of the Amazulu*, Tylor gave his evaluation of Callaway's study:

> It is scarcely too much to say that no savage race has ever had its mental, moral, and religious condition displayed to the scientific student with anything approaching the minute accuracy which characterizes the half completed works now threatened with an untimely end.[28]

Callaway apparently was already in touch with Max Müller while he was collecting his Zulu stories. He had read Müller's *Survey of Languages,* and had, corresponded through a friend with Max Müller on the questions of a more uniform orthography and was willing to adopt Müller's suggestions.[29]

With the publication of the first part of *Izinganekwane (Nursery Tales)* in 1866, Callaway's reputation in anthropological circles began to emerge. He was recognized as the local secretary for Natal of the Anthropological Society of London.[30] Professor Max Müller, fellow at All Souls College, Oxford and one of the foremost authorities in comparative mythology, reviewed Callaway's promising collection of Zulu folklore for an 1867 issue of the *Saturday Review*. Müller apparently regarded Callaway's work as having enough significance to include the essay on Callaway's "Zulu Nursery Tales" in his four-volume work of collected essays, *Chips from a German Workshop* (1871).[31]

While Callaway was working on his second book, *The Religious System of the Amazulu*, one of his letters, written in 1868, indicates that he was eager that Max Müller look at the first part of his *Unkulunkulu: The Tradition of Creation*, because "there is much information in it utterly unknown to others, even the oldest missionaries in South Africa."[32]

There appears to have been considerable mutual respect and appreciation between Max Müller and Henry Callaway. There is a note in Callaway's diary of February 8, 1872, indicating that he had read Müller's *Lectures on the Science of Religion*. Müller had argued in this essay that missionaries are apt to look at all other religions as totally distinct from their own. He hoped the *Science of Religion* would produce a change in missionaries, that they would look "more anxiously for any common ground, any spark of true light that may still be revived, any altar that may be dedicated afresh to the true God."[33] Callaway felt that Müller had articulated a position he had held for years, namely that

> the opinion which restricts the knowledge of God, God's gracious saving grace and efficacious operation among men, to Christian countries, is a godless heresy. Whoever maintains it, and not only so, but I feel very strongly, that whoever maintains it does thereby prove that he does not understand the Christian revelation, and that he is most effectually barring the way against its light.[34]

Callaway contributed a valuable paper, "On Divination and Analogous Phenomena Among the Natives of Natal," to the Anthropological Institute in

1871. The Anthropological Institute was formed that year from the merger of the Anthropological Society of London and the Ethnological Society. Callaway's article appears in Volume I of the Anthropological Institute's journal.[35]

Callaway returned to Britain in 1873. During that year he was not only consecrated bishop of St. John's, Kaffraria in Edinburgh in November 1873, but he also received an honorary D. D. from the University of Oxford on February 2, 1874.[36] This was in recognition of his philological and ethnographic work. During the same year he wrote a pamphlet, *A Fragment of Comparative Religions*, which was published in London in 1874. In an address "On the Religious Sentiment Amongst the Tribes of South Africa" given at Kokstad in 1876, he summarized his research and findings in relation to the religious life of the Amazulu by making a comparative study with other South African societies.

As an astute and sympathetic observer of Zulu society, Callaway provided valuable field data during the early formative years of the emerging sciences of comparative religion and anthropology.[37] In addition to providing a significant body of original descriptive data on a society without a written tradition, Callaway was associated with and in touch with the leaders at the center of linguistic and anthropological study in Britain.

Edward Burnett Tylor

The publication of E. B. Tylor's *Primitive Culture* in 1871 marked the turning point at which ethnology, or anthropology, became a science. Here was a mastery of a vast mass of material collected from missionaries, travelers, and colonial administrators, set forth in a clear analytical form, on the basis of a consistent and clear definition of religion and a theory of evolution. Tylor's theory of animism stressed the idea of the soul. Animism is the belief, ascribed to primitive peoples, that not only human beings and creatures, but also inanimate objects have life and personality, sometimes with an additional sense that they also have souls. Tylor's theory consisted of two main theses, the first of which accounted for the origin and the second for the development of religion. Tylor contended that primitive people reflect on experiences such as death, disease, trance, visions, and above all dreams, which lead them to the conclusion that there is some immaterial entity, the soul, apart from the body. The soul, being detachable, could be thought of as independent of its material home, and from this thought arose the idea of spiritual beings. The idea of spiritual beings constituted Tylor's minimum definition of religion. The belief in spiritual beings led to the reverence of ancestors, who developed into gods. This evolution then moves on from polytheism to monotheism.[38]

The other dominant figure in British anthropology during the last decades of the nineteenth and early twentieth centuries was James Frazer. In 1879 he became a fellow at Trinity College in Cambridge, where he taught until 1922. From Cambridge he kept up a large correspondence with a number of workers on the field, to whom he circulated a comprehensive questionnaire consisting of 213 questions.[39] His major contribution, *The Golden Bough*, is a work of immense industry. It is devoted to primitive superstitions. The first edition of two volumes appeared in 1890. The third edition of 1910 contained twelve volumes. Frazer's aim in *The Golden Bough* was to do a study of comparative religion. According to Frazer, societies everywhere in their evolution pass through three stages of intellectual development: from magic to religion, and from religion to science. This is a scheme influenced by Comte's phases: the theological, the metaphysical, and the positive.[40] Frazer did not add much to Tylor's theory of religion but introduced two new suppositions; the one was pseudo-historical, the other psychological. The pseudo-historical assumption was that the simpler the culture, the more magic and the less religion was present. Evans-Pritchard however has pointed out that hunting and collecting societies have both magical and theistic beliefs and cults. The psychological dimension of Frazer's thesis was his placement of magic and science in opposition to religion. In magic and science the world is subject to invariable natural laws which human beings by proper techniques can manipulate and control; religion, however, is marked by fear and trembling, awe, respect and submission.[41] According to Frazer, humankind everywhere, sooner or later, passes through these stages of intellectual development: from magic to religion and from religion to science.[42]

The nineteenth century evolutionary theories regarding the origins of religion were only just being challenged at the turn of the century. Tylor's and Frazer's theories were based on the assumption that the religion of the tribal societies of their day represented the primitive mode of thought out of which civilized religion had evolved. G. F. Moore, at the turn of the century, astutely pointed out:

> The Australian black or the Andaman Islander is separated by as many generations from the beginning of religion as his most advanced contemporaries; and in these tens or hundreds of thousands of years there has been constant change, growth, and decay — and decay is not a simple return to the primal state. We can learn a great deal from the lowest existing religions, but they cannot tell us what the beginning of religion was, any more than the history of language can tell us what was the first human speech.[43]

E. E. Evans-Pritchard felt that, broadly speaking, the intellectualist theories of Tylor and Frazer could not be refuted or sustained for the simple reason that there is no evidence about how religious beliefs originated. The evolutionary stages constructed by Tylor, Frazer, and others may have had a certain logical consistency, but they provide little or no evidential proof. However animistic theory, in various forms, remained unchallenged for many years and left its mark upon the anthropological literature of the day.[44]

These decades of the high imperialist era witnessed several outstanding examples of ethnological studies by missionaries working in tribal societies. Frazer's questionnaire and the theoretical frameworks of comparative religion developed by Tylor, Frazer, and Max Müller contributed to an advance in collecting more accurate field data in the last decades of the nineteenth and early twentieth centuries. Missionaries with anthropological interests made a significant contribution to these collections. They also began to provide the field data that challenged some of the predominant theories and assumptions of anthropology. Two particularly outstanding examples are the Right Rev. Robert Henry Codrington (1830–1922), missionary to Melanesia from 1863–1887, and Rev. John Roscoe (1861–1952), a missionary with the Church Missionary Society in Uganda.

The most prominent influence of Frazer on missionary anthropology is to be seen in his relationship with Rev. Lorimer Fison of the Wesleyan Mission in Fiji and with John Roscoe (1861–1932), an Anglican with the Church Missionary Society, who worked in Uganda among the

Baganda. Frazer acknowledges in the foreword to the second edition (1900) of *The Golden Bough* that he had incorporated most of Fison's notes and a selection of Roscoe's customs and beliefs of the Baganda.[45] Roscoe went to Uganda in 1884 and in 1899 became the principal of the theological school at Mengo, the capital of the Baganda, a position he held for ten years. For eighteen years Roscoe was in touch with Frazer. During these years he published a series of articles in the *Journal of the Anthropological Institute*. Roscoe returned to England in 1909, no longer in complete sympathy with the CMS. In 1910, Cambridge University, where Frazer was teaching, conferred on Roscoe an honorary M.A. degree for his services to ethnology and anthropology. He became a curate at Holy Trinity in Cambridge and lecturer to the University on Anthropology in Africa. His book, *The Baganda: An Account of Their Native Customs and Beliefs*, was published in 1911. In 1919–1920 Roscoe returned to East Central Africa as leader of the Mackie Ethnological Expedition.[46] In his research among the Baganda, Roscoe received important aid from his friend Sir Apollo Kagwa, the prime minister in the Court of the Kabaka, in Uganda. Sir Kagwa was not only knowledgeable of the lore of his people but also brought informants from all parts of the country acquainted with the ancient traditions and customs, which even at the beginning of the twentieth century were passing out of use and memory. Roscoe arrived in Uganda just after the powerful Kabaka (king) Mutesa had died and therefore saw the weakening or disintegration of a great African Kingdom.[47]

Tylor's Critics: Andrew Lang and R. R. Marett

The most radical and damaging attack on Tylor's premises came from two of Tylor's own students, Andrew Lang and R. R. Marett. Marett's book, *The Threshold of Religion*, drew heavily upon R. H. Codrington's *The Melanesians* for illustrative material for a proposed pre-animistic religion.[48]

In 1898 Andrew Lang published *The Making of Religion,* in which he argued the case for the existence of high gods in the religion of primitive peoples. His book represented the first real challenge to the dominance of Tylor's evolutionary theory, which regarded the religions of tribal people on the lowest level of the evolutionary scale. Tylor's interpretation of animism had no room for belief in a high god.

Lang had not unearthed new sources of information; the material he used was no different from that of other theorists, but he had a new way of interpreting existing information.[49] Lang pointed out from existing sources that the idea of a high god was to be found among the culturally simplest peoples. The Supreme Being was thought of not only as a spirit but rather as some sort of "person." Lang clearly thought that monotheism was prior to animism and was corrupted and degraded by later animistic ideas.

Partly because the animistic origin of religion was so generally taken as self-evident, the new insights which Lang pointed out were ignored.[50] Lang was later supported by Wilhelm Schmidt's *Der Ursprung der Gottesidee,* a twelve-volume work published over a forty-three-year period, 1912–1955. Schmidt carefully traces the monotheistic ideas in primitive societies. This work, however, never became popular among scholars. Only with the research pioneered by E. E. Evans-Pritchard was the "high god" that Lang drew attention to recognized as a genuine feature of primal religions.

R. R. Marett, who was appointed Reader in Anthropology at Oxford in 1910, had a very different critique of Tylor from Lang. He advocated a pre-animistic stage or dynamism, using the concepts of "mana" and "tabu." Pre-animism was a "supernaturalistic" stage in which an impersonal religious force was felt rather than reasoned out. Marett also challenged Tylor's reasoning: religion, he said, does not arise from rational intellectualizing, nor from reflection, but from the affective states. Marett took a psychological approach based on the experience of the individual, with attention to affective and emotional aspects. "Savage religion is something not so much thought out as danced out."[51]

Marett acknowledged that his critique of Tylor's theory of animism and of Frazer's theory of magic and religion drew heavily for illustrative matter on two authorities, R. H. Codrington and E. Tregear.[52] Although Codrington did not participate in or contribute to the Edinburgh 1910 report on animistic religions, he had a significant influence on missionary thinking. He was widely read in missionary circles and his work was used to critique the mainstream of Tylorian animism. It is also significant that Marett's book, *The Threshold of Religion*, which draws heavily upon Codrington's work, appeared just prior to Edinburgh 1910.[53] It is therefore necessary to include a look at Codrington in our assessment of the anthropology that informed the Edinburgh 1910 report.

Robert Henry Codrington

Robert Henry Codrington, D.D., was an Anglican missionary to Melanesia, 1863–1887, and a scholar of Melanesian languages. He was regarded by social scientists as the first systematic ethnographer of Melanesia.[54] Codrington was educated at Wadham College, Oxford. His high church views suggest that he may have been influenced by the Oxford movement. In 1857, two years after he was ordained, he moved to New Zealand. He accompanied Bishop John Coleridge Patteson in 1863 on a voyage to the Solomon Islands and New Hebrides on the mission ship, *Southern Cross*. In 1867, he joined the Melanesian Mission, which advocated a policy of racial equality and minimal interference in traditional native culture.[55] Codrington directed the mission school on Norfolk Island, where young Melanesians were brought for training as teachers. Codrington also took over the linguistic studies Patteson had begun. Patteson had begun the study in part from stimulus by the Oxford philologist and scholar of comparative religion, F. Max Müller. Codrington acknowledged his indebtedness to Lorimer Fison, a Wesleyan missionary with anthropological interests in Fiji, for his ethnographic sensitivity. Codrington quotes Fison as saying:

> When a European has been living for two or three years among savages he is sure to be fully convinced he knows all about them, when he has been ten years or so amongst them, if he is an observant man, he finds that he knows very little about them, and so begins to learn.[56]

It was through Fison that Codrington established a relationship with the social evolutionary anthropologist E. B. Tylor. By the year 1880, Codrington had begun to send ethnographic material to the *Journal of the Anthropological Institute*. One of Codrington's major contributions to the anthropology of Oceania was his analysis of Melanesian languages. He was able to speak many

Melanesian dialects. His analysis grows out of first-hand experience rather than the linguistic analyses performed by other Westerners.[57]

Codrington returned to England in 1883 to complete the translation of the Bible into Mota, the Melanesian *lingua franca*. While he was in residence for two years at Oxford, he attended lectures by E. B. Tylor, and in 1885 he wrote an article on the "Languages of Melanesia," which elicited the admiration of both Professor Tylor and Professor A. H. Krane of Oxford.[58] That same year, 1885, saw the publication of the first of his two major works, *The Melanesian Languages*. It has remained a standard reference to this day. The companion study, *The Melanesians: Studies in Their Anthropology and Folklore*, was published in 1891, after Codrington returned from a truncated final term of service with the Melanesian Mission.

Codrington's contribution to anthropology is based on twenty-four years of field work (1863–1887). Codrington's knowledge of a number of Melanesian dialects enabled him to work from a strong linguistic base. Like Henry Callaway, Codrington emphasized the importance of folklore as a means of interpreting Melanesian life and thought. Codrington conceived of his task as "setting forth what natives say about themselves, not what Europeans say about them."[59]

Codrington had early recognized that the islander is not an individual in the same sense as the Westerner. Therefore Codrington began his book *The Melanesians* with a long section on social organization and kinship systems, rules of property and inheritance, crisis rites, and age-grade societies. Only after this description does he examine the religious life. It should be noted that *The Melanesians* was written about the same time that Robertson Smith (1846–1894) was working on *Kinship and Marriage in Early Arabia*, a work that was formative in moving the study of religion toward a sociological orientation and away from the psychological emphasis of Tylor.[60]

Codrington was the first to recognize and analyze the important details basic to the concept of *mana*. He describes *mana* in the following words:

> It is a power or influence, not physical, and in a way supernatural; but it shows itself in physical force, or in any kind of power or excellence which a man possesses. This mana is not fixed in anything, and can be conveyed in almost anything; but spirits, whether disembodied souls or supernatural beings, have it

and can impart it; and it essentially belongs to personal beings to originate it, though it may act through the medium of water, or a stone, or a bone . . .[61]

Codrington saw *mana* as the basis of all Melanesian religious beliefs. It is the key to our understanding of how the pre-literate societies of Melanesia explain aspects of life that involve sickness, magic, dreams, prophecy, divination, and events that may otherwise be incomprehensible and frightening. By analyzing the mystique of *mana*, Codrington paradoxically provided a significant clue to the rationality of a pre-literate world view.

Although Codrington had been in touch with Tylor, he remained much closer to the philologically oriented ethnological tradition of Max Müller. Codrington had originally described *mana* in a letter to Max Müller.[62] Müller used this material in his Hibbert Lectures of 1878, which were published as the *Origin of Religion*, to challenge Tylor's rationalist and psychological views regarding the basis and origin of religion in animism. Unlike his friend Lorimer Fison, Codrington was little concerned with evolutionary problems. He questioned the evolutionary interpretation of socioreligious concepts in totemism and in the doctrine of animism.

As we have already noted, R. R. Marett adopted the concept of *mana* as the basis of his theory of pre-animistic religion, which played an important role in the critique of social evolution that developed in British anthropology after 1900. Codrington's interpretation of *mana* as a supernatural power belonging to the region of the unseen, a power that is emotionally experienced rather than rationally worked out, comes close to the ideas of the *mysterium tremendum* that Rudolf Otto would later develop in his book, *Das Heilige*.[63]

Codrington takes two chapters to describe the general social structure and the function of secret societies and clubs which are a characteristic feature of Melanesian social rank and status. His description of their functions in checking the limits of hereditary chiefs, redistributing wealth, protecting property rights, and maintaining social order in the community has been enlarged by subsequent field work. Codrington's description constituted a step forward in the theory of social structure, a foreshadowing of functional anthropological theory.[64]

In arriving at an assessment of E. B. Tylor's influence on the Edinburgh 1910 report, it has been recognized that he was the most widely read anthropological theorist on religion of the time. His concepts of animism and the evolutionary development of religion had popular appeal in an era immersed in the ideas of progress and development. For example, many people felt that Western culture represented the apex of human culture and civilization. The idea of beginning at a primitive level seemed logical.

We have noted that Tylor drew heavily upon Bishop Henry Callaway's research. Callaway, as the foremost authority cited by the writers of the Edinburgh 1910 report on animistic religions, did not subscribe to Tylor's evolutionary analysis but was influenced more by Max Müller's approach of comparative mythology. Furthermore, by 1910 the work of missionaries, like Bishop Codrington's *The Melanesians*, was being used by Tylor's students, Andrew Lang and R. R. Marett, to seriously challenge Tylor's ideas of animism. Although Tylor's term and his definition are used to identify the religious traditions of tribal societies, it would be a mistake to assume that his evolutionary theories were completely dominant in the report. In terms of theoretical impact, Max Müller appears to have been more influential upon missionary leaders writing on religion in tribal societies.

Henri Alexandre Junod

The second missionary anthropologist who plays a part in the "Animistic Religions" report at Edinburgh 1910 is Henri Alexandre Junod (1863–1934).[65] As a missionary of the Swiss Romande Mission, he spent twenty-six years among the Thonga tribes of Southern Africa. His book *The Life of A South African Tribe* (1912) has been widely recognized as one of the great early monographs in African ethnography. Junod brought to his missionary calling not only a devout and spiritual life, but also a scientific perspective of broad interests and an inquiring mind given to detail. He was born of Swiss Protestant parents in the canton of Neuchatel, Switzerland. His father, who had staunch free church convictions, founded the Independent Protestant Church and was an advocate for the separation of church and state in Switzerland. Henri was the eldest of five children. The three sons were ordained to the ministry and one of the two daughters became a deaconess.

Junod's teachers at the Gymnase in Neuchatel expected him to have a brilliant career in science and natural history. He, however, dedicated his life to the service of God and studied theology at the Independent Protestant Church School, College of Neuchatel. He also attended two semesters at the universities of Basel and Berlin before obtaining his degree. In 1885 he was ordained and served in the parish of Motiers-Boveresse. After two years he was accepted by the Swiss Romande Mission and was sent to Edinburgh for two years to study English and medicine.

The Swiss Romande Mission had also sent Paul Berthoud and Ernest Creux, the founders of its work in Southern Africa, to Edinburgh in 1870 to study English and medicine before starting their work in Transvaal. Originally the founders worked under the aegis of the Paris Evangelical Mission. They eventually began their own independent work among the Thonga of the Transvaal in 1875 and two years later moved into Mozambique to establish the Rikatla Mission, eighteen miles north of Lorenço Marques.[66] Rikatla was one of the primary locations from which Junod was to carry out both his mission work and anthropological research.

The early missionaries of the Swiss Romande Mission cooperated with a remarkable African church known today as the Presbyterian Church of Mozambique. This church was initially founded through the work of Africans. The founders were an ordained black missionary, Yosepha Mhalamhala, his prophetic sister, Lois Xintonmane, and a wealthy black businessman, Jim Ximungana.[67] During the 1880s this team of Africans led a movement of thousands into contact with small cells of Christians in Mozambique. This gave the church its firm African character. The French-speaking Swiss missionaries were invited to help this emerging Christian community in Mozambique.

Junod arrived in Mozambique at the age of twenty-six, and in 1889 began his work giving theological instruction at a school for evangelists in Rikatla. These were troubled political times. The Zulu military power in the region had been broken barely ten years earlier, and the resulting disorder was finally brought under some control with British occupation of Zululand in 1887. Open warfare flared up with the Ronga-Portuguese War of 1894–95, at which time the mission at Rikatla was burned. During his second term of service, Junod established the evangelists' school at Shiluvane in the Transvaal, despite the difficulties imposed by the Second Anglo-Boer War (1899–1902). In 1907 he moved back to his original mission station at Rikatla in Mozambique. The reason for the change was that mission schools in the Transvaal were subsidized by the local educational authorities, and Junod found that this arrangement would restrict the amount of time he would be permitted to spend on religious instruction.[68] These two locations of his school permitted him to study locally the Thonga, who were northern clans from the Transvaal, and the Ronga, who were southern clans located in Portuguese territory. While giving religious instruction at the school for evangelists in Rikatla and later in Shilouvane, Transvaal, he kept careful records of the traditional stories his students told him and the customs they described.

During his early years in Africa he pursued his scientific interests in natural history. He collected plant specimens, beetles, and butterflies, of which he discovered the species *papilio junodi* and *Eumeta junodi*. His collections of southeast African butterflies are preserved in museums in Lausanne, Lourenço Marques, and South Africa.[69]

Junod also applied his scientific skills to the study of African society around him. With the help of an illiterate informant, Junod made a systematic analysis of Ronga, one of the numerous Thonga dialects. Beginning around 1895, his major scientific interests shifted from entomology to ethnology. In 1896, his first book, *Grammaire Ronga,* was published. It was a grammar and conversation manual with vocabularies in Ronga, Portuguese, French, and English, together with an ethnographic introduction, and was published under the auspices of the Portuguese government. His first furlough in Switzerland in 1886–89 was a time of intense writing. He published a collection of more than one hundred traditional stories in *les chantes et les contes des ba-Ronga de la baie de Delagoa.* He also wrote *les ba-Ronga: Etude ethnographique* (Neuchatel, 1898), regarded as one of the very best ethnographic works of that time. This work was foundational for his best known work, *The Life of a South African Tribe.* Junod was back in Switzerland from 1909 to 1913 preparing this book, which was published by Neuchatel, 1912–1913. This two-volume work was one of the great anthropological works of its time, and still is one of the most comprehensive studies of an African tribe.[70] It won Junod an honorary membership in the Royal Anthropological Institute. It was while Junod was in the midst of writing this work that he was a participant in the First World Missionary Conference, Edinburgh 1910. The second edition

(London, 1927) was significantly expanded to a work over 1200 pages long. It represents some of Junod's most astute observations and incorporates much of his best writing in the periodical literature. A third edition was published in 1962 using photographs which are much better than those Junod was able to supply for the earlier editions.[71]

During the last fourteen years of his life, Junod delivered a series of lectures at the Universities of Lausanne, Geneva, and London. In 1925, the year of the jubilee of the Swiss Romande Mission, he was awarded an honorary Doctorate of Literature by the University of Lausanne. He also served as the president of *Bureau International pour la Defense des Indigenes.* He was particularly concerned for the abolition of the system of forced labor in the colonies.[72] He was able to continue his writing until his death in 1931.

Motifs in Junod's Anthropology

Junod was familiar with the work of Frazer, Tylor, Marett, Gobineau, Schmidt, and Levy-Bruhl, his major contemporaries in anthropology. We know that in 1909 Junod was conducting his research regarding the question of taboo, using a set of questions prepared by Frazer. Throughout *The Life of a South African Tribe*, one notices Junod testing general anthropological theories against the factual material he was accumulating. Junod pointed out that Levy Bruhl had made the contrast between the mentality of "primitive" people and western mentality more dramatic by presenting the latter as positivistic and the former as "pre-logical" or superstitious. Junod, in fact, points out that emotional factors often interfere with logical reasoning in "non-primitive races." In regard to the mechanism of reasoning, he declares, "I do not think there is any great difference between the Bantu mind and the mind of the more civilized people."[73] Junod bases these claims on the structure and clarity of African languages, which are able to express subtle distinctions.

Junod was a product of his times. He analyzed and interpreted the customs and religion of the Thonga in the light of the prevailing evolutionary theory. Having found among the Thonga the coexistence of a belief in a sky god or heaven, which was a form of monotheism, and also a belief in ancestral spirits, Junod attempted to assess the respective antiquity of the two religious concepts. To do so, he compared these beliefs with others found among southern Bantu-speaking societies. He followed the assertion of Henry Callaway that the forebearers of the Swazi and Zulu prayed to the sky god before the worship of ancestor spirits was introduced. Though Junod called this change from primitive monotheism or a high god concept to the veneration of ancestors "evolution," he realized that this succession was contrary to the schemes of orthodox evolutionism.[74]   Junod's scientific approach provided a valuable framework that contributed to his deep sense of history.

Junod's use of evolutionary language reflects the care of an experienced researcher trying to combine his research with the predominant theoretical framework of the times. He uses evolutionary language not so much to search for origins of religions or the human race, as to strive for a more historical study of a particular African religion. The driving force behind Junod's research is a deep sense of history and an awareness of the profound changes that were revolutionizing African cultures and societies. Beyond his scientific interest in the Thonga, he devoutly desired to help them, and he clearly articulated this concern in his perspective and stance as a Christian missionary. He also recognized that he himself represented one of the agents of change.

Junod was convinced that he was, in 1909,[75] at a favorable vantage point for his investigation. He indeed was at a watershed in African history. The age of African exploration symbolized by Livingstone and Stanley was over. The age of empire and colonialism represented by Cecil Rhodes and Sir Harry Johnston was in progress. The Transvaal mining interests had determined that the port of Lourenço Marques in the Portuguese colony of Mozambique was the shortest route overseas for shipping the gold mined on the Rand. The port of Lourenço Marques would only be permitted to develop in return for the right of South African mining interests to recruit contract labor in Portuguese territory, where the Bathonga had provided a substantial labor pool for the South African mines. Junod believed that the great bulk of Thonga still maintained the traditional social and belief systems; but he saw the radical demise of traditional Thonga society just over the horizon.

The occasion for the writing of Junod's book reflects both his historical and scientific interests. In 1895 he had the privilege of meeting Lord Bryce, then British ambassador to Washington, in Mozambique. Bryce remarked that the British would have been extremely grateful had the Romans taken the trouble to record the ways and habits of their Celtic ancestors, but this they failed to do. Junod realized there was not a single African people for whom such a record had been accurately compiled. It was this that he set himself to do.[76]

Junod set for himself a dual task: to be both scientific and practical. In being scientific, he attempted to depict the life of the Thonga tribe as objectively as "biological phenomena" can be described. He wanted to leave a record of Thonga culture and society at this particular point in their history.[77] He felt that even though some of the "biological phenomena" would be repulsive to Westerners, particularly dimensions from the sexual life that shocked Western missionary moral feelings, they could not be left out in a "truly scientific work."[78] Junod discreetly places some of these observations in an appendix written in Latin called "Latin notes for medical men and ethnographers."

"Scientific," for Junod, also meant that the description must be limited to one defined ethnic group, and all data must be localized. Because customs vary from clan to clan, data must be classified geographically. Only after a sufficient number of trustworthy monographs have been written can a comparative study be undertaken. Junod was therefore critical of his contemporary Dudley Kidd, whose book *The Essential Kafir* (1904) was not, he felt, based on sufficiently scientific and thorough studies.[79]

The second of Junod's aims was to be practical; he intended to write for colonial Native Commissioners and missionaries. The British colonial policy of indirect rule both encouraged and relied upon social anthropology. Junod remarks, "How many native wars might have been avoided if the Native Commissioner had better knowledge of Bantu ethnography, and on the other hand, how much good has been done by those who have taken the trouble to study the Natives with sympathy in order to be just to them."[80] As a delegate and contributor to the World Missionary Conference in Edinburgh in 1910, Junod came away with renewed vision for the ethnographic study he was already engaged in. In the "General Conclusions" of the report of Commission IV, *The Missionary Message in Relation to Non-Christian Religions*, there is strong affirmation of Johannes Warneck's work on the

Batak in the East Indian Archipelago and Junod's work in southern Africa. Both are cited as examples of the kind of ethnographic work that needs to be done in other areas.[81]   He heard Edinburgh 1910 call for both a sympathetic study of indigenous beliefs and customs and for thorough ethnographic field research, the purpose being

> that the message of the Gospel may be presented in such a way as will appeal to those aspirations after the truth which reveal themselves in the religion and social rites of the Natives. How superior is this conception to that of former times, when heathenism was looked on as a creation of the devil through and through! We see better now that amidst darkness and sin, the heathen mind is often seeking light and righteousness, and that these rays of truth, these presentiments of a higher life, must be infinitely respected and utilized in the preaching of the Gospel of Jesus Christ.[82]

How Junod conceived of the relationship between Thonga religious concepts and the Gospel will be pursued later in this chapter. Junod conceived of his work as an instrument, not only for a more just colonial administration, or a more profound religious understanding, but also for the moral responsibility and possibility to "contribute to the peaceful solution of our great practical problem there, the Native problem."[83] The racial prejudice and the impact of a western civilization which he described as "depraved and unscrupulous" was, he felt, as dangerous for the peace of the country as the defects for which whites reproach the "Natives."

> Let those who are prejudiced against the black race study more carefully its customs, its mind, such as it reveals itself in the old rites of the Bantu tribes. They will see that these natives are much more earnest than they thought and that in them beats a true human heart. . . Should I succeed in eliciting a new and more enlightened sympathy amongst the whites for our native brethren, should this book prevent the gulf which separates the races from becoming wider, I think it will have been worth while writing it.[84]

In summary, Junod combined his scientific observation with both his moral and religious perspective. He states, "To work for science is noble; but to help our fellowman is nobler still."[85]

Junod never concealed that he was a missionary, that his one concern was that his Bathonga friends should come to know the Lord Jesus Christ. He devoted an appendix to the question of the capacity of the Bathonga to understand the Gospel, and expressed his own belief that only through the acceptance of the Gospel could African tribal life with its many beauties be preserved from the forces that would destroy it. But in his scientific work, he was the friendly and objective observer. He was aware of his own Christian convictions and therefore tried to keep them from obtruding on his descriptions of Thonga society. Junod's detailed knowledge of an African people has not been frequently attained by a white person. The great value of Junod's work is that it sets down a benchmark in the first decade of this century for the historical and comparative study of African religions.

Attitudes Toward African Religions

Junod's attitude toward Thonga traditional religion and his conception of the relationship of the Christian Gospel to Thonga beliefs and world view were shaped both by his scientific perspective as an ethnologist and by his moral sensitivity as a Christian missionary. Two ethnological perspectives informed and influenced his views: an evolutionary concept of the development of religion, and the tension between religion, magic, and science. The primary tension was between the "scientific mind of the West" and the "Bantu magical conception of nature."

The following analysis draws upon the final and climactic section of Junod's *Life of An African Tribe*, "Religious Life and Superstitions," and on three articles: "God's Way in the Bantu Soul,"[86] "The Magic Conception of Nature Among the Bantu,"[87] and "The Fate of the Widows Amongst the Ba-Ronga."[88]

Junod stated that the theory of evolution gave him a perspective on Thonga traditional religion and morality different from that of the previous generation of missionaries, who, Junod claimed, believed that "the rites and customs of African savages were the work of the devil."[89] In Junod's view the science of anthropology had shown that primitive and semi-primitive peoples were passing through a phase of development which the ancestors of Western peoples had also passed through, and that within Western civilized societies there also remained survivals of animistic conceptions. Junod thus concluded,

"These pagans are our brothers, brothers whose growth has been delayed, brothers still wrapped in the mists of earliest infancy . . ."[90]

Junod's evolutionary ideas were rooted in Christian theism, which viewed humanity as growing up like a child in his father's house. Junod felt entitled to search for "traces of this divine education among primitive peoples" and felt that in studying the African soul sympathetically one could "find points of attachment for the high and pure conceptions of Christianity."[91]

> I do not despise the childish rites of Animism nor the absurd representations of Naturism. In them I see not only an attempt on the part of man to know God, but an attempt of the part of God to make Himself known to man.[92]

Even though the evolutionary perspective helped Junod develop a new respect and appreciation for African religious rites and customs (without having to view them as works of the devil), his comparisons of Africans to children still reflects a paternalistic attitude.

Junod selected examples from three principal areas of the "psychic life," by which he meant religion, magic, and taboo, to illustrate the fulfillment of Thonga beliefs and hopes by the Christian Gospel. He defined religion as "essentially the feeling of man's dependence on higher, supranormal powers to which he has recourse to help him in his distress."[93] Central to Junod's understanding of religion was "a belief in personal or semi-personal spirits endowed with the attributes of Deity."[94] From this definition, Junod observed that Bantu religion exhibited a dualism. On the one hand, the Thonga revered ancestors and spoke of them as *shikwembu* (plural *psikwembu*), ancestor-gods, who were personal but not transcendental. On the other hand, the Thonga believed in a high god, Tilo, conceived of as the heavens or sky, which was hardly a being, but seemed rather to be a personification of nature.[95]

The Thonga solemnly consecrated the firstfruits of the fields to the ancestors, praying to them to bless the village. These gods were essentially personal; they were the father, grandfather, uncle, grand-uncle whom the living had known. Indeed these gods were the whole pantheon of the dead whose memory had been preserved. Junod pointed out, however, that these ancestor gods of Thonga manism did not possess the transcendence and moral excellence which Christians attribute to Divinity.[96]

In addition to the animistic cult of ancestors, there existed among Bantus a belief that resembled deism. Among the Thonga the deity was referred to as Tilo, the sky, a formidable power manifested in unusual phenomena such as storms. This god was transcendent, but hardly personal. Junod regarded this dualism as a valuable preparation for the acceptance of Christian theism. Christian theism, Junod was convinced, had a way of absorbing and destroying previous ideas. Junod claimed that when the Thonga proclaimed the God of Heaven, the Being who was at once Father and the Creator who resides in heaven, the native united in a living synthesis his vague conceptions of the ancestor gods and the sky god. A combination never before affected took place; the notion of the heavenly Father captured the mind with such power that it could never be relinquished.[97] The concept of God became both personal and transcendental.

Junod seemed to suggest that the combination of the idea of the ancestor god and that of the sky god, produced when faith in the heavenly Father was born, so illumined the mind of the convert that a revelation took place which could never be forgotten. Junod was convinced that this was one reason why the Bantu accepted the Christian God so easily.[98] The discovery of monotheism within Christianity or Islam has had a profound impact on the religious life of many African traditional societies.

The second example of fulfillment was taken from the realm of magic. By magic, Junod meant all those rites and practices by which the Thonga strove to deal with hostile influences, impersonal forces of nature, living humans acting as wizards, or personal spirits taking possession of their victims. "Among certain tribes these forces are conceived rather in a pantheistic fashion, that is as *mana*."[99]

Missionary Christianity had been absolutely opposed to magic practices. Junod, for example, regarded magic as being based on connotations of deep-seated ignorance and anti-scientific outlook, and on frequently amoral and irreligious ideas. However, he observed that there was one point at which Christianity approximates to magic: Christians believe that there is a power given to the believer, namely the Spirit, the Spirit of God, the Spirit of Christ—not merely an influence void of personality, but the power of

regeneration, of salvation, of new life. Junod testified that the converted
Bantu believed in the Spirit with all his heart. Thonga converts waited for the
Spirit, somewhat as they waited for their charms, to bring them victory and
success. Junod wondered if it was not easier for Thonga converts to
surrender themselves to the working of the *Moya* (Spirit) due to their old
belief in the existence of independent forces and powers than it was for
Western Christians. The predominance given to the Spirit in the religious
experience of African Christians has been a striking feature observed not only
by Junod, but also in the literature describing the African Independent Church
movements which began in the nineteenth century and which have become a
prominent part of African Christianity in the twentieth century.[100]

Taboo is another element of Thonga belief that Junod regarded as a
potentially fruitful dimension to which the Christian Gospel could bring
fulfillment. Taboo, which Junod regarded as on the whole an "absurd code of
prudential prohibitions," also revealed divine preparatory action. According
to Junod, in reference to Thonga society, if

> any object, any act, any person is accounted taboo or *yila*, that implies a danger for
> the individual or for the community and that must consequently be avoided, this
> object, act, or person being under a kind of ban.[101]

Of central importance to most taboo prescriptions was the notion of
defilement. Defilement could come from menstrual flow and bodily
secretions, from contact with a corpse, from sickness, or from defilement of
certain inferior stages in life, such as infancy or adolescence. The extrication
from a defiled state was achieved by costly rites. Junod observed a real
aspiration for purity, and was amazed at the seriousness with which strange
and repulsive ceremonies were carried out. Junod was convinced that the
enlightenment of the Bantu by science and the instruction of Christian
revelation would help Africans to understand that physical defilement was of
little importance, but rather moral defilement was the great taboo of infinite
peril for human life and the human soul. If once the Bantu sought no more
than physical purity, there now could be an aspiration to true holiness.

Junod claimed that in his interpretation of Thonga culture and religion he
followed the example of the second century Christian theologian, Justin

Martyr. Junod agreed with Justin Martyr, who contended that paganism was not simply a mixture of "gloom and vice," but that in the obscurity there were "discernable streaks of light which foretold the advent of full day."[102] The Gospel, Junod contended, ought to be presented not merely as antagonistic to pagan error but also as fulfillment of former aspirations. The concept of fulfillment and development was a stance from which the missionary studied the pagan systems with wholly "new interest." The missionary's stance was no longer "the theorist teaching the ideas of a superior race, but the elder brother guiding his younger brethren towards the hill of holiness where the Father bids all His children gather."[103]

The Tension Between Science and Magic

Junod, like his contemporary social anthropologists, was unable to make a clear distinction between magic, religion, and science in Thonga society. These three elements, magic, science, and religion were particularly intermingled in the medical arts of the Thonga and in the composite character of those individuals who practiced the medical or magical arts.[104] In distinguishing between religion and magic, Junod broadly followed the guidelines, now largely abandoned, that James G. Frazer had suggested. In this view, religious practice and belief express supplication and submission to a personal or semi-personal deity, whereas magic operates by constraint and the control of nature, through living persons acting as wizards, or ancestor gods or hostile ghosts that take possession of individuals. Junod regarded as scientific those practices and conceptions which were inspired by a true observation of facts.[105] He included in this category certain medical treatments, as well as observation of botany and zoology.

Junod pointed out that the native physician (*nanga*) was not purely a scientist; he also exercised magic, praying to the ancestors who transmitted their charms to him. The magician (*mungoma*) functioned as a priest when he undertook to exorcise the spirits of possession. The diviner (*wabula*), whose art was totally based on magical concepts, also prayed to the ancestor-gods to help him in throwing the divining bones. Nevertheless Junod remained convinced that the three domains are essentially distinct and that there was a dim perception of this distinction also among the Thongas.[106]

Underlying both Thonga religions and magical rites and beliefs, Junod identified what he called the "axioms of primitive mentality." Magical rites rested upon a set of assumptions shared by the members of Bantu society. Junod identified three such shared axioms: (1) like acts on like and produces like (sympathetic magic); (2) the part represents the whole and acts on the whole (contagious magic); (3) the spoken, or even contemplated, wish produces the desired physical result (the immaterial has power over the material).[107]

It is this set of axioms or assumptions, Junod believed was at the basis of the fundamental difference between the scientific spirit of the West and the Bantu magic conception of nature. The scientific mind works from observation to causality. Observation, testing, examination and analysis are made prior to judgments of causality. The Bantu world view, Junod felt, accepted the world as it was, without asking who made it, but was prepared to believe that the world was manipulated and used by spiritual agents like human beings themselves. The self-evident basic principle of magic was that similar things act upon and influence each other. Sympathetic magic, therefore, was the basis of pharmacopoeia, hunting, and agriculture as well as being an integral part of religion.[108] For Frazer and for Junod, magic was akin to science in that it sought to control nature, even though it was done through a false or bastard science. Frazer attributed magical beliefs to faulty and immature reasoning.

Junod reserved some of his severest criticisms for the magical conception of the world in Thonga culture. For him it was an absurd and false view of the world based on ignorance, the antithesis of science.

> In perfect ignorance of the true succession of causes and effects, and never having scrutinized scientifically the processes of nature, they believe in the existence of forces which they seek to subdue, in order that these may be forced to contribute to their happiness or at least not plunge them in misfortune.[109]

For Junod, the darkest dimensions of Thonga society were associated with witchcraft and its dependence on sympathetic magic, with its unveiling of dark intrigues, denouncing the accused to receive either public punishment or rigorous trials by ordeal.

> Here we plunge into superstition at its worst, and assuredly magic is the dark side of paganism. For magic, basing its practices as it does on certain absurd axioms (such as the action of like upon like, or of the part on the whole,) is absolutely anti-scientific, and frequently anti-moral, and anti-religious.[110]

Junod regarded the practice of divining and the underlying magical framework as detrimental. He felt that it paralyzed the use of reason or experience in practical life, and it annihilated moral conscience and made reflection useless.[111]

Junod regarded the scientific and magical worlds to be in opposition to each other and therefore a barrier to true communication. This was not to say that remnants of magical practice no longer remained in Western societies. However, education, scientific training, and higher moral and religious conceptions had delivered most Europeans from magic. Therefore, Junod regarded Christianity and education as the tools to bring about change in the magical conception of nature among Bantu peoples.[112]

Callaway's Fulfillment Model

Earlier in this chapter Bishop Henry Callaway's methodology was described and set within the context of his missionary work. Missionaries in Southern Africa referred to Callaway as a model of Christian understanding of Zulu religion. The editors of the report on "Animistic Religions" also noted the creativity of his approach. This final section describes more carefully how Callaway conceived of the relationship between Christianity and Zulu religious life and mythology.

Callaway was attuned to a number of Anglican voices that were addressing the relationship between Christianity and other religions and appears to have kept in touch with major writers in the area of comparative religion through *Frazer's Magazine*, even while at his mission station at Springvale in Natal.

The Anglican theologian F. D. Maurice had been influential in Callaway's move back into the Anglican Church from the Society of Friends before he went to South Africa as a missionary. Maurice's Boyle Lectures of 1845–6, *The Religions of the World and Their Relations To Christianity* (1st edition, 1846; 6th edition, 1886) exhibited a breadth of sympathy, together with a desire for accurate and up-to-date information, that was unusual at the time. In spite of the fact that Maurice's information frequently was flawed, he succeeded, according to Eric Sharpe, in presenting the non-Christian religions not as systems of falsehood, but as evidence of the deep-seated desire of human nature to worship.[113] The fulfillment of this desire, Maurice believed, was to be ultimately found only in the church. Nevertheless, Maurice could speak of Christians as "debtors" to Buddhism, Hinduism, and Islam, a "wonderful testimony . . . borne from the ends of the earth".[114]

While Maurice had considerable influence upon Callaway's colleague and supervising Bishop J. W. Colenso, Callaway wrote in his diary of November 19, 1885, "I do not agree with Maurice as he [Colenso] does."[115] Callaway seems to have been somewhat independent in moving out to start his own mission station at Springvale.

The other Anglican voice which stands in contrast to Maurice is Charles Hardwick's *Christ and Other Masters* (1855–1858; 3rd ed. 1874). Hardwick was far more informed about Asian religions than Maurice and as such was Callaway's chief source for Indian mythology. Callaway used Hardwick's work for a comparative study of Zulu folk tales.[116] The tone of Hardwick's book is far different from that of Maurice. He sharply criticized the idea that religions are mere expressions of the fundamental beliefs inherent in our spiritual nature. And he also took an uncompromising position with regard to the claims of Christianity.

> Christianity will tolerate no rival. They who wish to raise a tabernacle to some other master . . . must be warned that Christ, and Christ alone, is to be worshipped.[117]

In the late 1860s and early 1870s, while Callaway was editing and publishing his two volumes of Zulu folktales, he was reading Darwin's *Descent of Man* and E. B. Tylor's *Early History of Mankind*. Callaway was scientist enough to be able to see the gaps in the evidence of Darwin's theory of evolution, and therefore regarded it as a mere theory and not a proof. But Callaway was also astute enough to know that we are on the eve of great changes which I believe will be for the better. We have been accustomed to regard the Bible as the only revelation made by God to man, . . . and now increasingly knowledge of man has brought out clearly to the light that God has not left himself without witness among them, but that God's testimony in nature and in human spirits has aroused men to such a knowledge as is really Divine . . . We have been accustomed to despise all religious knowledge formed without Christianity, thus raising up an image of a horrible God and consigning to perdition the masses of mankind. I have no doubt that new views which are now being rapidly developed will in many respects very materially alter men's notions of Christianity; but Christianity as the highest of God's revelations will stand and the accretions of human imaginations be taken away from it.[118]

Callaway recognized that the theory of evolution opened up a new view of history, and he foresaw a need for compromise between the conservative orthodox theologians on one side and philosophers such as Darwin and Spencer on the other.[119]

Eric Sharpe has pointed out that the pattern of orthodox opposition intensified as evolutionary judgments became more common. There was a basic shift in Christian theology from a belief in the authority of a Book or Church to a belief in the authority of God, actually revealed in the process of history. Liberal Protestantism was exchanging transcendent doctrines of God for immanentist doctrines—a God revealing Himself in the evolutionary theory which people were engaged in tracing.[120]

Callaway can hardly be thought to have bought fully into evolutionary theory, but he certainly was prepared to keep an open mind on this question, the implication being that God has not left Himself without witness among the peoples of the world, and that the Bible is not the only revelation made by God to humankind.

Resonance with Max Müller

It was with the German Lutheran romantic convert to Anglicanism, Max Müller, that Callaway found the most resonance. Callaway read Müller's "Lectures on the Science of Religion" in *Fraser's Magazine* in 1872. Callaway remarks, by instinct and *a priori* reasoning, I have for years held the position now taken up by Max Müller, and have regarded that position as absolutely necessary on Scriptural grounds. The opposite opinion which restricts the knowledge of God, God's saving grace and efficacious operation among men, to Christian countries, is a godless heresy whoever maintains it; and not only so, but I feel very strongly, that whoever maintains it does thereby prove that he does not understand the Christian Revelation, and that he is most effectually barring the way against its light.[121]

The basic axioms that undergird Max Müller's Science of Religion[122] also seem to have informed much of Callaway's interpretation of Zulu mythology and religious life.

Müller's first axiom was that common to all humankind and forming the substratum of all religion is the "perception of the Infinite."[123] There is, he said, a third faculty coordinated with sense and reason, the faculty of being able to "perceive the Infinite" which is the root of all religions. Müller described this faculty in German by the word, *Vernunft*, and sometimes referred to it as the "faculty of faith."[124] Müller's view of religion was immanentist and rationalist, influenced by the Romantic tradition of Schiller and Goethe. Müller used the Vedic scriptures as an example of an early form of the "perception of the Infinite". The hymns of the Rig Veda are expressions of surprise and suspicion that behind the visible and perishable world there must be something invisible, eternal, or divine. The origin of Aryan religion and mythology are seen in the names of the deities which are the great phenomena of nature: fire, water, rain, storm, sun, and moon, heaven and earth.[125] Müller argued that mythology arises out of the attempt to use language to express the "perception of the Infinite."

Callaway used a parallel concept to Müller's "perception of the Infinite" which he referred to as "religious sentiment." In his view, the instinctive nature of the religious sentiment is common to and shared by all human beings. The "human mind as to religious matters is not a mere passive *tabula rasa*, but a prepared *tabula*, like photographic film—prepared to receive the impression of light."[126] Like Max Müller, Callaway was convinced that Zulu mythology was a bearer of religious insight, perception, and experience.

The second of Max Müller's axioms was that the science of religion demonstrated that the history of the world in its religious dimensions was progressing towards Christianity. Non-Christian religions were preliminary stages.[127] The unconscious progress toward Christianity, therefore, even in the lowest expressions of religious instinct, had its legitimacy. There never was a false religion, unless one called a child a false man. The true religion of the future would be a fulfillment of all religions. It would go beyond Christianity, yet would be called Christianity.[128]

A third axiom in Max Müller's scheme was that the further one moved from the origin of a particular religion, the more corrupted it became. Müller argued that the worship of fetishes was a corrupt and degraded form of a previous higher religion. As soon as a religion was established, especially when it became the religion of a powerful state, foreign and worldly elements encroached more and more on the original foundation.[129] One implication here was that we must distinguish between 19th-century Christianity and the religion of Christ. True Christianity therefore must be the religion of Christ.[130] The study of religions called for a return to the origins. The nearer one got to the original spiritual perception of the founders, the more authentic it was. There seemed to be some internal tension in Müller's scheme. On the one hand, he had an evolutionary view of progress toward Christianity; on the other, there was a process of corruption and degradation that was somehow taking place simultaneously.

The practical implications emerging from these axioms, which Müller directed to missionaries, was a new approach:

> To the missionary, more particularly, a comparative study of the religions of mankind will be, I believe, of the greatest assistance. Missionaries are apt to look upon all other religions as something totally distinct from their own, as formerly they used to describe the languages of barbarous nations as something more like the twittering of birds than the articulate speech of men. The Science of Language has taught us that there is order and wisdom in all languages, and even the most degraded jargons contain the ruins of former greatness and beauty. The Science of Religion, I hope, will produce a similar change in our views of barbarous forms of faith and worship; and missionaries instead of looking only for points of difference will look out more anxiously for any common ground, any spark of the true light that may still be revived, any altar that may be dedicated afresh to the true God.[131]

Callaway resonated with Müller on the missionary application of the comparative method which Müller advocated in his Preface to *Essays on the Science of Religion* (1871). Müller called missionaries to this new perspective. Callaway seems to have agreed with Müller, for he suggested that "the wise philosopher or missionary will trace in the faintest feeling after God . . . an evidence that man is a religious being and made to know and hold communion with the unseen."[132] Indeed, he recognized that there may be serious errors in a religious system but argued that this should not lead one to a total rejection of it. Callaway went on to quote Schelling, "Honour the religious instinct even when manifest in dark and confused mysteries."[133]

In his survey of the writings of missionaries in southern Africa, written in 1876, Callaway stated that there was a general belief that an "endemic atheism" existed among African peoples, the possible exceptions to this view being the poet-missionary Pringle and the great traveler and medical man Livingstone.[134] However, from his own work, *The Religious System of the Amazulu*, Callaway concluded that "the Kafirs manifest as distinctly as other people the existence of the religious sentiment. . . there is no nation so debased but that it has some notion of God."[135]

While Callaway does not seem to use the language of "progress toward Christianity" in a religious evolution sense, his belief in the universal "religious sentiment" certainly came through in his writings. His analogy of photographic film would suggest that the human mind required the presence of light before any delineation can be produced. He stated that "man is naturally and differentially religious," but maintained that

> the facts of history prove that the masses of mankind are unable of themselves to make themselves truly religious either theoretically or practically, any more than they can make themselves mathematicians or geologists without the guidance and instruction of the wiser and more instructed few.[136]

Callaway saw the movement toward Christianity therefore as a matter of exposure and an educational process that built upon what was already present in the African religious experience.

Callaway felt strongly about the "knowledge of God, God's saving grace and efficacious operations" beyond the confines of the "Christian countries," but confessed that he had "been shy of being too forward with this teaching."[137] He hoped Max Müller's advocacy of a position like his own would encourage a more general shift in theological thinking.[138]

After reflecting on the Zulu tales and folklore, Callaway became convinced that they "point out very clearly that the Zulus are a degenerated people"[139] who were not in the intellectual or physical condition they were during the legend-producing period of their existence. He questioned whether the Zulus could regain the stature of previous generations, but felt confident that under the influences coming to Zulu peoples (one assumes here that Callaway means Christian missionaries), they were capable of regeneration. While Callaway did not give us the evidence for his judgments on Zulu society, one suspects that the impact of colonialism and the deterioration of traditional African societies were significant factors. Callaway found in Zulu legendary lore evidence of intellectual powers not to be despised, and throughout the tales he found evidences of tender feeling, gentleness and love common to all people.

Beneath the present traditions, Callaway discovered a "substratum of truth" which showed that the Zulu ancients were more astute than the present generation. This substratum provided the starting points with which missionaries might link the Christian message.[140]

An insight which comes through in Callaway's comparative study of Zulu mythology and religion is the conviction expressed in his preface to *Nursery Tales, Traditions and Histories of the Zulus of 1868*:

> If carefully studied and compared with corresponding legends among other people, they will bring out unexpected relationships, which will more and more force upon us the great truth, that man has everywhere thought alike, because everywhere, in every country and clime, under every tint of skin, under varying social and intellectual condition, he is still man,—one in all the essentials of man, one in that which is stronger proof of essential unity, than mere external differences are of difference of nature,—one in his mental qualities, tendencies, emotions, and passions.[141]

Max Müller, reviewing Callaway's first volume of *Nursery Tales, Traditions and Histories of the Zulus* in March, 1867, remarked:

> it is certainly surprising to see so many points of similarity between the heroes of their kraals and of our own nurseries. The introduction of animals, speaking and

acting the parts of human beings, was long considered as an original thought of
Greek and Teutonic tribes. We now find exactly the same kind of "animal fables"
among the Zulus, and Dr. Bleek had actually discovered among the Hottentots
traces of the story of Renard the Fox.[142]

The common shared human experience also seemed to have impressed those
who listened to Callaway's lecture on "Divination and Analogous Phenomena
Among the Natives of Natal" before the Anthropological Institute of Great
Britain and Ireland, May 15th, 1871. One of Callaway's objectives was to
demonstrate that the psychology of the "savage" Zulu did not differ from the
"civilized" European nearly as much as was assumed.[143]

Müller's Comparative Methods

There are two good written samples that illustrate how Callaway
implemented Müller's approach to the comparative study of religion among
the Zulu. The first is "On Divination and Analogous Phenomena Among the
Natives of Natal," which appeared in the first volume of the *Journal of the
Anthropological Institute*.[144] Callaway was then serving as the Local Secretary
of the Anthropological Institute in Natal. The second was a lecture given at
Kokstad in 1876, "On the Religious Sentiment Amongst the Tribes of South
Africa."[145]

Henry Callaway, as a medical doctor, linguist and missionary, attempted
in the article "On Divination . . ." to reconcile two contrasting world views.
These were the late nineteenth-century western scientific positivism of
Callaway's fellow social scientists, and the Zulu world view that perceived
behind the physical reality a parallel spiritual world which interfaced with it.
Callaway proposed to discuss before his fellow social scientists of the
Anthropological Society "Certain Mental Phenomena, occurring among the
Natives of Natal and which form the Basis of their System of Divination."[146]
He went on to speak of dreams, sympathy, and presentiment.

Callaway began from a position of respect, in which he refused to
belittle divination as "a system of mere imposture and deceit practiced by
intelligent men on the credulity of the ignorant."[147] In his description of
divination, Callaway was careful to point out parallels between the old
Egyptian hermits in Christian history and Zulu diviners who, in their

initiations, used techniques and processes such as fasting and bodily austerity, the results in both cases being similar: visions, inner voices, and clairvoyance.148 Also, there was among the Zulu, a certain power of divining using self-mesmerism. Callaway observed, "It is extremely interesting and remarkable that to excite this inner power into activity the Zulu use a plan precisely similar to that of certain Christian mystics when they are waiting for inspiration."149

The Zulu world interpreted and attributed dreams, self-mesmerization and various forms of divination to the activity of the spirit world. Callaway, as a medical doctor and social scientist, affirmed an absolute harmony of the universe, and therefore regarded it as a mistake to refer any peculiar phenomenon, either in the outer world or in the human mind, to the direct agency of supernatural good or evil powers, supposing that these powers override and set aside the ordinary laws of the universe. He felt no disposition to call in spirits to explain such phenomena. At the same time he held it to be "utterly unscientific" to deny the existence of spirits, or to refuse to allow them to play any part in the affairs of humans.150 It was this stance which permitted Callaway both to be sympathetic and to interpret Zulu divination from psychological and sociological perspectives. The *iziniyanga zesitupa* (thumb-diviner) related to his clients in a succinct and connected form the information he had gathered from questions in a disjointed and disconnected manner. The *iziniyanga ezadhla* held the same position among the Zulu as prophets, seers, and oracles have held among other peoples. Callaway found these diviners generally to be sensitive people who through illness, suffering, and famine discovered a latent power similar to that found among seers in other parts of the world, where one also finds mistakes mixed with truth.151

The discussion which followed Callaway's presentation to the Anthropological Institute is instructive. One respondent regarded Callaway's paper as an infliction!152 "The idea of spiritual influence over the true savage was an illusive fallacy, which no man of real science ought for a moment to entertain."153 One the other hand, another respondent remarked,

> One thing is already clear, namely that the psychology of the savage does not differ from that of the civilized man, nearly so much as might be supposed. His

susceptibilities to, and consequently his impressions from the supersensuous sphere are radically the same as those of his more highly organized and more educationally-developed brother.[154]

Callaway's lecture given at Kokstad in 1876 used a linguistic and etymological approach to the intricate ways African languages wrestle with philosophic questions. Among the Zulu and related peoples like the Gqika, the primary objects of reverence, prayer, and sacrifice were the spirits of the dead ancestors of the last few generations. There existed, however, an undercurrent of thought of "a great overruling Spirit or Power, which in some way they conceived to be the Author and Preserver of all things."[155]

When Callaway inquired of a Gqika informant from south of Kei River about the origins of things before missionaries came among them, he received the answer:

> Inyange ka'Nyange is Uhlanga, Uhlanga sprang from Uhlanga (ohlangeni). He came out of a hole.[156]

Inyanga meant a Great-Great-Grandfather and was equivalent to the Zulu *Unkulunkulu*.[157] *Inyange ka Nyange* therefore meant the Great-Great-Grandfather of the Great-Great Grandfather. The intention seemed to be to carry creation backwards as far as possible from the present time.

On one level *Uhlanga* meant a reed, but it could also be used as a personal or proper name. Callaway suggested that at first it was used as a metaphor for the Supreme Being (in much the same way we use the metaphor Spirit, and forget its material origin). Therefore the legend that man and other things have sprung from a reed was the metaphorical language by which the Zulus expressed their faith in the Primal Stem of Being. Callaway suggested that the answer he was given could be read, *Uhlanga* sprang from the Reed, the Primal Stem of Being.[158] Furthermore, Callaway observed that South African accounts of the origin of things frequently held in common the statement, *Uhlanga* was said to have sprung from *Uhlanga*. This appeared to be a contradiction, but Callaway suggested it was a necessary consequence of speculation in such questions, which urged the intellect to attempt to grasp a beginning, but in vain, because it was always pushed back, asking "and what was before?" into eternity, until it rested at last in the One Source who has no

Source, the underived being—the Great *Uhlanga*—the Primal Stem of all created things.[159]

Callaway made another projection regarding anthropomorphism from his observation that the worship of African peoples "belongs to that form which is called *ancestral*."[160] Ancestor worship is the most common form of worship throughout the world and is to some extent part of all religious traditions. The names for God among South African peoples frequently imply anthropomorphism. Among the Amaxhosa, *Umvelatanqi* implied the man *owa vela tangi*, the one who first came into being. The Gqika speak of the one who begat the *Uhlanga* which first came into being. The Zulu use the term *Unkulunkulu*, the Great-Great Grandfather.[161] Callaway noted that all our expressions used for religious notions, including the names for the Divinity, are metaphorical.[162] The human spirit urges one to pass onward from all one sees and handles, to something that belongs to another order of things. But to express what one believes of that other order, one must use words and symbols which are more or less known to be inadequate. The ancestral form of religion which applies the term "man" to the Supreme, Callaway remarked, may be regarded by some as the mistake of partially instructed minds. But they apply to God, the name of the highest form of Being with which they are acquainted.[163]

Callaway may have been projecting onto African religious language a western philosophic interpretation and understanding. However, this philosophic interpretation reflected Callaway's attempt to place Africans and Westerners in a common human religious quest. His position stood in sharp contrast to that of E. B. Tylor, whose 1891 article, "On the Limits of Savage Religion," maintained that monotheistic ideas among the "lower races" were not genuine developments of native theology but were the effects of borrowing and influence from "civilized" peoples, especially from missionaries since 1500.[164] Tylor's concept of animism as the lowest form of religion on the evolutionary scale tends to distance and differentiate the human religious quest in a manner which Callaway's experience and analysis of Zulu mythology would deny.

This chapter has traced the tension and interplay between two different agendas of missionaries and anthropologists in the study of African religions. Anthropologists of the late nineteenth century were interested in the questions of the origin of religion in human culture, while missionaries were more interested in the hermeneutical questions of communication and coming to terms with another world view.

The work of Henry Callaway, E. B. Tylor, and Henri Junod has provided evidence from the history of the development of the sciences of anthropology and comparative religion that missionaries in the imperialist era contributed significant new methods of research and understanding of religion in tribal societies. Their methodologies yielded a more sympathetic interpretation of these religions than did the earlier nineteenth-century reports or the evolutionary theories of the development of religion being articulated by such noted anthropologists as E. B. Tylor and James Frazer. Animism associated with an evolutionary theory tended to emphasize the differences between "primitive" tribal peoples and "civilized" western cultures. Evolutionary theories of religion, which have been associated with the imperialist era, lend themselves to more paternalistic attitudes and carry the potential for derogatory implications of inferiority.

The preference of the writers on animistic religions at Edinburgh 1910 was for anthropological understandings based on missionary experience and studies done by missionaries such as Callaway and Junod. Their actual field research contributed to an understanding of tribal religious traditions that was more accurate and faithful to tribal religious experience.

The missiological contributions of Callaway to the question of the relationship of Christianity to Zulu religion were developed around the concept of fulfillment. Callaway's research led him to emphasize the common and shared dimensions of the human religious experience.

Junod's contribution regarding the relationship of Christianity to Thonga religion is expressed by transformation. Religious ideas in the tribal world view which conceived of a world dominated by numerous powers and spirits is transformed into the Christian belief in the presence of the Holy Spirit. The concepts of fulfillment and transformation are not without implications of paternalism, but they move missionary theology of mission in the imperialist era toward a more human understanding of tribal peoples and toward sensitivity to the common human religious experience.

IV. German Lutheran Missiology

Missionaries of the imperialist era developed a number of different models of the relationship of Christianity to tribal religions that permitted them to affirm and integrate elements from tribal religions, as well as to reject and dissociate the two. These models reflect the definitions or understanding of religion which the missionaries employed. Furthermore, they are helpful in clarifying which aspects of traditional religion were incorporated and those that were clearly rejected. Each model had a different way of drawing that line of distinction. The models discussed here operate at two levels of Christianity, corporate and individual. On the corporate level the emphasis is on continuity; on the individual level it is on radical change.

Warneck's Contribution to the "Animistic Religions" Report

Johannes Warneck perhaps had the largest individual impact on the shape of the article entitled "Animistic Religions." Warneck was one of twenty members of Commission IV who, under the chairmanship of professor David S. Cairns, were asked to report on "The Missionary Message in Relation to the Non-Christian Religions."[1] Commission IV was divided into five sub-units to address the Commission's mandate: Animistic Religions, Chinese Religions, Japanese Religions, Islam, and Hinduism. Warneck served on the subcommittee on Animistic Religions, along with Ds. Jan Willem Gunning,[2] an administrator of the Nederlandsche Zendeling Genootschap of Rotterdam, Holland, and the Rev. Professor W. P. Paterson, D.D., University of Edinburgh, Scotland, who chaired the subcommittee. Professor Paterson was a special delegate appointed by the British executive committee.[3]

In terms of missionary experience on the field and writing on animistic religions, Warneck was the most qualified of the three.[4] He would likely have served as the chairman had it not been for the policy of the conference that for the sake of linguistic convenience, every chairman should be an English-speaking person.[5]

Johannes Warneck, at the time of Edinburgh 1910, was Missions-Inspektor for the Rheinsche Missions-Gesellschaft, in Barmen, Germany.

Warneck had been a missionary with the Batak church in Sumatra for fourteen years, from 1892 to 1906. For the first four years, he was a pioneer on the island of Samosir in Lake Toba. During the next ten years he taught and was the director of the seminary for pastors at Sipholon. He was appointed in 1908 to direct the Indonesian program from the home office in Barmen. He later returned to Sumatra in 1920 to serve as Ephorus (Superintendent) of the Church there until 1931, when he returned to become the Director of the Missions-Gesellschaft.[6] Just prior to Edinburgh in 1910, Warneck had made a significant contribution to missiology through his research into the language, literature, and beliefs of the Batak people. He published *Die Religion der Batak* in 1908. The same year, his book *Die Lebenskräfte des Evangeliums* was issued in which, through a broad psychological perspective, he traced the religious change of animist peoples. *Die Lebenskräfte des Evangeliums* was translated into English in 1909, the year after its publication in German.[7] The work exists under two English titles, *Living Forces of the Gospel* and *The Living Christ and Dying Heathenism*. The fact that this work has undergone numerous reprints[8] in both German and English, as well as translation into Danish, commends it as a work that has been recognized as a classic[9] of Protestant missionary literature. David Cairns in his "General Conclusions" to the findings of Commission IV commends Warneck's monograph, *Living Forces of the Gospel*, for its usefulness to students of comparative religion and to missionaries on the field. Cairns felt that the psychological study that Warneck had done in analyzing the influence of the Gospel on an animistic society and the process of transformation and conversion for the Batak in the East Indian Archipelago needed to be done by others in their work with animists.[10]

Warneck himself completed the questionnaire which Commission IV mailed out to select missionary leaders on the field. Among the twenty-five correspondents who completed the questionnaire regarding animistic religions, Warneck wrote the fullest and the longest of the responses—his response covered twenty-six typewritten pages.[11] It is probable that Warneck had a fuller understanding of the intent of the questions due to his position on Commission IV. W. P. Paterson, who finally collated and synthesized the twenty-five missionary responses into the article entitled "Animistic Religions," gave Warneck the most prominence, in terms of both the number and the length of quotations.[12] Both Warneck's book and his report seem to have influenced significantly the theological and missional perspectives of Paterson himself while he was editing the report on animistic religions. Paterson supplemented the twenty-five missionary responses with Warneck's *Living Forces of the Gospel* and also with Junod's study of the Bantu tribes of Delagoa Bay.[13] Evidently Junod had made available to Paterson some of the early drafts of his book, *Life of an African Tribe*, which he was in the process of writing at the time of Edinburgh 1910. We have seen earlier that Junod was acquainted with the city of Edinburgh, having been sent there by the Romande Mission as part of his orientation. Paterson used Junod as a counterpoint to Warneck at several crucial points. For example, Warneck's interpretation of Batak society was that it lacked a moral point of view; a sense of sin and conscience hardly seemed to exist.[14] On the other hand, Junod saw in Thonga society a rich folklore that taught patience, modesty, and wisdom, and illustrated the voice of conscience.[15]

On the crucial question of the attitude to be taken toward animism, Warneck seemed to stand in some tension to the consensus that Paterson discerned in the missionary reports. Paterson summarized: "Christianity is not antagonistic to other religions but is a fuller revelation of what the people instinctively groped after."[16]

Warneck, on the other hand, stated clearly, "The missionary should of course, never agree so far with the heathen religion that he presents Christian faith as a higher form of their own religion."[17] Paterson tended to tilt the consensus more in the direction of fulfillment motifs, whereas Warneck seemed to be coming from the perspective of greater distinction and otherness. Warneck's image was one of discontinuity, rather than fulfillment. He required displacement rather than fulfillment of animist traditions. One senses a tension also in his interpretation of "points of contact." For Warneck, they were not simply insights that could be expanded and fulfilled in Christianity; they were forms that needed new content. Warneck acknowledged that one should find connections for Christianity in high god concepts, such as prayer, sacrifice, etc. However, he felt that even the highest religions furnish no basis for Christianity, no equivalence, only thorough opposition to Christianity. "The one God creator of heaven and earth stands over against the vast multitude of spirits."[18]

The Development of National Churches

From the mid-nineteenth century, German, Dutch, and Swiss missionary societies were involved with a number of people's movements in tribal societies in which there were not simply individuals but families, clans, and villages that became Christians as a social unit.[19] The pietistic principle of missions had been directed to individuals, not the conversion of nations. For example, "brands to be plucked from the burning" was a motif Zinzendorf and the early Moravian missionaries often used. Most of the early German missionary societies felt the ultimate purpose of mission was to lead "heathen" individuals to God and to gather them into small communities isolated from heathen surroundings. At best, only a great number of *"ecclesiolae"* would have been possible. However, Professor Carl Mirbt of the Mission Der Brüdergemeinde, in his address to the Edinburgh 1910 Assembly, pointed out that since the second half of the nineteenth century the aim of German Missions had been the founding of national churches (*Volkskirche*).[20]

The concept of the national church had been articulated and promoted by Gustav Warneck, the father of Johannes Warneck. Indeed, German theology from Schleiermacher on had affirmed an essential relationship between nationality and the Kingdom of God on earth. Similarly, Karl Graul, founder and director of the Lutheran Leipzig Mission Society (1844–1860) and Gustav Warneck, Missions Inspector at Barmen from 1871 and Professor of Science of Mission at Halle from 1896, called for the creation of indigenous churches. National indigenous churches were to be developed, taking into account the social and ethnic structure of a people. Gustav Warneck has been called the founder of the scientific study of missionary principles. He articulated the concept of the national church in the missions journal he founded in 1874, *Allgemeine Missionszeitschrift*. Warneck's *Evangelische Missionslehre* (Evangelical Theory of Missions, five volumes 1892–1903) grew out of the pietist doctrine of Jacob Spener's *"ecclesiolae in ecclesia."* In essence this was the "small flock" within the Christian environment, in tension with the national church, which was the less than fully committed mass church. Warneck's main contribution to the theology of mission was the attempt to combine the salvation of the individual and the Christianizing of nations (*Volkschristianisierung*).[21]

Gustav Warneck's theory saw no contradiction between the two objectives, the individual and the national church. The founding of the church in a missionary setting, he declared, was at least a two-stage process. The first stage was the conversion of individuals. In this stage the highly committed individuals within a church, "the little flock," often found themselves alienated from the culture and society. The second objective was the development of "people's churches" (or a national church) which should lead to such a Christianization of whole peoples that in the end people live in a Christian atmosphere. The Christianization of nations followed the conversion of individuals. The church, "the little flock," of already converted, was God's instrument for Christianizing the nation. The national church had two functions: it was a kind of school that instructed and familiarized the nation with the Gospel, taught the masses and led them to Christ. Secondly, the national church provided the framework within which the hidden or invisible church, known only to God, could be built like a cathedral within its scaffolding.[22]

The concept of the national church was not original or new with Johannes Warneck. It was a legacy of mid-19th-century pietist mission theology, which had been developed most fully by his father Gustav Warneck. Gustav Warneck was the Missions Inspector at Barmen in 1871, and became professor of the science of mission at Halle in 1896. He articulated the concept of the national church in his journal, *Allgemeine Missionszeitschrift*, founded in 1874, and in his *Evangelische Missionslehre* (five volumes, 1892–1903).[23] Gustav Warneck died in 1910, just before the Edinburgh conference, but his concept of building national churches had percolated through most of the German-speaking missionary societies and therefore was represented in the German-speaking participants and respondents to the questionnaire.

This German pietist theology of mission proclaimed, on the one hand, the need for independent indigenous churches; but it opened itself to the recreation of a Christianized society on the model of a Christian Europe.[24]

Ludwig Nommensen and the Batak

The Batak Church is an example of an independent indigenous church within this German Lutheran tradition. The emergence of the Batak Church has been regarded as one of the prime examples of the planting of the church through the conversion of a tribal society. The Batak are the largest and ethnically the most homogeneous Christian group in Indonesia, even though they are located between two strong Muslim groups. Presently to be Batak is synonymous with being Christian. Ludwig Nommensen worked among the Batak from 1861 to his death in 1918. In 1869 he moved into the Silingdung Valley, and in 1871 he carried the mission to Toba. These have been the two most prominent centers where the Batak are largely Christian, and therefore they have been the subject of close examination by missiologists and historians of Christian world mission.[25]

To appreciate Warneck's book, *The Living Forces of the Gospel*, it is necessary to acquire some understanding of the factors that contributed to the remarkable growth of the Batak church in the period up to Edinburgh 1910. Missionary work under the Rhenish Missionary Society of Barmen, Germany, was opened among the Batak in 1861 by Ludwig Nommensen. Thirty years earlier there had been an abortive attempt by American Board missionaries, Munson and Lymann, who died at the hands of the Batak.[26]

Nommensen's first converts, eight adults and five children, were expelled from their village. Their presence changed his mission station into a small village in the prescribed manner of a Batak *huta* (village). Although Nommensen had indeed hoped to establish a Christian community, he had serious objections to the enforced isolation of Batak Christians from the common life of their people. Nommensen found himself, according to *adat* (customary law), to have become a *radja* (village chief) responsible for the behavior of his villagers at *Huta Dome* (Village of Peace). Whenever possible, Nommensen sought to recognize the authority of *adat* in civil disputes, and accommodated the Batak *adat* into the Christian way of life, i. e., regulation of marriage customs, kinship structure, and the filing of teeth, a custom which he hoped would die out.

Nommensen discovered in his own experience that each village chief was the personified *adat*, who also personified the community, and whose responsibility was to preserve order and equilibrium. This harmony was embodied in the notion of *adat*, commonly translated as "customary law," but was much more complex, having religious meanings and being enforced by supernatural sanctions. Deviation brought infertility, disease, famine, and crop failure.[27]

The *adat* was the law governing the common life of the nation. Nommensen and Warneck found that it dealt with all the problems of family life as well as social, economic and political activities. In short, *adat* was the source of Batak identity. Merle Davis says, "The Rhenish Mission dug through the upper layer of dirt and cruel superstition to the granite in the Batak character and built on this foundation."[28]

Merle Davis, in accounting for the rapid growth of the Batak Church, claimed that the incorporation of *adat* within Christian teaching and practice by Nommensen and the Rhenish missionaries was a rare insight which emphasized the similarities to Christian practice and in this way harmonized the new life with Batak cultural heritage.[29] The Swedish missiologist and church historian Bishop Bengt Sundkler adds that Nommensen took the *adat* and attempted to give it a theological interpretation. While he rejected specific aspects of Batak culture which he felt to be anti-Christian, he generally "regarded *adat* as a *praeparatio*, or rather as an attempt to interpret the orders of creation and natural law."[30] The church became the cultural as well as the spiritual home of the Batak Christian community. Merle Davis identified two factors of vital importance which made it possible for the Rhenish missionaries to come to terms with the *adat*. The first factor was the minimum of idol worship and sacrifice to the gods which is so often bound up with the cultural inheritance of many non-Christian people. Second, *adat* enjoined fidelity in the marriage relationship and provided a strict code of public morals. The fact that this code was often broken did not impair the respect in which it was held by the Batak.[31]

Hendrik Kraemer, himself a missionary in Indonesia, articulated the political dimensions that contributed to the growth of the Batak Church. He saw the coming of the Dutch government as an external cause of the church's growth. In 1876, after twelve years of work, there were 2000 Batak Christians, but each year following thousands were added. Kraemer recognized 1876 as the turning point in the growth of the church, and pointed out that it was that same year that the Dutch government took possession of the Silindung Valley and a military expedition penetrated as far as Toba, the region of earliest response to Christianity.[32] The coming of the Dutch government impressed the Batak with the dawn of a new age. Kraemer states that when in 1883 the Bataks, led by Singamangaradja, were defeated by a small Dutch occupation force,

> the embodiment of the past lost the day to the new age embodied by the civil administration and missions . . . Paganism, inwardly defeated, witnessed the fall of its last stronghold: isolation . . . considering their pagan way of thinking, this fact must have greatly encouraged their willingness to accept the change.[33]

At the time of Nommensen's death[34] in 1918 the Batak community had 180,000 members and 510 schools with 32,700 pupils enrolled. The church was led by 34 ordained Batak *pendata* (pastors), 788 teachers, and 2200 elders.[35] Merle Davis, writing in 1945, eighty years after Nommensen began his work among the Batak, reported that more than 400,000 Bataks or one-third of the nation were enrolled in the Christian Church.[36]

Warneck's Two Levels of Conversion

Johannes Warneck's book, *The Living Christ and The Dying Heathenism*, which was highly respected at Edinburgh 1910, is helpful in understanding Warneck's theory of the process of conversion of tribal people. The book is a theological, missiological interpretation of the experience of German Lutheran Pietist missionaries from the mid-nineteenth century onward who suddenly discovered themselves to be participants in the large people's movements into the church from tribal societies. Three such groups will be included in this chapter: the Bataks in Sumatra, the Kols in India, and the Toradja in the Celebes.

Warneck and his colleagues were aware of and able to articulate the two very different understandings of religion operative between them and the

Batak. Warneck has articulated well the warmly pietistic understanding of religion in his vision of the mature convert, where the emphasis is upon personal experience of the forgiveness of sins, and the love of God embodied in the crucifixion of Jesus Christ. The accent is clearly upon the individual, and upon the committed community of the devout, the "Gemeinde," who are the *ecclesiolae in ecclesia*. They provided the moral tension for renewal of the moral tone in the Christianized society.[37] Religion is a response to revelation; and for the Pietists, this is centered in a personal relationship of the individual to the Living Christ.

On the other hand, for Warneck, "animistic and polytheistic heathenism" with all its religious forms is not a religion in the sense of revelation and a relationship to God.[38] Warneck characterized Batak religion as "tradition, and the religious person as one who observes the tradition and customs. The *adat* (custom) is the holy, though unwritten book, of which the ancestors were the authors, and now are the strict guardians."[39] Worship therefore is essentially reverence for the ancestors. There is no clear distinction between religion and social life.[40] Religion is thus worldly oriented and reflects the society. Or, to say it in the words of a Lutheran missionary in New Guinea, Christian Keysser, "Primitive religion is primarily religiously sanctioned group solidarity founded on the biological fact of blood relation."[41] Warneck's book, *The Living Christ and Dying Heathenism,* is an attempt to understand the "psychological processes" of transformation and conversion.[42] Warneck wanted to examine the "intricate paths along which a heathen heart pushes upwards because few converted Christians are capable of accurate analysis of their experience."[43]

The book is divided into three sections. Warneck first set out to present "as faithful an account as possible of the social, moral and religious practices of the Batak."[44] He then compared his observations with those of fellow missionaries to assess the religious beliefs characteristic of tribal cultures and to come to an estimate of the nature and power of animistic heathenism.[45]

In the second section, Warneck examined the conflicts between tribal religions and Christianity, particularly religion as a "national affair" opposed to personal experience, and the rejection of Christian morals. Warneck looked at the agencies that clear the way for Christianity: the desire in these societies for health and education; the recognition of the superiority of western technology, the influence of "Christian colonial powers," the personal life of the evangelist, and the special "truth seeking" individuals in traditional societies who were open to Christianity.

This was all prelude to the central part of the book, the third section, "The Victorious Forces of the Gospel." Here Warneck examined the steps of the transformation or conversion in a tribal society. Warneck summarized the process in three stages. There was first a break with the multitude of spiritual powers in their world; the chaotic interaction of spiritual forces that hold people in fear are replaced by a child-like trust in the one Living God. This often was seen as liberation or an experience of deliverance, and it was frequently accompanied by a people's movement into the church. At the second stage there was the apprehension of the love of God and of personal surrender. In the light of the love of Jesus Christ, there emerged a knowledge of sin and the longing for forgiveness. The third stage was that of moral renewal, which was felt not as demand but as an experience of faith.46

Warneck's negative view of the religious life of the Batak and tribal societies grew out of his conviction, rooted in Biblical models, that animistic religions were in a state of degeneration. Without serious exegesis, Warneck cited a number of Pauline texts and passages from Isaiah and applied them to animistic religions. He cited Romans 1:18–23, Ephesians 4:18, 5:7–8, Acts 26:18, Isaiah 42:7 and 9:5, which describe the Gentile world in darkness and a growing blindness in moral and religious matters. This style of exegesis was rooted in the *pietistische Biblizismus* which he inherited from his father Gustav.47 And indeed, as K. D. Garrison pointed out, the whole book, *The Living Christ and Dying Heathenism*, can be read as a footnote to the first chapter of the Epistle to the Romans: the early chapters show man in his estrangement from God, the later chapters show that in Sumatra also the Gospel demonstrates the power of God unto salvation.48

Several interlocking issues were the focus of Warneck's critique of Batak religion: the individual versus the corporate, and the interaction of fear and morality. Around these issues, the arguments of this book were woven. Warneck held the religious life of the Batak and animistic societies responsible for the moral and social misery, the widespread slavery, the low estate of women, the near universal poverty, and the tyranny of the chiefs.49 Warneck had a very negative view of life in tribal society:

Animistic heathenism deludes men as to the worth of his personality, of that within him which is Divine. It deprives him of his freedom, his personal spiritual life, and degrades him to a will-less, thoughtless number of a flock of cattle . . . It is not mere error into which the poor animist has fallen; a positive lying power has mastered the ignorant. Left to itself heathenism might have lost God and neglected His worship. But it could not have created such a caricature of religion for its own torment unless [there was] some lying evil power taking advantage of its ignorance . . . They give the impression of a people who are misled and deceived in the most shameful fashion and who all the while believe absolutely in the lies by which they are being hypnotised.[50]

Warneck's rather sharp and thorough critique of animistic religions demonstrated very little sympathy for the evolutionary hypothesis regarding the origins of religion being put forward in the science of religion by E. B. Tylor. Warneck caustically remarked that he had more confidence in the research and study of missionaries, who had a more thorough knowledge of the language and took the time to enter the sanctuary of the pagan. "Scholars who do not have first hand data of observation are in danger of constructing heathen religions at their study table."[51] In another passage Warneck continued the same thought:

Animistic heathenism is not a transition stage to a higher religion . . . Let them produce facts to prove that animistic heathenism somewhere and somehow evolved upwards towards a purer knowledge of God, real facts, not imaginary constructions of such an evolution. Any form of animism known to me has no lines leading to perfection, but only incontestable marks of degeneration.[52]

Also, in contrast to Tylor and the evolutionists, Warneck and all the other missionaries answering the questionnaires found evidence for a belief in a supreme or high god in tribal societies. This to Warneck was not an evidence of development from spirit worship. Rather he agreed with the Scandinavian Lutheran Bishop and Professor of Natural Theology, Nathan Soderblom, who stated:

We must not believe that the religion of the lower uncivilized peoples and tribes is a faithful picture of the earliest religion . . . their beliefs mark a fall from a more childlike, but purer and stronger, religious conception. That is especially the case

with those tribes and peoples among whom sorcery and magic have completely
stifled the religious sense of reverence and trust.[53]

In spite of his strong judgments against animistic religions, Warneck used a
quotation taken from a Japanese Christian convert to recommend the attitude a
missionary was to take toward people of another religious tradition:

> to Paul and people of kindred spirit, heathenism is not something to be laughed at,
> or even to be pitied, but something to be understood, something into which one
> must think oneself with consideration and Christian kindness.[54]

But beyond this sympathetic understanding, Warneck's view was not one
of fulfillment but of a decisive break. "The Christian faith should never be
presented as a higher form of their own religion."[55]

Ferdinand Hahn and the Kols

The development of Christianity among the Kols was one of the early
Lutheran experiences of the conversion of a tribal people. The Gossner
Mission[56] originally came to work in Calcutta in 1845. The missionaries soon
found they could not ignore the street sweepers outside their doors. These
people were neither Hindus nor Bengalis, but Kols from Chota Nagpur in the
State of Bihar. It was among these Kol people that the Gossner missionaries
were led to establish their ministry in the State of Bihar. The Kols consisted
of a number of distinct tribes, such as the Munda, Oraon, Ito, Santals, and
others living in the hills. (The word *Kol,* like *Bantu,* means simply "people".)
Together these tribes numbered roughly about one and a half million.[57] They
were the remnants of the "aborigines," *adibasi,* who had been pushed into the
hills by Aryan peoples moving into the Ganges basin from the north and
northwest. In the face of the encroaching *Zamindars* (foreign farmers and
landlords), the Kols were being threatened with loss of traditional homelands
and oppressed by illegal rents and forced labor.

The Oroans, like many tribal societies, were attracted by the great
freedom they found in the personal, ethical, and monotheistic faith proclaimed
by the Gossner missionaries. Hahn observed that the Oroan people's
movement into the church was motivated by a search for freedom from the

ever-present fear of malevolent spirits, and dissatisfaction with the "consequences of their foolish belief in witchcraft, which is such a terrible source of strife and enmity among them . . . "[58]

> But above these two special reasons for dissatisfaction with their own religion, there is the general desire of getting rid of the oppression they have to suffer socially from the hands of their Hindu landlords, and the conviction that ignorance, want of education, of soberness of morality has brought them to the condition of semi-slavery. This widespread dissatisfaction with their social condition, the desire for knowledge, for a human-like existence, has proved the principal motion (motive) with thousands of the Oroan and Munda people to embrace Christianity.[59]

To the Kols, despised and rejected by major segments of Indian society, the Lutheran Gossner Mission offered a new future. These tribal people, whose material future was menaced by the encroachment of more powerful communities, gave a willing ear to any evangelist who brought news of a Savior and friend who could cast out the spirit of fear and liberate from bondage, both material and spiritual. Schools, medical care, improved agricultural methods, and a new sense of community all accelerated a people's movement among the Oroan and Munda into the Lutheran Church at the end of the nineteenth and early twentieth century. The support of missionaries in court cases regarding land disputes between the Kols and the Zamindars was a critical factor in the missionaries gaining the confidence of the Kols.[60]

In 1857, the year of the Indian Mutiny, there were 600 baptized converts and 2000 unbaptized inquirers. When the missionaries fled back to Calcutta from Bihar during the mutiny, the Christian converts were severely persecuted, but held firm to their new faith. The next ten years saw a remarkable movement into the church. By 1868, there were over 10,000 baptized Christians.[61] A division among the Lutheran missionaries brought the Anglican Society for the Propagation of the Gospel into Chota Nagpur. By 1872, there were 17,000 Lutherans and 5000 Anglicans.[62] The Roman Catholics entered in the 1880s and were also engaged in the mass movement of these same tribal peoples into the church.[63]

At the time Ferdinand Hahn responded to the questionnaire, there was a Christian community of about a quarter million, and the Gossner Mission had a history going back about 65 years.[64] Hahn himself was a veteran missionary of 42 years, having come to Chota Nagpur in 1868. The first eight years he taught in the Gossner Mission Theological College in Ranchi, and from 1877–1901, he worked especially among the aboriginal tribe called the Oraon or Kurnkh, at Lohardagga. In his later years he served in Purulia as the Superintendent of one of the largest leprosy hospitals in India.[65]

Hahn was linguistically inclined, and he produced an extensive 697-page Oroan-English Dictionary, *A Grammar of the Oroan Language* of 311 pages, and later a book of *Oroan Folk-Lore*, published in 1905.[66] The following year Hahn issued a collection of sayings, fables, and songs, *Blicke in die Geisteswelt der Heidnischen Kols: Sammlung von Sagen, Märchen und Liedern der Oroan in Chota Nagpur.*[67] Hahn's writings on Oroan religion included an article, "Some Notes on the Religion and Superstitions of the Oroans,"[68] and a monograph, *Einführung in das Gebiet der Kols-Mission: Geschichte, Gebräuche, Religion und Christianisierung der Kols.*[69]

Hahn stated that in his responses to the questionnaire of Commission IV he drew upon his book, *Einführung in das Gebiet der Kols-Mission*, and his collection of Kol folklore published under the title, *Blicke in die Geistwelt der heidnischen Kols.* His approach to the religion of the Kols is one of compassion. He looked upon it as the attempt of fellow human beings to grapple with the great questions of life: whence evil, whence death, and how to overcome them? From whence does one receive comfort, hope, and secure peace for the afterlife? The missionary, according to Hahn,

> should closely study the religion of the people among whom he labors and try to find out the sparks of truth which he must expect to meet, because even to the heathen God has revealed himself in some way. Besides many of the nations of the earth possess something of the original revelation from the dawn of human history to the present time through oral traditions.[70]

Perhaps because Hahn was working amongst a self-conscious minority of socially disadvantaged people who experienced discrimination, he felt that

> The preacher should understand that he has to do with fellow men who are groping in the dark after the light, who are waiting in the dim light of stars for the rising of the sun, who are struggling to get out of the mire and to set their foot on a rock.[71]

Even in this setting, where the Oroan people's openness to religious conversion might have been primarily because of deep social needs, Hahn showed a human compassionate consideration for their religious traditions. He wanted to try to distinguish, in the ceremonies and usages of the religious life of the Oroan people, "the cry for God, the cry of the soul for redemption, the longing for eternal life and happiness"[72] rather than to focus on the dark and the demonic dimensions. Hahn was open to

> recognizing what is good in the religion of his people, and developing the small beginnings of spiritual life in them, gently leading them on to the full truth as it is in Jesus, bearing up patiently with their errors, exposing them principally by putting the full revelation before them, not by vehemently denouncing them, that's the attitude which to my mind the preacher should take toward the religion of the people among whom he labors.[73]

Hahn's study and collection of Oroan sayings, myths, and legends opened him to seeing many "points of contact" of similar and parallel religious motifs and ideas to which the Christian gospel could connect. Hahn's questionnaire had an extensive list of such motifs, beginning with the idea of a personal God who was good and "does no evil to men."[74] It is interesting that Hahn, who was the superintendent of a large leprosy hospital, included the Oroan story that God became a leper, and that he entered the fire of the furnace kindled by the Asurs, for the purpose of saving the world and killing those monsters.[75]

In contrast to Warneck, Hahn did not emphasize the radical break and discontinuity between the Christian faith and the religious world of the Oroans. The place where the experience of Hahn and Warneck came closest together is in response to the question, "What elements of the Christian Gospel and life have the greatest power of appeal?" Both of them found the idea of Christ as the deliverer from evil powers, demons and the devil, to be one that caught the attention of people who were in constant fear of evil spirits. Hahn went on to say that the Christ who heals the sick, feeds the hungry, and has compassion on the poor and despised was one who attracted the Oroans, who were poor, despised, and oppressed. Prayer was another element already present in Oroan traditional beliefs and practice, and within the church prayer was given a special place, especially prayers in times of sickness and affliction—the pastor was always asked to pray for the sick and dying, not only among Christians but among other Oroans also.[76]

Like Warneck, Hahn observed that Christ's death as atonement for sins, Christ as the Savior from guilt and from the power of sin were not understood until a later point when, as Christians, the people acquired some knowledge and sense of sin.[77]

Warneck saw the solidarity of the clan and the sense of corporate identity, belonging, and decision-making as the chief hindrance, while Hahn said, "As to the opposition among the aboriginal tribes, the preacher of the Gospel scarcely meets with it at all."[78]

Albert C. Kruyt and the Toradja

One of the more interesting questionnaire responses came from Albert C. Kruyt (1869–1949). Kruyt went out to Indonesia in 1890 as a missionary of Nederlandsche Zendeling Genootschap (Dutch Missionary Society). In his response to the Commission IV questionnaire sent to him in 1909, Kruyt said "We have no converts till now."[79] It was almost nineteen years since he had begun the work among the Bare'e Toradja in the Central Celebes around Lake Posso. Before the arrival of the Dutch in Indonesia, the Toradja were an isolated mountain dwelling people with minimal contact with the outside world. Their family and clan structures had not been significantly challenged by any outside forces. Kruyt had no converts, not because he could not persuade individuals to be baptized, but on account of his respect for the clan unity and the collective character of the tribe and its decision-making processes.

> An individual cannot accept Christianity, unless he is willing to be excluded from the communal life. The only way is to exert Christianizing influence on the whole clan en bloc till God in His time draws the clan as a whole to conversion to Christ.[80]

Although Kruyt was Dutch Reformed, and Warneck was Lutheran, both took seriously the social structures of the society in understanding religion.

Kruyt was joined by Nicolaus Adriani (1865–1926) of the Dutch Bible Society. Adriani was a linguist who had completed his studies of the

"Languages and Literature of the East Indian Archipelago" at Leyden University in 1903.[81] Kruyt and Adriani were close lifelong colleagues. Their "Christianizing influence on the whole clan" was guided by several principles. First, people cannot make the Bible fully their own if the linguistic form reflects that of the original or of a western version. The translator needs to use, as fully as possible, the linguistic and stylistic forms of the receptor language. In the telling of Bible stories, Kruyt tried to avoid the need for further explanation, therefore Pharisees, publicans, and sinners were represented to the Toradja as noblemen and slaves. Toradja noblemen were certain of a good place in the kingdom of the dead, and the disdain with which the nobility looked down on slaves equaled that of Pharisees toward publicans and sinners.[82]

The second emphasis, and the missionary's first and continuing task, was the sympathetic study of the people's central religious, cultural, and psychological concepts. Only if the missionary began with them would his or her message be in any way intelligible. Kruyt gave considerable attention to cultural and religious dimensions. In 1906, he published *Het Animisme in den Indischen Archipel*,[83] a work of over five hundred pages of rather meticulous observations and descriptions. Kruyt drew largely upon a wide range of sources. The major Dutch source was G. A. Wilken's *Het Animisme by de Volken van den Indischen Archipel* (Vol.I, 1884; Vol.II, 1885). Kruyt was acquainted with the leading English anthropologist James Frazer and E. B. Tylor's *Primitive Culture* and *The Early History of Mankind*. He also had read R. H. Codrington's classic, *The Melanesians* (1891).

Kruyt's attempt to maintain continuity and links between the belief structures of the Toradja and Christianity enabled Kruyt to see many points of contact and similarity, for example in their creation stories, sacrifice, and priesthood.[84] But the Toradja also challenged Kruyt's linkage in a dramatic incident. The Toradja referred to the creator or high god as "the Kneader." When Kruyt referred to the God of the Bible by the name of "the Kneader," his listeners answered, "Listen, white man, you are still young, but when you have been with us longer you will realize who the Kneader is, and what he is like. For he is not at all like your description."[85] Kruyt concluded:

> When we tried to teach the people who God is, calling Him by their name, they generally contradicted us, saying that their god was not such as we described, and proved this by telling stories from their own mythology. So we were obliged to find a new name for God.[86]

Kruyt distanced himself from the viewpoint of missionaries of former days which condemned and regarded the heathen religion as an inspiration of the devil. Kruyt preferred to "consider this religion as a deviation, an alienation of the true knowledge of God."[87] He preached to the Toradja that he and his fellow missionaries had

> come to bring them the true religion of their ancestors, not anything new, but something very old; God has always been the same, but men have fallen off from Him. They did not see God; they forgot Him and clung to men, who came on the foreground and were made gods after their death.[88]

Kruyt worked from a concept of an original revelation from which there has been a process of degeneration. He therefore attempted to go back in history to find common ground. Going back to the beginning was the basis for the belief that God was universal, for He was the God of their ancestors, who are also our ancestors. It is interesting to note that Kruyt used linguistic data from neighboring tribes to demonstrate the relationship of Toradja to their neighbors and by analogy, therefore, the oneness of the human race. Once persuaded of the oneness of the human race, the Toradja were obliged to come to the conclusion that all these people could only have one God. One of the principal arguments for rejecting Christianity, the supposition that each people must have their own god, was shaken. The Christian teaching on the unity of God, Kruyt claimed, had a "strong and deep impression on the Toradja."[89]

Kruyt and Adriani tried to work from a perspective of respect. "We take the utterances of heathendom in earnest, and we try to understand their foundations."[90] On the key ethical issues of slavery and polygamy, Kruyt claimed the Toradja instinctively felt polygamy and slavery to be incompatible with Christianity, although the missionaries never spoke against these evils.[91] Kruyt did work from the positive side, demonstrating and teaching the principles and beliefs of Christianity. Women in particular were attracted to

Christianity by the teaching of monogamy. The Dutch missionaries did, however, express their strong disapproval of the annual raids against tribes considered the Toradjas' arch enemies. However, the missionaries' outspoken views about intertribal warfare, according to Kruyt, did not make the slightest impression.[92]

Schools, medical services, and a conscious policy of respect for the collective character of the tribe and the people's fear of the vengeance of the ancestors, were ingredients of change. At the same time, the Dutch colonial administration was establishing "law and order," regulations, and prohibitions that caused breaches in Toradja society for the missionary to enter and which opened the way for collective acceptance of a new faith.

On the other hand, it was Kruyt's sensitivity to the central value placed on community solidarity that gave him perspective and patience to work for a corporate decision of the clan to become Christians all together. Kruyt encouraged the enthusiastic individuals attending his school who wished to become Christians to wait for the whole tribe.

> In 1908 . . . a great festival was held in honour of the ancestors. It took the form of a farewell feast, in which the tribe together bade farewell to their hereditary faith. At a great service on Sunday, July 4, 1909, the supreme chief Papa in Wunte issued a proclamation: 'Clan chiefs and village head men, gather together all your groups and speak to them about the word of the Christians. Then we shall be able to arrive at a decision together.' On Christmas Day, of the same year hundreds were baptized, the supreme chief first of all. It was a decisive breakthrough, since then the tribe has become wholly Christian.[93]

Kruyt spoke of the "gradual appropriation of Christianity." He recognized that in a group conversion the Toradja would go through a period of "magical or superstitious Christianity" because they had no other mental framework. The missionary could not promote the magical interpretation of baptism and communion, or the fertility rites associated with the ancestors at Easter. Yet missionaries, Kruyt claimed, should not treat the magical and superstitious in a rough manner or exterminate it by force.[94] Kruyt felt it was better to have magical Christianity, and to recognize the magical dimensions associated with Christianity, rather than having certain magical conceptualizations and practices condemned by the missionary and then go underground. The danger, as Kruyt saw it, was that unless the magical interpretation was an open option at first, new Christians would be Christians only in certain habits or ceremonies which did not touch the heart and life, and for the rest they would remain heathen.[95] Kruyt would rather recognize areas where a dual life was being lived, than have people accept certain ceremonies and customs of Christianity, while the really meaningful dimensions and center of their lives were still controlled by the structure and values of their traditional religion.

Perhaps the key question in the emphasis on continuity and the gradual process of Christianization that Kruyt envisioned was whether there was that central transformation of a world view around which the other elements of a culture or religious system could be tested and reoriented. Unfortunately, Kruyt does not clarify whether that kind of transformation took place, nor whether that controlling vision rested with the missionary or with Toradja leadership.

This chapter has described the German Lutheran approach to tribal religious traditions articulated by Johannes Warneck at Edinburgh 1910 and illustrated by examples from the work of Ludwig Nommensen, Ferdinand Hahn, and A. C. Kruyt.

Perhaps the two missionaries who contrasted most in this group were Warneck and Kruyt. Warneck worked from a strong sense of discontinuity between Christianity and tribal religious traditions. He saw the fundamental breaking point as the acceptance of a monotheistic understanding of God who overrules the spiritual powers that appear to dominate the world in tribal religious traditions. For Warneck, the "points of contact" with other religions were not the points of commonality of theological ideas or concepts, but those points of human need and search. He uses the analogy,

> The point of connection is like a hook that will hold the picture, but the picture is something totally different. There may be a dim sense of a Supreme Deity, but the picture of God is completely different. The one God creator of heaven and earth over against the 8 million lays the axe at the root of superstition.[96]

Kruyt worked from a more gradual approach and saw continuity which shocked even the Toradjas. Kruyt worked more from the concept of fulfillment.

For Warneck, the center was the personal discovery of a monotheistic faith that challenged and transformed all the other spiritual powers in an animistic world view. Kruyt, on the other hand, was prepared to respect the corporate decision making process of the tribe or clan. He was aware that group conversion did not lead to personal inner conviction, which he felt took place only in the minds of the few. Ultimately the people, Kruyt felt, must develop individuality before the full claims of a personal surrender could be laid on those who had become Christian in a group movement into the church.[97]

Johannes Warneck took a strong stance that called for a clear discontinuity and a radical break between Christianity and other religions. Christian doctrine regarding the fall and human degeneration apart from God figured more significantly in Warneck's view of discontinuity, whereas Kruyt worked from the common human experiences of life and emphasized the continuity and fulfillment themes. Warneck's stance on the individual God/human relationship could be seen as typical of the stereotype articulated in Sawyerr's comments in the opening chapter. The Lutheran understandings of the orders of creation helped him to see more continuity on the social level.

The general model which these missionaries used was a two-step conversion process. The Lutheran doctrine of the orders of creation provided a high respect and regard for the tribal structures and organization of society. There was respect for the solidarity and stability of the community, and also for those structures within the life of the church.

The founding of national churches in tribal societies aimed at the Christianization of the whole society and created in these societies a religious environment parallel to the Christianized Europe that the missionaries had known. There were two levels of Christian commitment in the pietist model of *ecclesiolae in ecclesia*.[98] The first level was sympathetic to the corporate understanding of religion in tribal societies. The second level of the conversion process grew out of the pietist distinction between the *ecclesia* and the *ecclesiolae*. The movement was toward a more individualist, personal, and ethically oriented religious experience. This second level moved toward an understanding of religious experience more in keeping with the missionaries' own understanding of religion as a personal relationship with

God. The polarity of this two-level approach held in tension the individual versus the corporate understandings of religion.

V. British and American Missiology

Edinburgh 1910 was predominantly an English-speaking conference. One thousand of the twelve hundred delegates were British and American. It should be noted that of the twenty-five missionaries responding to the questionnaire, nineteen were speakers of English, of whom thirteen were British and three were Americans. While numerically the British still dominated Commission IV, the German and Dutch missionary societies were represented to a much higher degree on this commission than their representation in the conference generally.

The Lutheran Pietist approach to religion in tribal societies introduced a two-level conversion process. The initial level respected the solidarity, stability, and integrity of the community. The second level satisfied the personal, individual, and ethical dimensions of religion which were at the center of the missionaries' own religious experience.

By contrast, the British and American approaches to African societies emphasized human rights and justice-related issues. There was no single spokesperson for this group, like Warneck who articulated the German Pietist missiology. Rather, British and American missions in Africa at the turn of the century were still under the shadow of David Livingstone and the anti-slavery movement, committed to the transformation of African societies by the introduction of "commerce, civilization, and Christianity."

The impact of western economics, politics and culture on African societies provided the context and a significant driving force behind British and American missionary understanding and attitudes towards African traditional religion. This chapter is comprised of four different models of interrelationships between African traditional religion and the Christian faith from four respondents to Commission IV on Animistic Religions: Donald Fraser, W. D. Armstrong, Robert H. Nassau, and Godfrey Callaway.

Donald Fraser: Moral Reconstruction

Donald Fraser (1870–1933) was a typical example of a British missionary in the high imperialist era (1880 to 1920). Religious motifs like "moral regeneration"[1] and "construction rather than destruction"[2] run through Fraser's writings and are consistent with the missionary vision of the times, which integrated commerce, civilization, and Christianity. There is also a spirit of optimism and confidence that permeates Fraser's writings, and which is reflected even in the titles of some of his larger books, *The Future of Africa* (1910), *The New Africa* (1927), and *Winning a Primitive People* (1914).

Fraser's Background and Training

The high imperialist era was also the high missionary era.[3] There was at this time an explosion in the number of missionaries sent out[4] and a growth in the number of new missionary societies. A new kind of missionary began to emerge. The universities, Cambridge above all, produced a great number of volunteers. In fact, students began to see themselves as responsible for world evangelism. There emerged on university and college campuses in the U.S. in 1886 and Britain in 1892 the Student Volunteer Movement, which brought students into missions as never before. The movement's slogan was "The Evangelization of the World in this Generation."[5] Among its leaders were John R. Mott, Robert E. Speer, and Donald Fraser. It was a time when evangelical piety placed a new emphasis upon consecration and sacrifice. As an example of this, evangelicals of all denominations were finding one another and developing vision and encouragement at the Keswick Conventions, which were annual meetings "for the promotion of Scriptural holiness."[6]

British missions in Africa during this era concentrated in areas that were, or were to become, part of the British Empire. In Uganda, Nyasaland, and Bechuanaland, missionary occupation was intimately associated with the establishment of British rule. These missionaries were products of their time; "almost without dissent they believed in the essential beneficence of the empire."[7] In Nyasaland, the Scottish missionaries asked for the extension of the British Protectorate to prevent the Portuguese from claiming territory they did not hold and to halt the ongoing slave trade of the Sultan of Zanzibar with the Yao slavers.[8] The missionary grounds of the call for the extension of the British Protectorate in Nyasaland thus appear to have been practical and missionary, rather than imperial.

Donald Fraser was the son of a pastor of the Free Church of Scotland and was educated at the University of Glasgow at the Free Church Hall. Fraser studied moral philosophy there under Edward Caird, but Fraser's wife, Agnes, claims that he was untouched by Edward Caird's powerful influence, which forced many others to examine and re-fashion familiar and traditional beliefs. Fraser spoke more enthusiastically later in life of Principal John Caird's sermons.[9] Fraser was drawn much more to the evangelical tradition represented in the Keswick Conventions. He first went to the Keswick Convention in 1891, where 3000 people of evangelical persuasion gathered from Anglican and Free Churches, many of them university students. These meetings also attracted the upwardly mobile classes in industry and business, like Carlisle, a director of the London and Northwestern Railway Company, and the older Evangelicals, such as the granddaughter of Sir Fowell Buxton, one of the leaders of the successful anti-slavery movement of the previous century. The chief message was the need for holiness of life, the surrender of heart and life to God, and the resultant gift of the Holy Spirit.[10] Although Fraser was an evangelical, he held what were then advanced views on Old Testament criticism. He was certainly not a narrow evangelical. He was open-minded and ready to accept all the light which scholarship could shed on the Bible. But his own supreme interest was the Christian life and its expression in Christian service.[11]

While Fraser was a student, he became one of the pioneers of the Student Volunteer Missionary Union. As its traveling secretary he visited universities and colleges all over the British Isles, 1893–94. Fraser's student ministry culminated in the Liverpool Student Volunteer Missionary Conference of January, 1896, when he presided over a convention of 715 students from 26 nations. His spiritual and administrative gifts were recognized. Fraser maintained strong links to the Student Christian Movement all his life. That same year, 1896, Fraser was appointed a missionary of the Free Church of Scotland to the Livingstonia Mission in Nyasaland.[12]

The Livingstonia Mission

The Livingstonia Mission was the result of the efforts of the missionary explorer David Livingstone and of James Stewart of the Free Church of Scotland. Stewart was associated with Lovedale, the pioneer educational institution in South Africa. Stewart was also an early advocate of university education for Africans. With a view to prospecting for a mission station in Central Africa, Stewart made a trip up the Zambezi and Shire Rivers and joined Livingstone from 1862–64. Stewart was unable to make a recommendation at that time for the start of a new work, but following Livingstone's funeral in Westminster Abbey in May of 1874, Stewart reintroduced the idea to the General Assembly of the Free Church of Scotland. He proposed a memorial to Livingstone, an institution of an industrial as well as educational nature strategically placed in Central Africa to become a center for commerce, civilization, and Christianity.[13]

The outstanding leader of the Livingstonia Mission in the early years was Robert Laws, an ordained medical doctor, who left London in May, 1875. The group he led assembled their steamer at the mouth of the Zambezi, dismantled it at Murchison Rapids, reassembled it on the Upper Shire and sailed into Lake Nyasa, October 11, 1875.[14] Laws was primarily responsible for developing a hospital and a central educational institution at Livingstonia, where training was offered in many branches of industry and handicrafts, particularly in the building trades.[15] Three years later Scottish businessmen, in support of the missionaries, formed the African Lakes Corporation to introduce legitimate trade as an alternative to the slave trade. One of the central doctrines in missionary strategy in Africa during the nineteenth century was the development of an alternate economy, "legitimate trade," to counteract the slave trade. It is through the perspective of the "anti-slavery" ethos that we must understand the attitude toward African societies and religious life of the Livingstonia missionaries and of Donald Fraser in particular.

The sphere of the Livingstonia Mission was in Northwest Nyasaland and Northeast Rhodesia, serving a population estimated in 1913 at about 400,000.[16]

At the time Robert Laws and the Mission entered this inland region, the tribal system was in constant turmoil of war. Most of the ethnic groups were related to the Nyanja or Tumbuka groups, which at that time had no strong civil organization or powerful chief. The Arab slavers had established themselves at several points on the shores of Lake Nyasa. On the plateau to the west of the lake, the dominant tribe was the Ngoni. The incursion of the Ngoni Zulu from south of the Zambezi River, beginning in the 1830s, created a state of unusual turmoil. The Ngoni were a people formed from many ethnic groups. They were organized into a cohesive nation by the discipline of war and the genius of great military chiefs.[17] During the 1850s and 1860s under Mpezeni and Mombera,[18] the Ngoni settled in the fertile grazing country to the west of Lake Nyasa.[19] Ngoni armies annually raided the weaker remnants of the original inhabitants, the Chewa, the Tonga, and the Tumbuka, known as the slave population.

The invasions had broken the Tumbuka and allied peoples into a vast number of smaller clans which owed no allegiance to one another. There was no recognized chief, and there was a loss of social custom and arts, for example the smelting of iron and production of iron tools by the Tumbuka.[20] There were stretches of fifty miles through rich valleys that were uninhabited, where villages once had been located.[21] The population had been decimated by the two slave raiding tribes, the Yao and the southern Ngoni. "It was inevitable," wrote Roland Oliver, "that a large portion of the mission's recruits were either fugitives or slaves who had more than once to be defended by force against their irate pursuers."[22]

Slave trading and intertribal warfare made this a restless region. The opening decades were difficult, and after fifteen years of work, there were only sixty indigenous people who were communicants.[23] At Livingstonia, Dr. Laws, in contrast to other missionaries from the University Mission to Central Africa and the Church of Scotland, tried to adopt native law and practice in the governing of the emerging Christian community, and attempted to make the central institution to be the nucleus of a wide network of evangelistic stations and schools, penetrating and reaching into the life of traditional African communities, rather than drawing Christians out of their communities to a central station.

Roland Oliver has perhaps summarized well the attitude of missionaries toward African traditional societies:

> They were not, as many recent critics have suggested, attacking an ideally functioning tribal system, but mopping up in the name of humanity that system's septic overflow, to which Livingstone and others had so forcibly drawn attention.[24]

For years the early missionaries and the associated and supportive commercial enterprise, The Livingstonia Trading Company, witnessed the activity of slave-traders along the Lake and were threatened by the aggressive activities of the Ngoni. Meanwhile the Arabs were pressing down from the north into the region. The incursion of a Muslim slave-trading empire on defenseless tribes looked like a menacing threat to the progress of the missionary objectives of legitimate commerce, civilization, and Christianity. In 1888 when fighting erupted between Arabs and the Livingstonia Trading Company at Karonga on Lake Nyasa, the Free Church of Scotland missionaries were particularly supportive of the trading company. Lord Salisbury was not interested in the Arab War and extending the Empire. But when news that the Portuguese had begun to take advantage of the troubles in the interior and were about to claim for their nation parts of this region, the Directors of the Livingstonia Trading Company and the General Assemblies of the Church of Scotland and the Free Church started a campaign in the British Press with the intent of rousing the public to the danger and loss.[25] Slavery was a slogan of proven power with the British public, and the Portuguese reluctance to taking strong anti-slavery measures on the Zambezi added to the agitation. The British government was called upon to establish a protectorate over Nyasaland. The Foreign Office was slow to undertake further responsibilities overseas, but Lord Salisbury cautiously laid down a policy that eventually settled the future of Nyasaland as a Protectorate. The decisive factor, according to Roland Oliver, was that in 1889 Cecil Rhodes was in London seeking a charter for the British South African Company and offered to contribute 10,000 pounds a year towards the cost of administration if the British government would establish a protectorate.[26]

In June, 1889, Sir Harry Johnston was sent as consul to Central Africa armed with powers to declare a protectorate. He sent a dispatch to that effect to the Foreign Office early in 1880. Johnston credited this British Empire expansion to the effort of the missionary societies.

> He stated unequivocally that the 'chief hold which we have over these regions comes from the quite extraordinary work done by these four missionary societies' ... They [the missionaries] strengthen our hold over the country, they spread the use of the English language, they induct the natives into the best kind of civilisation, and, in fact, each Mission Station is an essay in colonisation.[27]

However, once the Protectorate was established, some of the missionaries began also criticizing the colonial administration.[28] Donald Fraser, writing in 1911 following Edinburgh 1910, maintained that the churches' duty toward the European governments that had assumed the protection of Africa was to "purify and ennoble the ambitions of colonial governments."[29] The task of colonial government, on the other hand, was to provide the stability under which these societies could restructure. The task of the missionaries was to remind the colonial governments that they had not come to exploit and enrich themselves, but rather had "undertaken a great trusteeship, that these people may learn under their tutelage to appreciate the blessings of Christianity and civilization."[30]

Fraser was also well aware that the impact of Western civilization, money economics, migrant labor for industries and mines,[31] introduction of cash crops, and the establishment of European administration contributed to the rapid disintegration of ancient tribal organizations and social custom. But, he wrote, "this very disintegration was preparing a way for the messengers of the Gospel."[32]

The advent of British administration led to a rapid decline in the power and prestige of the Ngoni invaders and overlords. Missionaries began to use the Tumbuka language instead of Ngoni and therefore were brought closer to the serfs, who were the original inhabitants of the land and composed the greater part of the population. There was a recovery of Tumbuka customs and a resurgence of traditional skills such as iron smelting and an increased integration of the Ngoni and Tumbuka peoples.[33]

Fraser's Work Among the Tumbuka and Ngoni

Fraser arrived in Nyasaland in 1896, just as the pioneer stage with the Ngoni was giving way to the constructive work of building a church. After fifteen years of mission work in 1890, there had been sixty indigenous communicant members. But the extension of British rule in the form of a Protectorate in 1891 had brought significant changes in African responses to the mission. Political order and stability, British prestige, and a history of fifteen years of faithful education, vocational training, and medical work combined to produce a movement at times *en masse* toward the new faith. Schools and churches multiplied. By 1915, eight languages had been reduced to writing, and in each language educational materials and Scripture portions were being sold in editions of thousands. There were 850 schools with 1500 teachers serving 51,000 pupils. Few villages were without the opportunity of education. The church claimed 9200 communicants and nearly as many candidates for baptism, and 41,000 called themselves Christian. The leadership of the church was in the hands of 230 elders, and there were three ordained African ministers working with the Scottish missionaries.[34]

The Ngoni Chief at Hora in 1901, Mzuku-zuku, was in the process of relocating his people farther south in search of better agricultural land due to locusts and drought. Fraser and his wife, who was a medical doctor, had been stationed at Hora. Mzuku-zuku was building his new village of Embangweni and invited the Frasers to build a mission station at the new location. He offered Fraser a square mile of land and the labor of his people to construct the main buildings.[35] Fraser believed the move of the mission was necessary both to hold the Ngoni together as a people and to keep the mission at the center of the population.[36] Fraser called the new station, which opened about 1902, Loudon, after the friend and physician of Dr. Livingstone who had generously supported Fraser's work.[37] The Tumbuka-Ngoni, however, knew it as "Mzuku-zuku's Mission." This was to be the center of Fraser's work for the next twenty-two years until he was recalled to Scotland to serve as one of the foreign mission secretaries in 1925.

In 1900, there were 800 church members among the Ngoni. The first two decades of the century saw a dramatic growth in the church. At the time of Fraser's retirement, Loudon was the center, serving an area of 2000 square miles, with over 200 substations. The schools had 370 teachers and 10,000 students, and there was a Christian community of over 10,000.[38]

Fraser's policies established a distinctive style in the churches in the area of Loudon. Fraser viewed the schools as the essential evangelistic agency. He abolished school fees and was willing to open schools with teachers of limited training. Three years after establishing Loudon, Fraser had begun 142 schools. These schools provided catechumen and hearers classes. Fraser baptized up to 75% of those whom he examined, whereas some of his older colleagues such as W. A. Elmslie averaged about half Fraser's rate. Between 1905 and 1909, Fraser baptized almost twice as many adults at Loudon than at the older mission station Ekwendeni.

This evidence could suggest that Fraser had a more sympathetic attitude toward Ngoni culture than did his colleagues. Thomas Thompson in his research on Fraser and Livingstonia missionaries and their attitude towards Ngoni culture concludes

> the Livingstonia missionaries were not universally sympathetic to Ngoni culture—far less that the Ngoni were always satisfied with missionary attitudes. They were not. Furthermore, the Scottish missionaries, Fraser included, made no attempt to accept Ngoni culture as a viable unit, but judged individual aspects of it against their own standards or right and wrong, or sometimes against similar customs among surrounding tribes.[39]

Despite these limitations, the Scottish missionaries in general, and Fraser in particular, had a more sympathetic attitude than that displayed by missionaries in other societies elsewhere in Nyasaland.[40]

Fraser was highly attracted to the Ngoni as a people and expressed his appreciation for the hospitality, respect, and friendship with which he was received even by strangers. Fraser adopted a more sympathetic attitude towards Ngoni culture and aspirations than many of his colleagues. He encouraged African music and hymnody. He also gave his approval to one of the major dances, the *ingoma*, and distinguished it from dances he considered immoral and unacceptable.[41] Fraser took a more supportive view of the Ngoni custom of marrying a deceased brother's widow (the custom of *chokora*) than did some of his colleagues. The Presbytery discussed the issue three times, May 1900, November 1907, and January 1908, and came to the decision not to allow a man to take the widow of a deceased brother as a second wife. Fraser, supported by an African, Edward Bothi Manda, pressed for an amendment to read "considering that marriage with a deceased brother's widow is a common native custom, and is not clearly contrary to Biblical law, the Presbytery, while discouraging the custom, do not think such a marriage sufficient cause for discipline."[42] Fraser's amendment carried 19 to 9. The following year while Fraser was on furlough, more conservative missionaries were able to rescind Fraser's amendment. Thompson suggests a new factor may have been the legal opinion from the colonial government that such a marriage was illegal in the Protectorate.[43]

Though Fraser was basically sympathetic, he opposed individual parts of the culture, particularly polygamy, excessive beer drinking, and the reliance on the "trial by ordeal" to determine guilt or innocence in questions of morality. Fraser was also opposed to most traditional doctors. Though he admits that some herbal medicines were effective, he regarded the traditional doctors, notably the *Kayeyi*, as shams and frauds who deceived the people.[44]

When one examines the statistics of the Livingstonia Mission for 1914, there were ten major mission stations similar to the Loudon Station. Europeans were located at eight of the stations. Each was a center around which there was a network of schools that totaled 787 in 1914, according to figures given in *Winning Primitive People*, and 860 schools in 1915, according to details in Fraser's book *Livingstonia*.[45] In the forty years of the mission from 1875–1915, there were a total of 93 missionaries, of whom 25 were ordained ministers, 17 were teachers, five were medical doctors and nine were nurses, and 36 were tradesmen including carpenters, engineers, agriculturalists, seamen, weavers, printers, and surveyors.[46] Loudon, which in 1914 had a history of only twelve years, was a relatively new station in comparison to some that had a history of almost forty years. Loudon was the center with the largest number of schools and the most rapid growth of the church. Loudon served 194 schools. Bandawe, the nearest competitor, had 130 schools. There was a comparable number of communicants, 2647 and 2463, respectively, for Loudon and Bandawe. But the great difference was that Loudon had 2341 candidates for baptism, the next largest group being 1109 at Kasungu. Loudon had a total Christian community of 11,530, Bandawe had 7038. In fact Loudon had over 25% of the total Christian community of 46,283.[47] These statistics indicate that there was a special attractiveness to Fraser's approach.

In the 25 years from 1890–1915, remarkable changes took place in the Livingstonia Mission. The total Christian community increased from around 60 to over 41,000.[48] Thompson, working from census figures of 1911, estimates that 15% of the population considered themselves Christian.[49] Fraser said of this era, "Christianity is becoming the nominal religion."[50] Fraser himself was amazed at the "extraordinary advance which our religion has made."[51] He credited it to a combination of commerce, good government, and civilization (education) as the primary evangelistic tool. Fraser felt the white men's influence had been altogether out of proportion to their numbers.[52]

Fraser also felt that Europeans had to help provide strong and permanent social bulwarks in place of those crumbling away. Fraser was aware that in the conscious attempt to alter the economy, education, and religion of the people, there were also unintentional modifications.[53]

The most apparent influence of Europeans was in the arena of industrial and commercial changes. The introduction of urban money economies broke the individual loose from religious and communal prohibitions of village life without providing new restraints in the religious life. New wealth generated new needs and wants, particularly in the area of clothing. Blankets, soap, cloth, and books also became very desirable items. The introduction of money economy resulted in greater individual freedom from social restraints in village life, which without new ethical guidelines, led to new freedom which in turn contributed to "immorality and debauchery."

The translation of the Bible had a great influence in establishing the common vernacular of the people. The missionaries chose, for example, to change from Chi-Ngoni, the language of the minority overlords, to Chi-Tumbuka, the language of the majority of the population, who were serfs.

The growth of schools and education eroded and withered reverence for the traditions of the past and the elders, especially among the young. Belief in magical powers that had helped to prop up the social order were weakened and parental authority declined. Fear of penalties and consequences, which in a magical world view were supposed to follow certain sins against society, no longer exercised their restraints.

The intertribal and Arab hostilities during the nineteenth century had eroded the fabric of African societies by external forces. The introduction of Western economic patterns, migrant labor, education, and medical practice encouraged an individualism that eroded tribal societies internally. It was this combination of forces that made it imperative for Fraser to work toward a vision of social and moral restructuring of society from a Christian perspective.

Fraser recognized the irony in the fact that the introduction of commerce and primary school education and the establishment of the British Protectorate over Nyasaland which brought political stability had also brought on a radical disintegration of Ngoni and Tumbuka societies. Economic, educational, and political changes were eroding the social and religious authorities that had held traditional societies together.

It was the continuing and expected disintegration of African cultures and traditional world view that may have kept Fraser from making more than a surface study of African traditional religion. There is no evidence that he examined in any systematic way, like Henry Callaway or Henri Junod, the religious or social structures of the African societies among whom he worked. However, he frequently wrote on the topic of religion. His writings on African religion have a generic character, especially in his book, *The Future of Africa*. Fraser was anticipating the demise of traditional African cultures and religions, which he regarded as the preparation for the Gospel:

> The advance of civilization and the establishment of European administration are rapidly disintegrating the ancient tribal organizations and social customs, and by this very disintegration are preparing a way for the messengers of the Gospel.[54]

Fraser was not alone in this opinion; it was shared by the leaders of Edinburgh 1910. The title of Johannes Warneck's book, *The Living Christ and the Dying Heathenism*, issued before Edinburgh 1910, expressed this same conviction. But more significantly, the idea that the religions of the East and Africa were in decline and disintegration was endorsed by Robert Speer. Speer was the co-chairman of Commission IV at Edinburgh 1910, Secretary of the Board of Foreign Missions of the Presbyterian Church in the USA, and along with Fraser had been deeply involved in the leadership of the Student

Volunteer Movement. Just prior to Edinburgh 1910, Speer had argued for the uniqueness of Christianity from the three great elements of religion, namely, dependence, fellowship, and progress. The element of dependence is present in other religions, he stated, but it is frequently distorted by fear. Christianity alone supplies fellowship and progress. Non-Christian religions in their popular and applied forms are in a state of degeneration. Christianity, however, has the power to regenerate. Speer argued that Christianity alone "begets progress and is the only religion that can live with progress. . . Western Civilization is disintegrating both the customs of the 'savage nations' and the more stable civilizations of the East."[55]

At the International Missionary Council meeting at Jerusalem in 1928, Speer took this argument one step farther when he wrote:

> These religions are going to be smashed anyhow, perhaps not quickly, but surely, and what is going to do it—indeed is already doing it—is modern science, modern commerce, and modern political organization. These are the things that the East wants from us; and on the whole it does not want our Christianity. It will have them and they will destroy its religions, its customs, and its social organizations. It doesn't seem to me to be really worth while to attempt to save from the wreck what seems to us good and valuable in the older non-Christian civilizations . . .[56]

Speer did not view as a priority the attempt to preserve the good in these traditions and civilizations from the inevitable "wreck." But once the wreck happened, he felt the values of the non-Christian religions were to be salvaged by the grace of Christ and baptized. Only thus could these religions survive. Fraser and Speer were not alone in this view, as the quote by Speer from the proceedings of the International Missionary Council at Jerusalem in 1928 illustrates:

> When the old systems of life have become a mere memory—as Rome and Greece have for us,—then all that is of permanent value in them will be ripe and available for educational purposes. At the moment the good and the bad are so thoroughly intertwined, so unified in a common concrete way of life, that the destruction of the system must precede the rescue of its valuable elements.[57]

Speer then went on to summarize his own thinking on this matter:

But the time element is not so sharply edged. The movement is a living process. Christianity enshrines in its present forms a great deal that it took over from the thought and life which it met in the world. It is now to repeat this work of redemption. The values of the non-Christian religions are to be salvaged by the grace of Christ and baptized into Him. Only so can they survive. Their value, like all other values, is as material for Him that the works of God may be manifested in the world.[58]

In the L.P. Stone Lectures at Princeton Theological Seminary 1932–1933, published as *The Finality of Christ*, which is perhaps Speer's most mature work on Christianity in relation to other religions, Speer expressed this conviction that oriental civilizations and African cultures were doomed to crumble everywhere before the forces of Western scientific, social, and industrial ideas and influences. [59]

It is instructive to notice that at first Fraser was positive about the disintegrating impact which modern science, commerce, communication, and colonial political structures were having on pre-literate and pre-industrialized societies. However, he was discouraged to discover the negative side of modernization as shown by the devastating effects the modern world had on Christianity in his homeland, Scotland, when he returned in the 1920s.

Fraser's view of Tumbuka-Ngoni society and religion was premised on the conviction that traditional African societies and religion were in a state of disintegration. At the time that Fraser completed the questionnaire for Edinburgh 1910, the two African societies he was associated with were undergoing rapid social changes and there was a strong influx of people into the church. Fraser was aware of how this milieu of change made it difficult for missionaries and Africans to talk about religious beliefs. He found few Africans who could define or distinguish what their faith, or belief was. At the outset of the questionnaire Fraser made the statement,

The two tribes among whom I work have less religion than any others possibly in Central Africa and there is now little of the old religious observances. What there is is not observable on the surface, and is rather disowned . . . there is practically no formal religion.[60]

Fraser tended to make a distinction between religion and faith: religion refers to formal worship, ritual and the cult, whereas faith refers to belief and the world view. In his chapter on the "Religion of the Tumbuka," Fraser said:

> They themselves are scarcely conscious of any religious belief. But after patient investigation their atmosphere is found to be charged with religion, and although few can define and distinguish what they worship, their lives are surrounded by spiritual powers which they acknowledge, and which play a great part in their common life.[61]

Fraser felt that for the Tumbuka, "religion is an atmosphere rather than a creed."[62] Fraser followed E. B. Tylor's definition that religion is a belief in spiritual beings. In this sense Fraser recognized that Africans were very religious, for the unseen world was never far from their thoughts.

Fraser understood African cultures as a composition of independent identifiable elements, rather than a viable unity with an integrity and integration of the various elements. At the time of Edinburgh 1910, the integration and unity of a tribal society was an insight yet to come from the functionalist school of British Social Anthropology. Fraser was therefore freer to identify elements that he could affirm and those dimensions that he clearly rejected, particularly excessive beer drinking, polygamy, and immoral dances and initiation ceremonies for young adults.[63]

One can identify two basic principles that appear to guide Fraser's approach to the Ngoni "religious atmosphere." He judged individual aspects of ethical behavior against the concept of fulfillment and the need to create new ethical foundations and structures.

Fraser's attitude toward African culture and toward the relationship of the Christian Gospel to the traditional faith and beliefs of the Tumbuka-Ngoni may best be summed up in an article he wrote for the Le Zoute Conference in 1926, toward the end of his career,[64] and in his book, *The New Africa*, which came out a year later in 1927.[65]

In these writings, Fraser expressed himself as cautious and fearful of the "evangel who denationalizes."[66] He felt that the idea of a complete break with the past has led Christianity in Africa to taking a very Europeanized form, down to dress and customs, which are not the necessary essence of the Gospel, and to making simple expressions of nationalism appear anti-Christian.

The fulfillment motif, as exemplified by Fraser and Speer, begins instead with the African experience and attempts to relate the Gospel to the African heritage. In response to the question "What attitude should the Christian take toward the religion of the people among whom he labours?" in the Edinburgh questionnaire, Fraser began by affirming that there has been revelation and light for all, that "God has not left himself without a witness among these people." Second, he affirmed that the God ignorantly worshipped "we declare fully by the revelation of Christ." Fraser identified three points of contact between Ngoni traditional religion and Christianity. First, the Christian belief in immortality he felt was implicit in the reverence for the spirits of the dead. Second, the intercession of the spirits of the ancestors on behalf of the living was a reaching toward the idea of the one intercessor, Jesus Christ. Third, among the Ngoni and Tumbuka people, there was a faith in one supreme God, though Fraser observed that it was the least influential of their religious beliefs.[67] He felt these points of contact indicated that the "Gospel is not antagonistic to their simple faith, but the clearer revelation of what they simply sought after."[68]

The fulfillment motif is developed rather extensively in Fraser's article, "The Evangelistic Approach to the African." Fraser spoke of the unfolding of the Gospel. He proposed to begin from the declaration that God is, and by logical extension of this to develop the character of God, and then to move from the creator to loving Father who cares for his children, and from these characteristics then move to holiness and goodness. Fraser's rational argument of the fulfillment concept rested on several assumptions: (1) that logical processes of reasoning are the way non-Western cultures go about making religious changes, particularly in their world view and (2) that one understands the development of culture and religion as a simple linear progression. This argument assumes an incremental development of religion somewhat independent of culture, rather than a systems approach in which the interacting elements form something of an equilibrium and balance each other to form a cultural unity and an integrated world view, in which the change of one significant element affects the balance of the whole system. (3) Fraser rationally moved from the known to the unknown. However, he began with what was crucial to him but peripheral to the Ngoni. Fraser took the belief in the high god, which he recognized as among the least influential beliefs of traditional Ngoni theology, and attempted rationally to move it towards ethical monotheism, which is central to Christianity. That which was on the periphery of traditional religion was brought to center stage in Christianity by a rational process. In contrast, Fraser's own experience of the encounter between missionary Christianity and traditional religion began not with what was peripheral and rational, but on something personal and existential, the question of health, healing, sickness. These were among the central religious issues with which African people wrestle and struggled.

Fraser observed that two main factors maintain the ethical fabric of African society: social or communal loyalty and a faith in magic. An evil act is against the community in that it destroys the harmony and well-being of the community. There is a deep sense of loyalty to one's own people. One does not steal from a member of one's own community or he becomes an enemy of his own society. But these loyalties do not apply to other communities. Thus, in an urban pluralistic society, without loyalties to one another, one of the great safeguards of life has been broken down.

The other great sanction of society is magic, which penetrates the whole idea of social loyalty, building the community into unity and continuity. Fraser pointed out that, although faith in magic is all-prevailing, there is no word for "magic" in African languages.[69] It is the mystic essence in the poison ordeal that unerringly detects and punishes the criminal. "Magic is the most unerring detective in the world."[70] It is the belief that an act against the harmony of the community will be punished by a calamity or sickness. A man who lives and works thousands of miles away maintains family loyalty, because he knows that should he be unfaithful, his wife and family will suffer. Furthermore, it is only when relationships have been righted that medical skills have effect. If a sickness is believed to be caused by the unfaithfulness of one of the chief's wives, it is only when she confesses that healing can proceed.[71] Traditional society is protected by communal loyalties and by the belief in magical powers to serve justice. Magic is the strong judge and punisher. "Social order was maintained by magical terror."[72] Animism, like all other phases of human development, has its lights and its shades. The magical view raises respect for government and helps to maintain civil order. In addition to the substratum of a type of moral order in the universe, the whole of life is surrounded by magical and spiritual powers over which traditional doctors exercise peculiar authority. But they have no monopoly on these powers since even the simple villagers can curse and kill a neighbor by magic.[73] Therefore magic of some sort is suspected at the root of nearly all sickness.[74] Fraser observed, "I have never known a chief to die without accusations of sorcery flying wildly about. A chief's life is the most precious possession of the people and magic is his guardian."[75] Fraser drew the conclusion that death does not seem to the African to be a natural and necessary end of life. All sickness and death are seen rather as the result of "black magic."[76] Of the five explanations of sickness and pain, natural causes were the least frequently cited, while more important were actions of sorcerers using magic as poison, retributive effects of the sins of others, poison, unfriendly spirits, and demon possession.[77] Fraser had his harshest criticisms for African societies at this point of their magical interpretation of sickness and death. "The evil of witchcraft cannot be exaggerated."[78]

> Magic has played her part in primitive society, by her terrors guarding property, and authority, and social order, and compelling temperance and abstinence. But when she has sat on the judgment seat, she has been a mad judge, unable to distinguish the innocent from the guilty, and hopelessly punishing the wrong party. More crimes lie to her charge than to passions.[79]

Even with these strong criticisms, Fraser states clearly,

> As we unfold our Gospel it is well to remember that we come not to destroy distinctive nationality, but to fulfill what men have searched after gropingly and . . . to retain and purify all that is not evil. Society has been safeguarded by many a social and magical tie, and none of these should be cut unless we give in their place surer bonds. If magic has visited anti-social acts with severe punishments, we must see that our Christian faith replaces the authority of magic and gives stronger sanctions. If we only denounce magic, we leave the society unprotected and unguided. But as we give a strong ethical Christian faith we create guardians of society who replace the magical safeguards with far greater ones.[80]

Fraser understood the importance of the maintenance and protection of morality which the belief in magical powers brought, but he also realized the limitations of replacing that world view with his own:

> Lift him out of these loyalties, break his faith in magic by the sight of your superior mechanical and scientific skill—then, unless you have given him new sanctions and safeguards of conduct in the higher faith of Christ, you leave him a derelict in a stormy sea.[81]

Fraser regarded the underlying difference between traditional communal ethics and Christian ethics as a major shift in world view from a magical perspective to modern scientific perspective. Fraser's theology therefore focused more on the establishment of Christian law and conscience than on the development of the church as the new community.

Construction Not Destruction

British Protestant evangelical mission perspectives, represented here by Donald Fraser, grew out of the heritage of the practical, ethical, and political concerns of the anti-slavery movement. This approach was guided less by a unified anthropological theory of African societies or a theology of religions than by the ethical, moral, and humanitarian concerns of "building up fresh social structures."[82]

Two themes have been noted. There was the theme of fulfillment or of "construction rather than destruction." Within this theme Fraser worked from the known to the unknown and sought to preserve the Africans' national integrity, to find linkage and continuity with the African religious search. "In spite of the gross superstition and cruelty bound up with the religion of Africa," Fraser could claim, "there are many things that are 'broken lights' of God."[83] The fulfillment motif gave Fraser a measure of freedom and flexibility even on the issue of polygamy, which he vigorously opposed. Fraser reflected on an old man for whom the Gospel message had come in his old age. He never did break with polygamy and therefore was never received into the Church. "I like to think that perhaps he was in the Kingdom of God. For . . . the Kingdom is wider than the church, and the names of some who have never been baptized may be written in the Lamb's Book of Life."[84]

The second theme is the recognition that "commerce, civilization, and Christianity" have contributed to the destruction of the "magical and communal" restraints in African traditional societies. The impact of the modern world has undermined the foundations of tribal social ethics. The ethical and social restructuring of society demand "the creation of Christian law and conscience."[85] It is the creation of a new foundation and not simply a matter of fulfillment of the old. We have noted that Fraser's confrontation with the magical world view was primarily in the areas of health, healing, and justice. It is significant too that Fraser regarded medical mission work as the greatest evangelist of all, particularly a hospital "scientifically and sympathetically conducted."[86] Medical work may only be regarded as a manifestation of a more potent magic, and do little to open closed doors, but when united to a spirit of loving sympathy its power is immense.[87]

It is also worth noting that in the history of African Christianity and especially in the rapid growth of the African Independent Church movements in the years following 1914, healing was a prominent issue. On this question a large body of literature has developed, particularly since about 1960.[88]

Fraser concluded his history of the first forty years of the Livingstonia Mission with the words, "Yet everything calls for sheer optimism. The past years have shown the invincible power of our message."[89]

Paul Bohannan, writing as an anthropologist in the 1960s on the interpenetration of cultures, missionary and African, credits the missionaries with being important carriers of new ideas because their contact was over a broad social range and they stayed in one area for longer periods of time than other foreigners.[90] "Missionaries brought not only religious ideas, they brought economic and political ideas."[91] Colonial administrative officers often relied on missionaries, who knew a different aspect of African life from administrative officers. Missionaries influenced policy profoundly. From the perspective of the 1960s, at the close of the colonial era when African countries were gaining independence, Paul Bohannan could affirm in part the restructuring vision of Fraser and the Livingstonia mission in the high imperialist era:

> The missionaries were, probably, the dominant importers of ideas because their contact with Africans was of a broader social range. . . Whatever the religious impact may have been, the initial impact was economic, and to a very real extent, political . . . Missionaries are very often blamed because they destroyed and misunderstood, and so they did. But so did everybody else. And missionaries are the only people who *built* [emphasis Bohannan's] below an institutional level.[92]

The institutional level Bohannan refers to is the school system which provided the means for African societies to rebuild and restructure.

More specifically, Thomas Thompson has evaluated Fraser's contribution and attitude towards Ngoni culture and religion:

> Fraser's attitude did not satisfy all Ngoni Christians, but his attitudes were sufficiently open to encourage the Ngoni to work out their own response to Christianity in the light of Ngoni culture, and to find an answer which gave that culture a place of some importance in the new way of life. . . That the Ngoni were able to preserve a distinctive and valid culture, while turning in large numbers to Christianity, was due mainly to their own inherent strength and cohesion, and partly to the sympathetic approach of Fraser.[93]

The characteristic feature of Donald Fraser's approach to Ngoni and Tumbuka societies of what was then known as Nyasaland, but now as Malawi, was moral reconstruction.[94] This can be seen in Fraser's emphasis on the restructuring of economic, educational, and political life within the mission village. Second, Fraser believed the most fundamental element of the missionary's task was to live from a new standard of ethics. He stated: "The new ethical standard of his [the missionary's] life is the first and most startling doctrine he brings."[95] Finally, for Fraser the great tension was between the magical view of ethics associated with tribal societies and a new view of ethics more compatible with a scientific world view and the social and political changes taking place in Nyasaland.

W. D. Armstrong: Radical Displacement

W. P. Paterson's summary of the questionnaires on "Animistic Religions" states several times that W. D. Armstrong of the Regions Beyond Missionary Union, who worked in the Upper Congo on the Lulanga River, represented a minority view among the missionaries surveyed.[96]

Armstrong, along with Elizabeth Chadwick of the CMS in Uganda, were particularly hesitant to apply the name "religion" to the beliefs and practices they observed. Armstrong's opening sentence in his questionnaire was "There is no religion in our district, simply heathenism."[97] And Chadwick stated,

"The pagans of Uganda and surrounding tribes can scarcely be said to have any definite religion; certainly not set forms of religious observance."[98]

On the question of "points of contact" and "preparation for Christianity," Paterson recognized that there was a wide divergence of opinions and views. Godfrey Callaway and a number of the Anglican missionaries spoke confidently of a preparation for Christianity. On the other hand, Armstrong denied the existence of any point of contact or preparation for Christianity in any of the African traditional beliefs and rites he observed. In fact, Armstrong indicated that there was an advantage here because ". . . there is practically no false religion to oppose."[99] He was also quick to recognize the hermeneutic problem:

> This in one way is a distinct disadvantage, however, since there is very little vocabulary in use to convey religious and abstract ideas. When missionaries first came there were no adequate words to express trust, faith, holiness, purity, repentance, and many other abstracts. . .[100]

Of all the missionaries responding to the article entitled "Animistic Religions", W. D. Armstrong and Elizabeth Chadwick have the fewest and briefest published records. Therefore, conclusions must be more cautious and limited. Our interpretation of Chadwick is based only on her questionnaire, one mission report of her boarding school, two letters, one dated December 9, 1899, another dated November 7, 1897, and one mention of her name in another missionary's letter.[101] W. D. Armstrong's anecdotes and reports were written primarily for the mission's supporting constituency.[102]

We are therefore left with meager resources to actually determine what kind of definition or understanding of religion was guiding Armstrong's negative religious assessment of the Lolo people at the great horseshoe bend of the Congo River. Elizabeth Chadwick's negative evaluation of African societies in Uganda must be held in tension with the more sympathetic and careful observations of her contemporary Church Missionary Society colleague, John Roscoe.[103]

How then can one understand the sources of this exclusivist view of Christianity and the negative attitude toward African religious traditions? Paterson offers the explanation that views of missionaries like Armstrong and Chadwick, in particular, who were unable to recognize any religion or religious observances, "arise from the idea that nothing deserves the name of religion which is false and unethical."[104] Because of the paucity of actual data from these two missionaries, one can only substantiate or corroborate Paterson's view from several passages in their respective questionnaires.

For example, Elizabeth Chadwick, the only woman included in the survey, responded forcefully and tersely to the question, "What do you consider the chief moral, intellectual, and social hindrances to the full acceptance of Christianity?"

> Undoubtedly the degraded position of women. Where women were bought and sold like cattle, and re-sold constantly from one master to another, and a man would marry a new wife "on trial" to see whether her cooking and digging pleased him or not, and if not, get rid of her promptly, it is very hard to inculcate ideas of personal holiness and purity.[105]

Chadwick was appalled and angered by the low social state of women among the Baganda. In response to the questions on the attitude the missionary was to take toward the religion of the people with whom one worked, and if there were points of contact, Chadwick, consistent with her earlier answer, stated: "The Christian teacher must almost ignore the old faiths of Uganda; . . .there is very little point of contact . . ."[106]

Armstrong served under the Regions Beyond Missionary Union, which was an outgrowth of the interdenominational East London Institute for Home and Foreign Missions (Harley College), founded in 1872. It was founded by Grattan Guinness, an Irish evangelist intimately associated with Hudson Taylor. Taylor had founded the first interdenominational faith mission, the China Inland Mission, in the 1860s.[107] Guinness helped establish the Livingstone Inland Mission on the Congo River before turning it over to the American Baptist Missionary Union. Guinness, from the East London Training Institute, then opened a new work in 1889 at the great northern bend of the Congo River among the Balalo. This work was incorporated under the Regions Beyond Missionary Union.[108]

In the scramble for Africa in the 1880s, which culminated in the carving up of Africa among the colonial powers at the Berlin Conference of 1884, Belgium emerged as a colonial power largely through the efforts of King Leopold II, who established the Congo Free State, in the hope of enlightened and civilized rule. Belgian colonialism degenerated, however, into cruel oppression and merciless exploitation. The Congo Free State, according to the British colonialist Sir Harry H. Johnston, was predisposed to the abuse of power for two reasons.[109] The Belgian Governor General in Boma on the Lower Congo was so removed from the interior having inadequate communication and transportation, that he could have administered as effectively from Brussels. Second, the commodities of value, first ivory and then rubber, were virtually a state monopoly from which Africans were forbidden and from which salaries of state officials derived a commission. In March 1896, Leopold created at the center of the state, the Royal Domain which was at his own disposal. Commercial concessions and the Royal Domain could not, however, be exploited without labor. It was at this point that the worst excesses appeared in the coercion and exploitation of the people. African societies were brutalized through forced labor, bloodshed and mutilations. H. H. Johnston estimates that the level of intensity equaled, if not exceeded, that of the Arab slave trade in the region earlier in the century.[110]

Missionaries of the Congo Balolo Mission, within the Royal Domain, along with the Southern Presbyterian Mission of the U.S., the American Baptists, and Baptist Missionary Society began to expose the atrocities.[111] Guinness joined forces with H. R. Fox Bourne of the Aborigines Protection Society and E. D. Morel,[112] a self-committed reformer with no particular commitment to the church. They collaborated from 1903 until 1908, pressuring the British public and House of Commons. The British pressure hastened the transfer of the Royal Domain to the Belgian Parliament and the implementation of reform.

In order to be more understanding of W. D. Armstrong's perspective of a rather comprehensive rejection of African traditional religions, one needs to keep in mind that the Christian missionary movement in Africa in the nineteenth century was closely associated with the anti-slavery movement. The presence of slavery in African societies, the exchange of bridewealth, polygamy, and human sacrifice kept ethical issues high on the missionary agenda and affected their understanding and interpretation of religion. One of the chief purposes of religion in society from the evangelical western perspective was the preservation of moral and ethical sensitivity.

The evangelicals who were at the forefront of the anti-slavery movement saw the function of religion as preservation of moral and ethical sensitivity and standards. Therefore where there was a lack of ethical and moral behavior, there was reason to doubt the presence of religious life.

W. D. Armstrong and Regions Beyond Missionary Union in 1910 were not interacting with a healthy African society, but one deeply wounded and brutalized and penetrated by fear and suspicion. Armstrong among the Balolo, like Donald Fraser among the Ngoni, was not attacking an ideally functioning tribal system but was addressing in the name of humanity the septic overflow of the systems of exploitation. African societies like the Balolo of the Upper Congo River had been subject to the cruelty and violence of the Arab slave trade. In addition, during the imperialist era, the Balolo had suffered the atrocities of bloodshed and mutilations from a system of forced labor in King Leopold's colonial Royal Domain. Because they were Europeans, the missionaries of the Regions Beyond Missionary Union, particularly in the early years, were the object of intense hostility and suspicion. In a climate of fear and distrust on the part of the Balolo toward the missionaries, and of moral outrage on the part of the missionaries toward aspects of Balolo society that appeared exploitative and dehumanizing, mutual understanding was nearly impossible. It is therefore not unexpected that Harry Guiness, in recording the history of the first twenty years of the Regions Beyond Mission, reports the brutality of a society in which Chief Molong of Bokenoylo killed thirty-three of his slaves within a week and missionaries record finding children thrown away by their masters because they were weak or ill. This violence controlled the missionaries' perception of religion and ethics among the Balolo.

> Our minds grew sick and our hearts tired of hearing and seeing these deeds of cruelty. Some of them formed part and parcel of their superstitious worship, while others were enforced by native law.[113]

It is not surprising that Armstrong had a more negative view of African society and religious life than some of the other missionaries on the question of "points of contact" and "preparation for Christianity."

Robert H. Nassau: Bridging by Affiliation

Dr. Robert Nassau's (1835–1921) philanthropic and humanitarian concerns wedded to a nineteenth-century Protestant religious definition resulted in an approach of affiliation to African culture and religion. Nassau, at the time of Edinburgh 1910, was a recently retired Presbyterian missionary who had spent 45 years (1861–1906) in Equatorial West Africa, primarily in Gabon.[114] Nassau was a graduate of Princeton Seminary in 1859 and went on to the University of Pennsylvania to become a medical doctor before beginning his missionary career.

Nassau had presented an essay on "Bantu Theology" before the American Society of Comparative Religions in 1893, and lent it to the Society for its use at the Parliament of Religions at the Chicago Exposition that same year. Nassau's interest in writing on African religions filtered back through Nassau's Princeton University connections to the Presbyterian Board of Foreign Missions. He was assigned in 1899 by Robert Speer, the secretary of the Presbyterian Board of Foreign Missions, to write up his research of 25 years on African religious beliefs and customs.[115] Nassau's fluency in three West African languages, Benga, Pahouin, and Fang,[116] gave him greater access to traditional African life than most expatriates. His two most significant works are *Fetichism in West Africa* (1904), and a collection of folklore, *Where Animals Talk: West African FolkLore Tales* (1912).[117]

The Feeling for God

Nassau stated at the outset of his work, *Fetichism in West Africa*, that the objective of his description of African traditional religion "is to show how degradingly false is that falsity, in its lapse from God, even though I accord it the name of religion."[118] Nassau began from a theological affirmation of an original revelation of God and conscience as its witness. He began his definition of religion with "a sense of infinite dependence," an idea similar to Schleiermacher's definition of religion as "the feeling of absolute dependence."[119] This awareness and knowledge of God was regarded by Nassau as an "original, donated component part of us."[120] All religions had but one Source, from which have degenerated all manner of perversions.[121]

Nassau was not completely closed to the idea of evolution in the natural world but affirmed a Divine act, the origin of creation. However, his belief in the degeneration of religion ran counter to the evolutionary ideas of religion in Tyler and Spencer, and Nassau rejected the idea that the belief in a Supreme Being evolved from lower forms of belief in spiritual beings.[122]

Nassau thought rather that religious thought degenerates from monotheism to polytheism and idolatrous sacrifices, to the worship of ancestors, to the third stage of degeneration which quietly disregards God, where worship is transferred to a multitude of spiritual agencies who are under God's power, but uncontrolled by God. This third stage is what Nassau refers to as fetichism.[123] The missionary task therefore is to separate the true from the false. On the one hand, Nassau maintained that African beliefs about God by and large reflect a divine revelation echoed in the conscience.[124] On the other hand, Nassau regarded the belief in spiritual beings, animism, as "almost pure superstitions . . . the outgrowth of individual imagination."[125] With the elimination of the "superstitions," Nassau conceded, very little is left of truth in African religions; nevertheless the superstitions point to God.[126]

Nassau was convinced that beneath the superstitions there still remained an African belief in the Creator. "When the overgrowth was cleared away one would find a prepared soil responsive to the message of the Gospel."[127] The belief in a Supreme Power, a Creator sometimes referred to as "The All-Father," led him to conclude that Africans were monotheists and not idolaters.[128]

Nassau's book is a vast catalogue of anecdotal experience lacking a clear scientific method of study.[129] Nassau was praised in reviews for his vast experience but criticized for his unscientific method and religious presuppositions. Andrew Lang was appreciative of Nassau's work because it gave strong evidence for a belief in a "high god." This was evidence that Lang used in his ongoing debate with Tylor challenging the evolutionary hypothesis on the origins of religion.[130]

In spite of the negative and low view of African religion that Nassau's "degeneration theory" would indicate, the study of Nassau's philosophy of mission done by an African doctoral student at Temple University suggests that Nassau "pioneered in the rapproachment mode."[131]

Nassau appears to have been motivated by a deep sense of justice. The experiences of slavery related to him by African American students while he was a student at Princeton, and the American Civil War classic, *Uncle Tom's Cabin*, factored into his intense hatred of American slavery and his call to missionary service.[132] His concern for justice and human rights made him a vigorous opponent of polygamy, not so much on legalistic biblical grounds but from the indignities that usually accompanied it. Nassau regarded polygamy as the chief hindrance to Christianity. It was the economic abuses of this social system that were particularly offensive to him.[133]

We have noted that Nassau spoke three African languages, and his vast catalogue of detailed information regarding religious issues indicates that he had gained the confidence and trust of his African informants and friends. Only where there is a bond of trust are Africans (or any other informants) prepared to share the deepest traditions of the spiritual life with an outsider. Teeuwissen points out that Nassau, in describing his approach to African peoples, referred to it as "affiliation," over against the domination he perceived in his fellow whites at the end of the nineteenth century.[134]

Regarding therefore the attitude of missionaries towards African religions, Nassau maintained that "the preacher commends his message, primarily, not by the excellence of that message, but by his own personality."[135] It was this personal dimension of rapproachment and affiliation that Nassau brought to Edinburgh 1910, which indeed may have itself been more significant than anthropological or theological theories or insights.

Godfrey Callaway: The Fulfillment of Ubuntu

Godfrey Callaway (1867–1942) was an Anglican missionary of the Society for the Propagation of the Gospel at St. Cuthbert's Mission near Tsolo, Transkei, South Africa, for fifty years (1892 to 1942). Callaway served in the Diocese of St. John's Kaffraria in which Dr. Henry Callaway had been the first bishop and from which he had retired several years prior to Godfrey Callaway's arrival in South Africa. Among the missionaries responding to the questionnaire of Commission IV on Animistic Religions, Callaway was perhaps the most articulate advocate of a theology of fulfillment. As a writer and poet, he cultivated and celebrated friendships with all people, black and white. His prophetic voice was a lament addressing the racism that robbed the African people and societies of personhood, dignity, and respect. He offered a missionary stance of humanity and presence, drawing upon the resources in the African concept of *ubuntu* (humanity). In this regard he was a forerunner of his fellow Anglican missionary, John V. Taylor, who articulated a missiology of Christian presence in the African setting in his book, *The Primal Vision*.[136] Callaway's biographer, R. H. Shepherd, described him thus:

> Those who knew him are agreed that (Godfrey) Callaway's chief contribution was in what he was in himself: a man of vision and of sound judgment. . . quick to word a resolution which would reconcile opposing views. His obvious sincerity and goodness inspired trust and confidence; touching humility, love of the world of nature, cheerfulness and deep spirituality were features of his character.[137]

Background and Training

Godfrey Callaway, like Donald Fraser, was part of that generation of university students who were profoundly challenged by the missionary movement in the high imperialist era. Callaway came from a religious family—his mother was the daughter of an Anglican rector. He entered Cambridge University to study medicine but decided later to take holy orders. He went on to study theology at Wells Theological College. Callaway's childhood and much of his later life were marked by poor health, which may have contributed to his sensitivity to human relationships and his poetic spirit. Browning, Wordsworth, and Dean Church were among the many whose works were his recreation and who shaped his mind.[138] Canon Alan Gibson, a brother to the principal at Wells, was the priest in charge of St. Cuthbert's Mission in the diocese of St. John's Kaffraria. Callaway responded to Gibson's challenge for priests in the Transkei.[139] He was ordained a deacon in 1889, and arriving in South Africa in December of 1891, was assigned to work with Canon Gibson at St. Cuthberts in Tsolo and St. John's Cathedral in Umtata.[140]

The Diocese of St. Johns Kaffraria became a separate diocese in 1873. Dr. Henry Callaway was the first bishop. He made Umtata the site of his cathedral in 1877. St. Cuthbert's Mission was thirty-six miles from Umtata in Tsolo. The land for the mission was a gift from the chief of the Pondomisi in 1880.[141]

Godfrey Callaway entered a diocese that had a history of bishops who were gifted and perceptive in reflecting on the Christian Gospel in relation to African societies. In 1865, Henry Callaway was planning a new mission among the Griqua, while Barnsby Key was initiating work among the Mpondo. Key was Henry Callaway's type of missionary, sympathetically disposed to the customs and culture of African societies. He was eager to keep converts integrated with their own people rather than to establish Christian enclaves. Henry Callaway together with his successor as bishop, Barnsby Key, laid the foundation for the new diocese. Henry Callaway resigned in poor health in 1886, six years before Godfrey Callaway arrived at St. Cuthbert's Mission.

Bishop Key had a deep influence on Godfrey Callaway. From the beginning Key attempted first to win the friendship and confidence of the people.[142] It appears that Callaway also came to know the Pondomisi elders intimately from continuous personal relationships. There was no great urgency to convert the people.

One of the principal litmus tests in the attitude toward African culture was the issue of polygamy. Key felt deeply about the domestic tragedies in polygamous households, especially when they faced the demands of monogamy in the teaching of the church. The family life of even polygamists was sacred—"Rash hands may not touch it in any form; we must deal gently even with this form of family."[143] In 1889, Bishop Key and Bishop Mackenzie of Zululand organized a missionary conference in which the consensus on the issue of polygamy was that "Under no circumstances should a Christian wife be told to leave her husband if he married another wife by heathen (traditional African) rites."[144]

Bishop Key would not encourage a polygamist to put away his wives to receive baptism. His idea and that of the 1889 Missionary Conference was not to modify the demands and standards of the church. However, keeping the sanctity of family life might require that a convert be prepared to forego baptism.[145] Polygamists could not be baptized, but they could join a guild of "hearers"; and at the Synod of Bishops in 1893 it was agreed that wives of polygamists could be baptized under certain conditions.146

Godfrey Callaway had an intimate and penetrating knowledge of Xhosa, a language he loved; and he received strong affirmation from Bishop Keys for his respect for the traditional structures of African family life. In 1893, Canon Alan Gibson resigned from St. Cuthbert's; and Callaway, then twenty-six, was appointed priest by Bishop Keys.147

Callaway's Anglo-Catholic Emphasis

Almost a century after the British occupation of the Cape of South Africa, in the period between the Boer War (1899–1902) and the World War I, the theological climate in the Anglican Church was predominantly Anglo-Catholic. Peter Hinchliff has described the Anglican Church of the Province of South Africa as the great "Catholic" part of the Anglican communion.148

Bishop Robert Gray, who replaced Bishop J. W. Colenso of Natal, sympathized with the Tractarians, while Colenso was a Latitudinarian. Clergy recruited by Gray for service in South Africa were predominantly Tractarian and Anglo-Catholic.

F. D. Maurice's theological opinions had been largely rejected by Anglicans in South Africa in part because of the use Colenso had made of them. But Maurice's Christian Socialism had great influence on the next generation of the younger Anglo-Catholics back in England who were being recruited at the turn of the century to serve in South Africa within the Anglican communion.149 In addition there was a renewed interest in England in religious communities.

Callaway shared that vision and gathered around him a group of fellow workers, among them his brother Robert. Callaway's thoughts were moving towards a more dedicated form of service which found expression in the formation of the Society of St. Cuthbert. He was encouraged by members of the Society of Saint John the Evangelist (SSJE). The Society of St. Cuthbert was inaugurated on September 14, 1900, when the Bishop, Barnsby Key, received the profession of the first three members, with Father Godfrey Callaway as the Superior. Callaway's health failed and the small community did not grow. Finally Bishop Key invited the Society of Saint John the

Evangelist (Cowley Fathers) with its Mother house at Oxford[150] to take charge of St. Cuthbert's Mission along with the remaining members of the Community of St. Cuthbert.

Callaway's hopes that African Christians would turn toward the religious life went without realization until close to the end of his life, when the first African made his profession.[151]

A Theology of Fulfillment

When one examines the questionnaire of Godfrey Callaway for Commission IV, one is struck by two features. The first is a reluctance to describe and speak of African religion and a preference to speak of the social and communal dimensions of Pondomisi and African society. Instead of using the language of "doctrines" and "religious observances" in the questionnaire, Callaway responds that "a vast number of observances are just customs which had at one time a practical reason in their origin but are now carried on merely as belonging to the past."[152] Whereas other missionaries were eager to identify a belief in a Supreme God as a contact point, Callaway is more reserved: "Whatever belief in a Supreme God the heathen people may give assent to in conversation, there is practically no sense of practical obligation due to such belief."[153] Reading his responses to the questionnaire, one has the impression that Callaway's understanding of religion goes beyond looking for those features such as gods and spirits traditionally associated with religion.

The second feature in Callaway's questionnaire is his positive and affirming attitude toward the African social system. He says that the social and family system

> is a system not dictated by the revelation of God, but largely based on the known needs and lights of men. Anyone with any knowledge of the Kafirs recognizes at once the remarkable excellence in some respects of much that is visible in the social system.[154]

This genuinely positive attitude to African culture is not surprising, given the clear and imaginative leadership of Bishop Henry Callaway, the first Bishop of the diocese of St. John's Kaffraria. Godfrey Callaway cited the canons and regulations of the diocese regarding the stance that missionaries were to take toward African societies: "Missionaries should be careful not to interfere needlessly with harmless customs or to act toward them as though they partook of the nature of sin."[155] In addition, Callaway pointed out that converts were not to live separated and isolated on mission stations but rather integrated back into society as far as possible. He concluded, "Such regulations imply a sympathetic attitude on the part of the missionary towards the heathen and towards the tribal life and customs which support it."[156]

Callaway articulated more explicitly his approach as a Christian missionary in *Sketches of Kafir Life* (1905), a work written after fourteen years of experience. His writing is pastoral, poetic, prophetic and occasional rather than systematic. Callaway was a regular contributor to the *Cowley Evangelist*, the organ of the Society of Saint John the Evangelist, and *The East and The West*, a predominantly Anglican missionary journal.

We have an insight into the understanding of religion from which Callaway wrote and worked in a brief passage in *Sketches of Kafir Life*:

> We go out to the heathen primarily to fulfill and not to destroy, and a personal knowledge of the moral consciousness of the heathen must be very important. We need to sound their moral and religious instincts, as a doctor sounds his patients with a stethoscope. We are looking for the 'altar to the unknown God', which is built up somewhere in every human heart. We dig for it underneath all the surface appearances of indifference, because upon it we want to see the sacrifice of prayer ascending to God, who has revealed Himself in Jesus Christ. We may not expect to find much positive religion. The 'Unkulunkulu' of heathen thought may very possibly be only a sort of deified ancestral chief. We may find more and more that the one desire of the heathen mind is not to formulate a belief in the unseen, but rather hide from it.[157]

What is significant in this passage is that it moves the understanding of religion to the deeper level of a search for the primary loyalties, the "instincts," the sources of the genius and creativity of life in an African culture.

> It may seem that it is impossible to give the name 'religion' to that which seeks to escape fellowship. But yet, in *moral instincts which are at the root of all that is good in social life;* (emphasis mine) in the sense of loyalty to their chief; in the honour which responds to trust; in the charity which is generous to the needy; in the affections which bind together the home, we find some of the stones of that

altar. Him therefore whom they worship in ignorance, it is our privilege to proclaim.[158]

Callaway's understanding thus seems to move towards a definition of religion as the primary loyalties or concerns of a people. Callaway was searching for a foundation in the fundamental fabric and orientation of African societies upon which there could be continuity and fulfillment. Callaway located that "moral and religious instinct" in the Xhosa concept of *ubuntu* (humanity). This is detailed in two articles, "Ubuntu (Humanity)"[159] and "Further Thoughts about 'Ubuntu.'"[160] Callaway moves beyond the Xhosa dictionary definition of *ubuntu* as "human nature or quality, humanity, kindness, manliness, manhood,"[161] to a certain respect for the dignity of human nature itself. It is the dignity of human nature inherent in every person. "Ubuntu is really nothing else than the image of God stamped upon man, and by failing to respect that image we fail to respect God."[162]

In an African society where the corporate outlook is strong, the qualities that make up *ubuntu*, as we would expect, are largely social. "The one essential law, the fulfillment and crown of all other laws governing native life is that man should be a neighbor."[163]

There is a kind of idealization of African culture by Callaway which was likely a result of the prophetic and poetic stand which he had taken against the policies of racial prejudice that permeated South African political and social life. Callaway saw in this clash two different value systems. He regarded the individualistic gospel of the West as running counter to all that was best in African traditions.

Europeans found particularly difficult the lack of a sense of responsibility in Africans because of the European value of devotion to duty. Africans recognized that whites value reverence for truth, respect for a promise, strict morality; but, Callaway remarked, "the eyes of the African are upon a quality dearer than any other—he wants respect for fellow-man."[164] Callaway observed that it was the complaint of Africans that the attitude of the white man towards himself denied his own *ubuntu*, because he did not respect the *ubuntu* (human nature) shared by all.[165]

In the contact with whites (missionaries were not exempted), Callaway asserted that this greatest treasure enshrined in the Africans' social life, *ubuntu*, was being lost. He felt that this greatest spiritual and social value was being threatened from two additional directions: (1) migrant labor and the purely wage contract had dissociated work from the rest of life; (2) home for the African, which united kin, land, occupation, and clans, was being lost. The loss of home threatened spiritual qualities-self-respect, respect for others, and manners which are the ways in which members of a community take an interest in each other and which spring from respect for humanity.[166]

It was obvious to Callaway that tribal societies did not have sufficient forces to meet the spoilers. Tribal custom, strong as it was, could not hold its own against the spoilers from modern society. Against this invader, Callaway regarded himself as a trustee of African societies, one of those who cried out the Xhosa warning and exclamation, "*Zemk'inkomo magwalandini!*"("The cattle have left us, ye cowards,") when a marauding party raided the cattle from the kraal.[167]

Callaway begins his book, *The Fellowship of the Veld*, with the twin questions: "To what extent may Christianity be presented as the fulfillment of the primitive social order? What is there in the primitive order which will dispose the people to accept Christianity?"[168] Callaway's own spiritual inclinations were toward community; he saw the "Ancient Kraal" leading to and fulfilled in the "New Kraal." The first word one learns as one enters is

> *Bavo wetu*—'our Father'. It is a word which not only stamps all the good fellowship of life with a divine sanction, it also teaches that every member of the 'New Kraal' who would have God for Father must have man for brother. As he learns the mysteries of the "New Kraal", he finds that God is revealed in Jesus Christ, not only as Creator, but also as *neighbour*. [emphasis Callaway's] He learns that the new tribe has no limits of race narrower than humanity, and, if he would have the neighbourly succour of Jesus Christ for himself, he must be a neighbour to all.[169]

This chapter has described a variety of the definitions and understandings of religion that informed the British and American missionaries' interpretations of African traditional religions. Four different models were identified: moral reconstruction, radical displacement, bridging by affiliation, and fulfillment/affirmation.

Donald Fraser's moral reconstruction model was guided by an ethical and humanitarian understanding of religion, both in terms of his own missionary motivation and vision, and of his understanding of the religious foundations of ethics in African societies. Fraser shared the ethical concern that motivated evangelicals in the anti-slavery movement: a comprehensive vision of the rebuilding of society and human dignity through "commerce, civilization, and Christianity." Thus, Fraser and the Livingstonia missionaries were prepared to encourage and cooperate in extending the British Protectorate over Nyasaland.

For Fraser the Christian understanding of law needed to replace two religious foundations of ethics in Ngoni society: (1) loyalty and solidarity which was limited only to the family, clan, or tribe, and (2) the magical concept of justice reflected in the trial by ordeal. There was both fulfillment and displacement in Fraser's model. Fulfillment took place when Christian law expanded the horizons of accountability and responsibility beyond family and clan and universalized those claims. On the other hand, Christian law displaced the magical conception of justice.

W. D. Armstrong's radical displacement model was in some respects a modification of Fraser's model. Both Armstrong and Fraser shared a vision and motivation from the humanitarian concerns of the anti-slavery movement. Their experiences with colonial governments contrasted, however. Instead of encouraging the colonial government to intervene for the purpose of stability and order, as did Fraser and the Livingstonia Mission, Armstrong and the Regions Beyond Missionary Union opposed the policies of King Leopold's Congo and advocated justice. Armstrong's definition of religion was far more closely associated with ethics than was Fraser's. Armstrong saw less evidence of ethical life in the Balolo society, which indicated to him that there was no religious foundation. He took the radical position that there was little or no linkage between Christianity and Balolo religious experience. Therefore the missionary task was to build a new foundation, and to displace what was previously there. The breakdown of African societies in the Congo River basin and their brutalization by the slave trade, together with the exploitative colonial policies, had created an atmosphere of mutual suspicion and distrust which made it more difficult for W. D. Armstrong and his fellow missionaries to appreciate the religious traditions that were there.

R. H. Nassau's model began from a definition of religion which may reflect influence from Schleiermacher, "the sense of infinite dependence." This definition made it possible for Nassau to make a clear distinction between African ideas of God and fetishism. Nassau associated religion with a belief in God. Although African ideas of God had been in a process of degeneration, there remained a "feeling" for God. Nassau was clear that he believed Africans were monotheists. This monotheism was rooted in an original revelation and was the foundation for Christian faith. Fetishism was a human invention and a distortion and aberration of religion which Nassau rejected. The recognition of the "feeling" for God in African traditional religions opened the way for the rich and genuine friendships Nassau enjoyed with the African people among whom he lived. Nassau regarded these affiliations as more significant bridges to convey the Gospel than the theological and religious ideas and constructs that missionaries look for.

The model of Godfrey Callaway was fuflfillment through affirmation of human nature (*ubuntu*). He began from the fundamental religious values that were the very foundation of Xhosa society. He located these in the African concept of *ubuntu*, the respect and dignity of being human. In an environment in which racial prejudice and economic exploitation threatened the very core of African life, Christian community was the preservation and fulfillment of *ubuntu*. Among the missionaries responding to the questionnaire on "Animistic Religions," Callaway was the most articulate advocate of the fulfillment model.

The models used by missionaries lead us to conclude that all the models described here, except that of W. D. Armstrong, had the capacity to discriminate between those elements of tribal religion that can be accepted, incorporated, transformed, or fulfilled and those that are clearly incompatible with the Christian faith. The idea that missionaries at Edinburgh regarded African religions as demonic and to be uprooted is a judgment which is unwarranted from this evidence. It is not true that the missionaries' judgments were categorical and the models they used were unable to discriminate. The fulfillment model, particularly as developed by Godfrey Callaway, lends itself to a more respectful posture appropriate for dialogue. However, this was a prophetic stance that appears from our vantage point to have been ahead of its time. The missionaries of the imperialist era who contributed to the article entitled "Animistic Religions" are their own best advocates. They are worthy partners with present-day Christians in tribal societies in the search for a more indigenous theology.

VI. The Legacy of Edinburgh 1910

The Animistic Religions Report

We began with the perception that missionaries of the imperialist era have been inadequately heard and represented. Their attitudes and actions have often been represented as lacking in understanding of and respect for tribal religions. Missionary attitudes and contributions of the era, 1880–1920, were examined by studying the Edinburgh 1910 Missionary Conference, in particular, the work and writings of the twenty-five missionaries who contributed to the "Animistic Religions" report. The questionnaire circulated by Commission IV was focused primarily on the issue of the relationship of Christianity to religion in tribal societies and the attitude and stance of the missionary toward these religions. Fourteen of the twenty-five missionary correspondents served in Africa, hence the focus on that continent.

Although the present research was not comprehensive of all missionaries in attendance at Edinburgh 1910, this book's findings parallel W. H. T. Gairdner's claim that the belief that "non-Christian religions are of the devil and to be eradicated"[1] was certainly not the major view represented by missionaries at the conference.

The present assessment of the stance and attitudes toward tribal religious traditions at Edinburgh 1910 centered around several questions:

(1) What kind of representation was there at Edinburgh 1910? How were tribal peoples, particularly Africans, represented?

(2) What theories and insights from the emerging sciences of anthropology and comparative religion contributed to the report on "Animistic Religions?"

(3) What understandings or definitions of religion shaped and informed the missionary correspondents' attitudes toward tribal religions?

(4) How did colonial history and policy influence the missionary correspondents' attitudes towards tribal religions?

Role of Delegates From Emerging Churches

Edinburgh 1910 was a conference with twelve hundred missionary leaders and administrators. Attendance was only by invitation or appointment. There was a small representation of Christians from the younger churches of Asia, but none from Africa or the homelands of tribal peoples. By the choice of delegates, the conference did not seem to be attuned toward conversation with peoples of other cultures. The watchword of the conference was "the evangelization of the world in this generation." Therefore the conference's agenda was primarily "how to do mission." The mood of optimism and confidence that "white men" had a burden to carry for the world did not lend itself to a posture for dialogue. The fact that there were no African delegates to the conference may be indicative of a move during the last decades of the nineteenth century to replace indigenous African missionaries with staff from Britain and Europe. The best known case was the replacement of Yoruba Bishop Samuel Crowther of the Church Missionary Societies' Mission on the Niger River. At the conference, Dr. Alexander Camphor, an African American missionary from Liberia, chided missionary societies for not giving Africa the same priorities afforded their work in Asia.

Nevertheless, Edinburgh 1910 marks a significant point in the mission and witness of the church. Bishop Azariah of India confronted western missionaries about their patronizing attitudes. Under the canopy of colonialism, Western missionaries in 1910 were associated with positions of power and privilege; without a strong counterbalance from people in Asia and Africa there was a very real danger that the Christian message might be radically corrupted and compromised into a kind of spiritual imperialism. Azariah pled with missionaries to be friends and colleagues of people in Asia and Africa. Edinburgh 1910 marks the turning point in which leaders from the emerging churches of Asia and Africa have had an increasingly greater voice in mission policy and the globalization of Christianity. This voice has the potential for revealing the biases of those in power and increasing the integrity of the Christian witness.

Initiatives in Anthropology

Animism was the most popular concept for understanding tribal religions in the era of the Edinburgh Conference in the late nineteenth century. The animistic theory of the origin of religion as developed by E. B. Tylor was generally taken as self-evident. It was assumed that tribal societies represented the "primitive" mode of thought out of which "civilized" religion had evolved. Tylor's evolutionary theory might have had logical consistency, but it lacked historical evidence about how religious beliefs originated. It was a theory that was not based on actual field research.

The concept of animism tends to distance and polarize Europeans and Africans. In fact, the term animism, particularly as part of an evolutionary theory of the development of religion, has attributed to African traditional religions some concepts that Africans regard as derogatory, prejudicial and paternalistic.[2]

Even though the term "animistic religions" was used to refer to tribal religions, there was no indication that E. B. Tylor's evolutionary theory of the development of religion from its lowest level, "animism," played a significant part in the report. It was balanced by Henry Callaway's linguistic study, which was cited by Commission IV as a model of missionary research and understanding of African religion. Callaway emphasized much more the common shared dimensions of the human religious experience.

Henry Callaway and Henri Junod both pioneered in providing creative ways to study African religions on the basis of actual field research. Callaway did this through the study of Zulu mythology, using a linguistic model similar to Max Müller's comparative mythology. He used an approach that permitted Zulu people to tell their own stories and traditions. Junod's contribution was a more comprehensive study of the life of a particular African tribe, with a methodology that was similar to that which was later developed by the functionalist school of British social anthropology. Junod did not see religion as a distinct element of culture but rather as part of the integrated life of the tribe. Junod's concept of evolution was not concerned with the search for the origins of religion as was Tylor's. Rather, he had an awareness that cultures and religious ideas are constantly in the process of change and therefore he had more historical regard for the integrity of both culture and religion. He also recognized the significance of the moment in which he lived among the Thonga at the confluence of two radically different cultures, one oriented to "magic," the other to "science."

Both Callaway and Junod conceived of Christianity as a fulfillment of African religions. Callaway, encouraged by Max Müller, was not able to limit divine revelation to Christianity alone. He believed that God had revealed himself in African religions as well as in Christianity. Callaway and Max Müller believed there was a form of Christianity towards which all religions were moving, as the fulfillment of the human religious quest, though it was not necessarily the Christianity of the West.

Junod was more practical and specific in recognizing how Christianity fulfilled African traditional religion. For example, the Christian concept of God in Christ transformed the African belief in a transcendent, distant Creator God and ancestral spirits into a powerful discovery of theistic monotheism and a personal, caring God. A second example was that instead of denying the African spiritual world view, Junod recognized in it the relevant connection to the Christian belief in the work and power of the Holy Spirit.

One of the significant issues in the meeting of Africans and Westerners in the late nineteenth century was the tension between religion, science and magic. To discriminate between religion and magic, Junod used a definition of religion similar to Schleiermacher's definition of religion as a feeling of absolute dependence, to discriminate between religion and magic. Junod could accept African religion when it was an expression of dependence on the divine, but he had much greater difficulty understanding and accepting the African magical world view.

This book has shown that the missionary contributors to the report had a preference for anthropological insights which were based upon actual field studies, such as those done by Henry Callaway and Henri Junod. The participants at Edinburgh 1910 recognized and appreciated the methodology of Henry Callaway. It was also used by others, such as Ferdinand Hahn among the Kols in Bihar, India, and Robert Nassau in Gabon, who had done extensive linguistic work and collected anthologies of folklore. These extensive collections reflect the missionaries' appreciation of these cultures, and the trust the people must have had in the outsiders to share these valued resources with them. Missionaries with anthropological interests made significant contributions to the study of African religions.

This attention to field study shows up particularly in the attitude of the missionaries toward other religions. Junod and Callaway conceived of the relationship of Christianity to African religions in complementary ways. Their concepts of fulfillment and transformation were not devoid of paternalistic overtones, but their intention was not demeaning or derogatory. This fact was especially significant given Junod's critique of the magical world view from his western, scientific orientation.

The writings of missionaries cited at Edinburgh 1910 in the field of African religion have been regarded as anthropological classics and have moved missionary thinking toward a more human and sensitive appreciation of the common human religious experience.

Approaches to Tribal Religions

The creativity and insight of missionaries who did not have the current tools of anthropology and comparative religion available to them is amazing. At least five models based upon their understandings of religion were operative in the writings of the missionary respondents. These five models can be divided into two basic approaches. We first examined the European missionaries who were influenced by Gustav Warneck's missiology, which focused on the building of national churches. These missionaries were much more intentional about respecting and preserving the corporate nature of tribal life and recognized the place of religion in preserving that solidarity. The second basic approach was that of the British and American missionaries whose nineteenth-century concerns in Africa were associated with the Evangelical anti-slavery movement in Britain and the United States. Their heritage from the anti-slavery movement and David Livingstone combined Christianity, commerce, and civilization. The moral restructuring of society and the role of religion in preserving and establishing social and individual ethics were central in these models. These two basic approaches gave rise to other models the missionaries used in relating to traditional, tribal societies.

The German Lutheran model called for a two-stage conversion process of continuity and change, which took into account the tension between corporate and individual ideas of religion. This German model drew upon the Lutheran doctrine of the orders of creation, which respected and preserved the social institutions of society, and the pietist doctrine of the *ecclesiolae in ecclesia*. This model maintained the group solidarity of tribal societies but kept it in tension with the ethical and individual emphasis of Pietism. This German Lutheran model was illustrated by the work of Johannes Warneck, Ludwig Nommensen, Ferdinand Hahn, and A. C. Kruyt.

The British and American missionaries were not as clearly unified in their approaches. Fraser's approach to religion focused on finding and restructuring a foundation of morality and ethics for a society in the process of demise. He worked to build Christian community and a new sense of law based on Christian principles. The Ngoni and Tumbuku societies were undergoing rapid social change, first because of the devastation of the slave trade, and secondly because of the impact of Western technology, economics, and colonial political structures. Fraser saw the need for providing a new foundation for ethics. He worked for the transformation of two Ngoni structures: their sense of community solidarity and community loyalty, and their magical view of justice, illustrated in the trial by ordeal. Fraser called for strong family and clan loyalties to become more inclusive and universal, and taught that Christian law, with its call for personal responsibility, held individuals far more accountable for ethical and moral behavior than did the system of magic.

W. D. Armstrong had a more exclusively ethical definition of religion than did Fraser. He regarded religion as the foundation of ethics. He saw the presence of polygamy, slavery, and human sacrifice as clear evidences of the lack of moral life in Balolo society. He felt therefore that their culture contained nothing worthy of being called religion. Our negative evaluation of Armstrong's position needs to be tempered by the realization that Balolo society had been devastated by the slave trade and Belgian colonial policies and exploitation.

Nassau's approach bridged the radical rejection and fulfillment approaches. His system tended to be dialectical, holding together the polarities of the fulfillment model of Callaway and the discontinuity models of Warneck and Armstrong. Nassau bridged this polarity by an affirmation of affiliation and deep personal relationships, which he regarded as having a mysterious ability to communicate religious ideas and feelings beyond rational, theological formulations. Nassau was able to hold these polarities in a creative kind of tension, using a definition of religion borrowed from Schleiermacher, that "religion is a feeling of absolute dependence." This definition enabled him to identify an implicit monotheism in the feeling for God which permeates African culture. Yet he criticized the development of fetishism as part of a process of the degeneration of religion.

Godfrey Callaway viewed religion as a humanizing force in culture. He saw this idea embodied in the African concept of *ubuntu*—the respect and dignity of human beings, an expression of which he saw in the Xhosa greetings and manners. He encouraged the preservation and fulfillment of *ubuntu*, which he regarded as a fundamental religious value of African culture. Callaway believed Christian community was the fulfillment and affirmation of the African understanding of being human in community.

In the South African environment in which racial prejudice and economic exploitation threatened the very core of African life, Callaway was an advocate of African traditional values. His stand often placed him in the minority among Europeans. He was the most articulate advocate of the fulfillment model among the missionaries responding to the questionnaire.

Each of the five models, except that of W. D. Armstrong, has the capacity to discriminate from the perspective of that model, between those elements of tribal religion that can be accepted, incorporated, transformed, or fulfilled, and those that are clearly incompatible with the Christian faith. Therefore the characterization that missionaries at Edinburgh regarded African religions as demonic and to be uprooted is a judgment which is not supported by the research. This kind of statement suggests that the missionaries' judgments were categorical and the models they used were unable to discriminate. The present exploration of Edinburgh 1910 has demonstrated that this is not the case. The ability to incorporate strengths and to discern places of incompatibility opened the door for them to engage in a conversational process in the interreligious encounter and witness.

In the missionary respondents and reports of Edinburgh 1910 prophetic voices are heard which call for a more respectful, dialogical stance of mutual learning. The missionaries who were the focus of this study were for the most part students of the culture, friends of the people, and advocates for their welfare. Missionaries were in the forefront of careful linguistic, literary, and anthropological research which helped to preserve the mythology, history, and customs of the people and assisted them in moving toward more indigenous or contextual expressions of Christianity.

The Interface of Colonialism and the Missionary Enterprise

The interaction of missionaries with colonial regimes and policies was marked by a dynamic tension even during the high imperialist era. On the one hand, the Livingstonia Mission in Nyasaland preceded the British colonial administration into the area and actively promoted the extension of the British Protectorate over Nyasaland. The missionaries' appeal to the colonial office helped to terminate the slave trade and to keep the Portuguese, who did not have a clear anti-slavery record, out of the region. The Scottish missionaries initiated and collaborated with the extension of British colonial policies in Central Africa. On the other hand, the Regions Beyond Missionary Union opposed the Belgian colonial regime and joined with other human rights groups in both the international and British political arenas to expose the atrocities of King Leopold II's Congo. It is significant that missionaries could co-operate with secular human rights groups on issues of justice. Godfrey Callaway and Junod also carried an advocacy role against the exploitative migrant labor policies in the gold and diamond mines of South Africa. Their work and writings encouraged the preservation of African culture and society. Godfrey Callaway regarded himself as a watchman warning Xhosa and Zulu people of the way European technology and migrant labor were "stealing" the wealth of their cultural values.

Thus this sample of missionaries' attitudes in the imperialist era indicates that missionaries were much more than a religious camouflage for the exploits of colonial governments. Although Christian missions often cooperated with and benefitted from colonialism, and were in positions of power and privilege in ways more significant than they probably recognized,[3] they were also often in tension with colonial administrations and policies. They critiqued colonial policies. They worked for justice and human rights, and stood in prophetic judgment of its policies and plans.

Missiological Significance

The theology of religions, how Christians relate to and address those outside the Christian community, and their posture toward people of other faiths, was a pressing issue for the missionaries and the people of Asia and Africa at Edinburgh 1910. Today the question is no longer far away; it is as close as our next door neighbor. In our contemporary pluralist urban environment, there is a new urgency to wrestle with a Christian theology of religions. The questions of Edinburgh 1910 seem once again relevant, for there are few places untouched by the religious pluralism of the contemporary world.

The early missionary encounter within primal societies shows us the priorities the Edinburgh missionaries set for themselves. Robert Nassau described this encounter as a relationship of affiliation, a friendship that penetrated beyond the ideas, concepts, and world views that often separate and divide. It was friendship that provided the grounds for true conversation. It was, above all, a decision of the heart to accept the person of another faith without resenting their presence or the views they held. This was dealing with mystery, the mystery of friendship. This commitment to the relational dimension was not unique to Nassau; it was present in all the missionaries we have met. However, there is a particularly personal dimension in the writings of Henry Callaway, Henri Junod, Ferdinand Hahn, Robert Nassau, Albert Kruyt, and Godfrey Callaway. It is reflected in the careful linguistic analyses and dictionaries of these persons, who gained mastery of the language and sought to communicate well and accurately. These collections in turn reflect the trust of their informants to share the wealth of their traditional cultural and religious heritage. The collection and preservation of folklore and mythology is a significant way of listening and learning. It opens the way for a two-way conversation, the mutual respect that comes from both giving and receiving.

In her biography of Temple Gairdner, the Anglican missionary in Cairo who compiled the historical account of Edinburgh 1910, Constance Padwick has described Gairdner's approach to Muslims, "Other teachers taught us how to refute Islam, he taught us how to love Muslims."[4] The contemporary missiologist from South Africa, David Bosch, has pointed out that conversation and understanding are possible if we proceed from the expectation of meeting God, who has preceded us and has been preparing people within the contexts of their own cultures and convictions.[5] Bosch presses even more articulately the direction the Edinburgh 1910 missionaries were reaching toward by affirming:

> God's Spirit is constantly working in ways that pass human understanding. We do not take God to others. God accompanies us and also comes toward us. . . We are not the haves standing over against the have nots. We are all recipients of the same mercy. Therefore we approach adherents of other faiths reverently, taking off our shoes as the place we are approaching is holy ground.[6]

The missionaries at Edinburgh 1910 held in tension the elements of continuity and change in their models of approaching tribal religions, but they began their theologies of religion by identifying elements they could affirm and respect as holy ground. In the missionary respondents and reports of Edinburgh 1910 prophetic voices are heard which call for a more respectful, dialogical stance of mutual learning. The missionaries who were the focus of this study were for the most part students of the culture, friends of the people, and advocates for their welfare.

A second area of missiological significance of Edinburgh 1910 is the contribution toward more indigenous or contextual theologies. The ethnographic, linguistic, and anthropological reporting of these early twentieth-century missionaries has historical significance not only for the missionary movement from the West, but for the understanding of Christianity within these tribal societies to which the missionaries went. Many of these societies had little or no tradition of writing. Prior to the missionary introduction of schools, they relied on oral tradition.

It is important for the church in Africa to see this encounter between the early missionaries and their societies as part of the larger history of the development of African Christian thought and ethics in the twentieth century. Both Junod's and Callaway's writings are particularly helpful in providing material from an era before there was major contact with the West. They are therefore instructive as to what approaches and concepts might be cogent to an Africanization of Christianity. A number of the religious issues they identified as central to the peoples among whom they lived have been articulated in the life and theology of African Independent Church movements. For example, the prominent role of the Holy Spirit, the attractive power of the concept of monotheism and law, and the practical applications in life of prophecy and healing are all central themes. The centrality of these themes, may well be related to the primal world view which sees nature and human societies as permeated with spiritual powers and beings. There needs to be even more encouragement for African Christians to develop more fully their own theologies of faith and evangelism and to discover valuable theological conversational partners including some of these early missionaries. With the present majority of Christians now living in the southern, non-white, non-Western parts of the world, their perspective and viewpoints urgently need to be heard.

One of the significant imbalances in the Christian world at present is the fact that the Christians of the West are the primary archivists of the Christian movement and its history. The churches in Asia and Africa need greater access to these historical materials and resources in order to gain historical perspective. For example, the multiplicity of models for approaching traditional religions at Edinburgh 1910 should provide freedom and perspective for the development of more indigenous theologies today.

It would also be significant to explore the models that were developed at the International Missionary Council in Jerusalem in 1928 and at Tambaram in 1938 in order to see what movement and development took place after World War I, with the demise of the nineteenth century's optimistic spirit and ideas of progress and development.

Persisting Questions

There are related issues which need to be addressed in the unfolding interpretation of Edinburgh and the ensuing twentieth-century missionary movement and the emergence of Christianity in the two-thirds world. There is a need to examine this material from a younger church's viewpoint. Mission history could, for example, be read with sensitivity attuned to the paternalism and prejudice that gave rise to the African Independent Church movement throughout much of the African continent. More could be done with the justice and humanitarian themes discussed in chapter 5. With the current political climate in a world where old categories of East and West are in flux, there is a new tension between the wealthier countries of the North and the poorer countries of the South. How might this earlier history of the meeting of two cultures, two religions, two peoples inform the current processes of becoming one world?

The reconstruction model of Fraser could be much further developed in light of other historical, political, and sociological research. If the western invasion of African societies threatened the fabric and social structure of their lives and culture, what has been the history of the alternative foundations Fraser and others had projected?

Some of the misreading of history has been unnecessarily negative. A more positive and honest evaluation could correct earlier misconceptions and accusations that contribute to racial tensions and feelings. It is important to note that Mbiti and Idowu, who have critiqued some of the missionaries, are advocates for fulfillment — the very same stance taken at Edinburgh 1910![7] Additional models could and should be developed, especially from non-western viewpoints. It would be particularly valuable to have an African scholar's response to some of the models developed from Edinburgh 1910.

An even more pertinent issue for our times is the question of a Christian theology of religions. The theology of religions that dominated the discussions at Edinburgh 1910 was that of fulfillment. One should ask whether these two polarities of discontinuity and fulfillment are false alternatives. This concept has roots that go back to Jesus' own words regarding his relationship to his Jewish and Old Testament heritage in law, "I came to fulfill and not to destroy", Matthew 5:17. The idea of fulfillment had a special resonance with people caught up in nineteenth-century ideas of progress and theories of evolution, and in the birth of the new discipline of comparative religion formulated by Max Müller. The stage was set for comparing religions on an ascending scale. There was no doubt that Christianity was at the pinnacle and that every other religion was a form of preparation pointing toward Christianity. Other religions could prepare the way for Christianity, but it was the crown. This was India missionary J. N. Farquhar's point in his widely read book, *The Crown of Hinduism* (1913). Ideas of fulfillment continued to be in the forefront of missionary thinking in the sequel to

Edinburgh, the International Missionary Council, which met in Jerusalem in 1928.

One question that persists is, how does one move beyond the implied paternalism in the models of fulfillment and discontinuity to one that is more humble, respectful, and open to dialogue. One should ask whether the polarities between fulfillment and discontinuity common to all the models examined here are in fact false alternatives.

A critique of the fulfillment concept was articulated by A. G. Hogg in his "selective contrast" in *Karma and Redemption* (1908). Hogg argued that Christianity fulfilled Hinduism, not by a linear evolutionary development, but by a transformation that meant a reorientation around a new center. Christianity addresses questions which are not being asked by Hinduism or by traditional African religions. Hendrik Kraemer and Lesslie Newbigin[8] have elaborated on this insight, recognizing that each religion is a system, a world with its own axis and structures. Christianity and other religions face in different directions and ask fundamentally different questions. As an illustration, we return to Jesus' words, "I came to fulfill and not to destroy" (Matthew 5:17). Jesus' intent was not simply a more rigorous application of the law, but a life lived in graciousness that addresses the spirit and intent of the law. Christianity offers a grace that goes beyond the law. Law defines the borders between persons, as does grace, but grace actively seeks the welfare and the healing of the neighbor, and indeed even of the enemy.

The fulfillment model kept in place the strong Protestant Christocentric emphasis and the idea of Christianity as the absolute religion. In this model, salvation comes only through Christ; but at the same time, one recognizes that Christian faith is not the only sphere of God's revelation, but it is only in Christ that revelation finds fulfillment.

The great limitation of the fulfillment models, as well as the discontinuity model, is that they all draw the line between truth and Christianity on one side and falsehood or partial truth and the non-Christian religions on the other. The stage is set for a conversation that moves predominantly in one direction, from those who have the truth to those who do not. Such models can hardly avoid a paternalistic spirit.

A Christian theology of religions ought to point in the direction of a more respectful and mutual conversation. The fulfillment model, as developed by missionaries of the imperialist era, begins but does not go far enough. Our theology of religions should lead us to recognize that the line between good and evil, between true and false, does not run between Christian and non-Christian, but lies within the midst of each religion and within each individual. The Pauline way of referring to law is instructive: Paul regards the law as God's revelation, but he can also refer to law as one of the *stoicheia*, the ruling spirits of the universe, in Galatians 4:8–9. The law is part of God's revelation, but it can also become a kind of legalism that distorts and enslaves. On the basis of this model, each religion has elements of good and evil. The recognition of the human capacity for distortion makes it possible to see the divine and the demonic within both Christianity and other religious traditions. This stance offers the possibilities of humility, openness, and repentance, on both sides. Godfrey Callaway called for repentance and issued prophetic judgment on the racial prejudice, exploitation, and policies of apartheid so often supported by his fellow Christians in South Africa. Repentance opens the way for a new mutual respect, for genuine dialogue and witness. This kind of witness can be characterized as "one beggar telling another where he has found food." From a stance of repentance one can give humble witness to where one is finding grace and truth in Jesus Christ.

In the pilgrimage back to Edinburgh 1910, one is gratefully aware of the vision, energy, creativity, and compassion of a people who were committed to communicating the Gospel without the tools of missiology and cross-cultural communication now at our disposal. This study helps us to see that in the quest for a more faithful Christian witness and genuine encounter with people of other faiths, we are not alone, but are heirs of a growing and rich heritage. We can take courage in our common task in the words of Henry Callaway's affirmation: "God is ever working and never tired; so His working is His rest. His rest and work are both eternal—He works and rests in the 'eternal now.' . . . 'My Father worketh hitherto and I work . . .'"[9]

Appendix A

The Questionnaire Circulated by Commission IV[1]

1. Kindly give your name, station, and the Church or Society in connection with which you are working. Name the non-Christian religion or religions with which you have to deal in your missionary work, and say with what classes of the population you yourself come into contact.

2. Can you distinguish among the doctrines and forms of religious observances current among these classes any which are mainly traditional and formal from others which are taken in earnest and are genuinely prized as a religious help and consolation?

3. What do you consider to be the chief moral, intellectual, and social hindrances in the way of a full acceptance of Christianity?

4. Have you found in individuals any dissatisfaction with their own faith on specific points? If so, give details.

5. What attitude should the Christian preacher take toward the religion of the people among whom he labours?

6. What are the elements in the said religion or religions which present points of contact with Christianity and may be regarded as a preparation for it?

7. Which elements in the Christian gospel and the Christian life have you found to possess the greatest power of appeal and which have awakened the greatest opposition?

8. Have the people among whom you work a practical belief in a personal immortality and in the existence of a Supreme God?

9. To what extent do questions of "higher criticism" and other developments of modern Western thought exert an influence in your part of the mission field, and what effect do they have on missinary work?

10. Has your experience in missionary labour altered either in form or substance your impression as to what constitute the most important and vital elements in the Christian Gospel?

11. What was it in Christianity which made special appeal to you? Did the Western form in which Christianity was presented to you perplex you? What are the dstinctively Western elements, as you see them, in the missionary message as now presented? Was it the sense of sin which enabled you to go behind the Western forms? If not, what was it?

Appendix B

List Of Correspondents:

Animistic Religions[1]

The Rev. W. D. Armstrong (Regions Beyond Missionary Union), Upper Congo.

The Rev. W. T. Balmer, B. A. (Wesleyan Methodist Missionary Society,) Sierra Leone.

The Rev. G. Callaway (Society for the Propagation of the Gospel), Briqualand East, South Africa.

The Right Rev. Bishop Cameron (Society for the Propagation of the Gospel), Capetown.

Mr. Andrew Campbell (United Free Church of Scotland), Manbhum, India.

Miss J. E. Chadwick (formerly of Church Missionary Society), Uganda.

The Rev. S. W. Cox (Society for the Propagation of the Gospel), Port Elizabeth, Cape Colony.

The Rev. Canon Dale (Universities Mission to Central Africa), Zanzibar.

The Rev. W. C. Dodd (Presbyterian Church in the U.S.A.) Laos.

The Rev. Donald Fraser (United Free Church of Scotland), West Nyasaland.

The Rev. R. S. Fyffe (Society for the Propagation of the Gospel), Madalay, Burma.

The Rev. W. Babrooke Grubb (South American Missionary Society), Paraguay.[2]

The Rev. Fred. Hahn (Gossnersche Missionsgesellschaft), Bengal.[3]

The Venerable Archdeacon Johnson (Society for the Propagation of the Gospel), Zululand.

The Rev. Copland King (Society for the Propagation of the Gospel), New Guinea.

Mr. Alb. C. Kruyt (Nederlandshe Zendeling Genootschap), Central Celebes.

The Rev. R. H. Nassau, D. D. (Presbyterian Church in the U.S.A.), formerly of West Africa.

The Rev. B. J. Ross, M.A. (United Free Church of Scotland), Transkei, Cape Colony.

The Rev. W. H. Sanders (American Board of Commissioners for Foreign Missions), Benguella Angola.

Missionar H. Sundermann (Rheinische Missionsgesellschaft), Borneo.

Mr. Carl Wandres (Rheinische Missionsgesellschaft), Windhuk, Ger. S.W. Africa.

Herr Missions-inspektor Lic. Joh. Warneck (Rheinische Missionsgesellschaft), formerly of Sumatra.

The Rev. Geo. Whitehead (Society for the Propagation of the Gospel), Burma.[4]

The Rev. G. A. Wilder (American Board of Commissioners for Foreign Missions), Rhodesia.

Missionar Dr. Joh. Winkler (Rheinische Missionsgesellschaft), Pea Radja, Sumatra.

Notes

I. Edinburgh 1910: A Retrospective View

1. Peter Walshe, *Black Nationalism in South Africa: A Short History* (Johannesburg: Raven Press, 1963).

2. Kwame Bediako, "The Roots of African Theology," *International Bulletin of Missionary Research* 13, no. 2 (April 1989): 58–59. See also Kwame Bediako, *Theology and Identity: The Impact of Culture upon Christian Thought in the Second Century and Modern Africa*, (Oxford: Regnum Books, 1992), where he develops more fully his critique of European ethnocentricism and its effects in creating the theological problem of relating to the African religious past in chapter six, "Christianity as 'Civilisation': The Legacy of 'The Third Opportunity' and the Making of a Modern Identity Problem," 225–266.

3. Desmond Tutu, "Whither African Theology?" in *Christianity in Independent Africa*, eds. E.W. Fashole-Luke et al. (London: Rex Collins, 1978), 366.

4. For a survey by a writer outside the Christian tradition, see Okot P'Bitek's book, *African Religions in Western Scholarship* (Kampala, Nairobi, Dar Es Salaam: East African Literature Bureau, n.d. [approx. 1975]). See also David Westerbund, *African Religion in African Scholarship: A Preliminary Study of the Religious and Political Background* (Stockholm: University of Stockholm, Almquist & Wiksell International, 1985).

5. Harry Sawyerr, "The First World Missionary Conference: Edinburgh 1910," *International Review of Mission* 67, (July 1978): 271. Sawyerr is quoting from W. H. T. Gairdner, *"Edinburgh 1910": An Account and Interpretation of the World Missionary Conference* (Edinburgh and London: Published for the Committee of the World Missionary Conference by Oliphant, Anderson, & Ferrier, 1910), 137.

6. Bediako, 50, citing World Missionary Conference 1910. *Report of Commission IV: The Missionary Message In Relation to Non-Christian Religions* (Edinburgh and London: Oliphant, Anderson & Ferrier, and New York, Chicago and Toronto: Fleming H. Revell, 1910), 24. Hereafter referred to in the notes as *The Missionary Message*.

7. W. H. T. Gairdner, *"Edinburgh 1910": An Account and Interpretation of the World Missionary Conference* (Edinburgh and London: Oliphant, Anderson, & Ferrier, 1910), 137.

8. Ibid., 137–138.

9.   *The Missionary Message*, 24.

10. *The Missionary Message*, "General Conclusions," 267.

11. Ibid.

12. Ibid., ix.

13. See Appendix A for a copy of the questionnaire circulated by Commission IV to the correspondents, *The Missionary Message*, 2.

14. See Appendix B for the List of Correspondents who answered the questionnaire on "Animistic Religions," *The Missionary Message*, xi–xii.

15. Ibid., x–xx, lists the following women correspondents: Miss J. E. Chadwick (formerly of Church Missionary Society), Uganda, xi; Mrs. George P. Pierson, Presbyterian Church USA from Hokkaido, xv; Mrs. Ferguson Davie, M. D. (Society for the Propagation of the Gospel), Punjab, xviii; Deaconess E. Goreh (Society for the Propagation of the Gospel), Burma, xviii; Pandita Ramabai (Mkuti Mission) Poona, xix; Miss de Selincourt (Zenana Bible and Medical Missionary Society), Lady Muir Memorial College, Allahabad, xx; Miss A. M. L. Smith (Church of England Zenana Missionary Society), Bangalore, xx.

16. R. Pierce Beaver, *All Loves Excelling* (Grand Rapids: Eerdmans, 1965), is a landmark study detailing the contribution of women's missionary societies. Beaver credits women with considerable initiative and leadership in the missionary movement, including financial responsibility. He also documents and describes many women who served as missionaries during the time of Edinburgh 1910 and following. Given the major role women played in early missionary zeal and participation, it is unfortunate that women played such a minor role in Edinburgh 1910.

17. Carbon copies of twenty-two of the twenty-five questionnaires dealing with "Animistic Religions" are in the files at Day Missions Library. It was this set of materials that was located and researched. Two additional questionnaires (George Whitehead and Johannes Warneck) were located through the microfiche collection of the International Missionary Council Archives 1910–1961, at Day Missions Library. The microfiche were produced by the Inter Documentation Company AG, Industriestrasse 7, 6300 Zug Switzerland. Rev. R. S. Fyffe's questionnaire is missing from both of these collections, apparently because his responses only dealt in part with animistic religions, so it is likely catalogued with another section of the report. Since then, the following additional sources have been noted: William Richey Hogg in *Ecumenical Foundations*, (New York: Harper Brothers), 1952, states on page 394, note 64, that materials from Commissions III, IV, VII, and VIII

are typed and in fourteen bound volumes on file at Edinburgh House, London. Eric J. Sharpe in *Not To Destroy But To Fulfil* (Uppsala: Gleerup, 1965), 278, states that the Edinburgh manuscripts are preserved in the Missionary Research Library, Union Theological Seminary, New York. I understand from a conversation with Andrew Walls, Director of the Department of History of Christianity in the Non-Christian World at the University of Edinburgh, that copies also exist at Speer Memorial Library at Princeton Theological Seminary and at the University of Edinburgh.

18.   A comprehensive (though not exhaustive) bibliography is to be found in the *Occasional Bulletin of the Missionary Research Library* 11 (June 14, 1960): 11–12. This issue marks the 50th anniversary of "Edinburgh 1910."

19.   W. R. Hogg, *Ecumenical Foundations* (New York: Harper & Brothers, 1952), 392. Printed and unbound minutes of Edinburgh's preparatory committees are on file at Edinburgh House, London, the Missionary Research Library, New York, and the Day Missions Library, Yale University, New Haven. The Day Missions Library is the repository for the John R. Mott Collection. Mott was the chair of the International Committee that planned the World Missionary Conference.

20.   Eric J. Sharpe is Professor of Religious Studies in the University of Sydney, Australia. He studied comparative religion at the University of Manchester under S. G. F. Brandon.

21.   Eric J. Sharpe, *Not To Destroy but to Fulfil: The Contribution of J. N. Farquhar to Protestant Missionary Thought in India Before 1914* (Uppsala: Gleerup, 1965). See also, *John Nicol Farquhar: A Memoir* (Calcutta: Y.M.C.A. Publishing House, 1963).

22.   Eric J. Sharpe, *John Nicol Farquhar and the Missionary Study of Hinduism* (Aberdeen: Department of Religious Studies, University of Aberdeen in association with the Scottish Institute of Missionary Studies, 1971), 2.

23.   Eric J. Sharpe, "The Legacy of A.G. Hogg," *The International Bulletin of Missionary Research* 6 (April, 1982): 65–69. See also Eric Sharpe, *The Theology of A. G. Hogg*, (Madras: The Christian Literature Society, 1971).

24.   Eric J. Sharpe, *Not to Destroy But to Fulfil*, 288.

25.   J. N. Farquhar, *Crown of Hinduism* (1913; reprint, London: Oxford University Press, 1920).

26.   J. N. Farquhar, "The Relation of Christianity to Hinduism," *International Review of Missions* 3 (1914): 417f.

27. Sharpe, "The Legacy of A. G. Hogg," 65–69.

28. Sharpe, *Not to Destroy*, 290.

29. Ibid., 290–292.

30. T. E. Yates, "Edinburgh Revisited: Edinburgh 1910 to Melbourne 1980," *The Churchman* 94, no. 2 (1980): 151.

31. Sharpe, *Not to Destroy*, 282–284.

32. Ibid., 289. Sharpe cites a letter from Cairns to Hogg of May 7, 1909.

33. *The Missionary Message*, 267.

34. Dr. T. E. Yates is the Rector of Darley Dale in Derbyshire. Earlier he was Warden of Cranmer Hall, Durham.

35. T. E. Yates, "Edinburgh 1910: Edinburgh 1910 to Melbourne 1980," *The Churchman* 94, no. 2 (1980): 145–155.

36. Ibid., 148.

37. Kenneth Cracknell, "The Theology of Religion in the IMC and WCC 1910–1989," *Current Dialogue*, 19 (January 1991): 6.

38. Ibid., 6. Cracknell cites Wesley Ariarajah's Ph.D. diss., 1987, *The Implications of Recent Ecumenical Thought for the Christian-Hindu Relationship*, p. 279. See also, Wesley Ariarajah, *The Bible and People of Other Faiths*, The Risk Book Series 26 (Geneva: World Council of Churches, 1987). Ariarajah's thesis is now published as *Hindus and Christians: A Century of Protestant Ecumenical Thought* (Grand Rapids: Eerdmans, 1991).

39. T. E. Yates, "Christian Approaches to Other Religious Traditions: The International Review of Missions, 1912–1939," *Mission Studies* 6, no. 1 (1989): 41–50.

40. Ibid., 42.

41. David Jonathan Mandeng, "The Philosophy of Mission of Robert Hamill Nassau in the Contemporary World," (Ph.D. diss., Temple University, 1970).

42. Ibid., 97.

43. Ibid., 197.

44. Raymond W. Teeuwissen, "Robert Hamill Nassau 1835–1921 Presbyterian Pioneer Missionary to Equatorial West Africa," (S.T.M. thesis, Louisville Presbyterian Theological Seminary, 1973).

45. Ibid., 93.

46. Robert H. Nassau, *Fetishism in West Africa: Forty Years' Observation of Native Customs and Superstitions* (New York: Charles Scribner's Sons, 1904).

47. Thomas J. Thompson, "Fraser and the Ngoni," (Ph.D. diss., University of Edinburgh, 1980).

48. Ibid., 214.

49. Ibid., 186.

50. Sawyerr, "The First World Missionary Conference: Edinburgh 1910," 271, quoting Gairdner, *"Edinburgh 1910,"* 137.

51. Gairdner, *"Edinburgh 1910,"* 137f. Gairdner's exact words are: "The non-Christian religions have been variously regarded by Christian men. Some have considered them as perfect specimens of absolute error. . . A closer study of Scripture itself, and also of the history of the earliest missions, has, however, convinced most people that this view is simply the exaggeration of one extreme aspect of a wide question. And while of course theories as to the origin and significance of the non-Christian religions still vary, there is a general consensus that, representing as they do so many attempted solutions of life's problems, they must be approached with very real sympathy and respect; that they must be *studied*, if only to bring the evangelist into touch with the minds of his hearers." Sawyerr chooses to quote only the negative portion of this statement, leaving out the preceeding and the following sentences, which gives a much different conclusion about the views and approaches of the missionaries being discussed.

II. The Setting and Background of Edinburgh 1910

1. Kenneth Scott Latourette, *History of the Expansion of Christianity* (New York: Harper and Row, 1941). The subtitles of volumes 4 and 5 refer to the 19th century as the "Great Century," meaning the great century of mission.

2. Ibid., vol. 4, 12–14.

3. Sir Frederick John Dealtry Lugard, *The Dual Mandate in British Tropical Africa*, Edinburgh: Blackwood, 1922. Lord Lugard was one of the main architects of

British colonial administration in Africa. He is particularly known for his concept of "indirect rule" in northern Nigeria.

4.   Philip Potter, "From Edinburgh to Melbourne," in *Your Kingdom Come: Mission Perspectives* (Geneva: World Council of Churches, Commission on World Mission and Evangelism, 1980), 6–21. This book is a report on the World Conference on Mission and Evangelism, held in Melbourne, Australia, 12–25 May, 1980.

5.   Lord Balfour of Burleigh's "Opening Address" in World Missionary Conference 1910, vol. IX *The History and Records of the Conference Together with the Addresses Delivered at the Evening Meetings* (New York: Fleming H. Revell, 1910), 145.

6.   Ibid.

7.   Gairdner, "*Edinburgh 1910.*" 10.

8.   Ibid., 10–11.

9.   Ibid.

10. World Missionary Conference 1910, vol. IX, *History, Records, & Addresses*, 7. Edinburgh was a missionary conference to set priorities and to articulate strategy. It was an action oriented, "how to do it," conference rather than being a reflective time to think through a theology of mission. This character of the conference was underlined by the fact that the 1200 participant delegates came as representatives of Mission Boards and Missionary Societies, not of Churches.

11. Ibid., 147.

12. Gairdner, 50–52.

13. World Missionary Conference, "General Account of the Conference," *The History and Records of the Conference*, vol. IX, 18–19.

14. Gairdner, 53. See also *World Missionary Conference History, Records & Addresses*, 11.

15. Kenneth Latourette in S. C. Neill and Ruth Rouse, *A History of Ecumenical Movement 1517–1948* (London: SPCK, 1954), 359. Latourette reports on the participation of younger churches in prior ecumenical missionary conferences:
     A   An Indian had taken part in the discussions at Liverpool in 1860. He declared more nationals must share in the work of Bible Translation.

B Six participated in the New York Ecumenical Missionary Conference of 1900.

C Younger churches seem not to be represented at the Centenary Conference of the Protestant Missions of the World held in London in 1888.

D Only six or seven Chinese were among the 1,170 participants of the Chinese Centenary Conference in Shanghai in 1907, and there only as visitors.

E There were only a few Indian members at the Decennial Missionary Conferences in their own country, for example at the Bangalore Conference in 1879, only fourteen out of 118 persons were Indian.

16. V. S. Azariah from India was chosen as a special delegate by the British Executive Committee. *WMC*, vol. IX, 40. T. H. Yun from Korea and Yoitsei Honda from Japan were special delegates chosen by the American Executive Committee. *WMC* vol. IX, 51.

17. Latourette in S.C. Neill and Ruth Rouse, *A History of Ecumenical Movement*, 359f.

18. V. S. Azariah of India had already launched the National Missionary Society in India five years before Edinburgh in 1905. Two years after Edinburgh he became the first Indian bishop of the Anglican communion. He was one of the prime movers in the development of the Church of South India and later Chairman of the National Christian Council of India.

19. Bishop Azariah is quoted in William Richey Hogg, *Ecumenical Foundations* (New York: Harper & Brothers, 1952), 126.

20. *World Missionary Conference*, vol. IX, *History, Records and Addresses*, 315. For an account of Azariah's speech and its aftermath at Edinburgh by a witness and long time associate of Azariah, see J. Z. Hodge, *Bishop Azariah of Dornakal*. The speech is recorded in World Missionary Conference, 1910, vol. IX (History, Records, and Addresses), 306–15. See also Hogg, *Ecumenical Foundations*, 126 f and Gairdner, *"Edinburgh 1910,"* 109–110.

21. Hogg, *Ecumenical Foundations*, 126.

22. K. S. Latourette, "Developments in the 'younger churches' since Edinburgh 1910," *Religion in Life*, 29, (Spring 1960): 352–362.

23. World Missionary Conference, *History, Records, and Addresses*, vol. IX. See pages 35–71 for the complete list of official delegates. W. R. Hogg, *Ecumenical Foundations* (New York: Harper, 1952), 396, also lists these delegates.

24.   W. R. Hogg, *Ecumenical Foundations*, 396. Sketches of the five Baptists from Asia are given in *Missions* 1 (1910): 189–90.

25.   Ibid.

26.   Gairdner, 56–57.

27.   Ibid., 58.

28.   W. R. Hogg, 396, and the "List of Official Delegates," in *WMC*, vol. IX, *History, Records, and Addresses*, 36.

29.   Walter L. Williams, *Black Americans and the Evangelization of Africa 1877–1900* (Madison: The University of Wisconsin Press, 1982), 10–11.

30.   Ibid., 12–13.

31.   Ibid., 14. Williams cites Alexander P. Camphor, *Missionary Story Sketches: Folklore from Africa* (Cincinnati: Jennings and Graham, 1909), 7–9, 21–22. See also: Willis J. Kings, "History of the Methodist Church Mission in Liberia," (Typescript, Lake Junaluska, NC: United Methodist Commission on Archives and History, Box 266, n.d.); *Official Journal of the Liberia Annual Conference, Methodist Episcopal Church* (2–7 Feb. 1898): 68–71. See also Edith Holden, *Blyden of Liberia* (New York: Vantage Press, 1966), 674, 700; and Donald R. Roth, "Grace not Race: Southern Negro Church Leaders, Black Identity, and Missions to West Africa, 1865–1919." (Ph.D. diss., University of Texas, Austin, 1975), 298–327.

32.   Camphor returned to the United States to raise more money for expansion of the mission, but finding little interest in his denomination he accepted the presidency of a Methodist Episcopal Freedman's Aid School, the Central Alabama Institute. In 1916, Camphor was honored by being chosen as the Methodist Episcopal Bishop to Africa, and he returned to Liberia. But again financial difficulties plagued his mission, and he died in Liberia in 1919, a discouraged man. This story is detailed in D. R. Roth's dissertation, "Grace not Race," 313–27.

33.   World Missionary Conference Report, vol. V, *Preparation of Missionaries*, 311.

34.   J. F. A. Ajayi, *Christian Missions in Nigeria 1841–1891: The Making of a New Elite*, (London: Longmans, Green & Co., 1965), 235, 250–254. See also: E. A. Ayandele, *The Missionary Impact on Modern Nigeria, 1842–1914: A Political and Social Analysis* (London: Longmans, Green and Co., 1966), 220–230.

35.   Ibid.

36. James B. Webster, *The African Churches Among the Yoruba 1888–1922* (Oxford: The Clarendon Press, 1964).

III.   Anthropological   Perspectives

1. World Missionary Conference, "Animistic Religions," in *The Missionary Message in Relation to Non Christian Religions*, (New York: Fleming H. Revell, 1910), 7. This volume is the report of Commission IV, and is referred to hereafter as *Missionary Message*.

2. The term "tribal society" is hard to define. Harold Turner's descriptive definition is that it "usually refers to a group of people who feel they belong together through sharing a common culture and set of values, a common territory and social organization, and probably a common language. They differ from modern societies in lacking a literary tradition and in being undeveloped in scientific knowledge, technological skills, and economic life. Turner also suggests the term "primal" to replace "primitive" in referring to "tribal" religions. "Primal" then means that these religions both anteceded the great historic religions and continue to reveal many of the basic or primary features of religion. Harold W. Turner, *Living Tribal Religions*, (London: Ward Lock Educational Ltd., 1971), 5–7.

3. Henri-Philippe Junod, *Henri-A. Junod Missionarie et Savant* (Lausanne: Mission Suisse Dans L'Afrique Sud, 1934), 45–47.

4. *Missionary Message*, 7, 13.

5. *Ibid.*, 6. The Report on "Animistic Religions" cites E. B. Tylor's work, *Primitive Culture*, vol. 1, 426.

6. Ibid., 7.

7. Henri Junod, *Life of a South African Tribe*, vol. 2, 2d rev. ed. (London: Macmillan, 1927). See chapter 4, "Taboo and Morality," 573–585.

8. *Missionary Message*, 13.

9. Ibid., 13.

10. Ibid., 271–172.

11. Ibid., 20.

12. Benjamin C. Ray, *African Religions: Symbol, Ritual and Community* (Englewood Cliffs, NJ: Prentice-Hall, Inc. 1976), 3.

13. Samuel Baker, "The Races of the Nile Basin," *Transactions of the Ethnological Society of London*, n.s., 5 (1867), 231, as quoted in E. E. Evans-Pritchard, *Theories of Primitive Religion* (Oxford: The Clarendon Press, 1965), 7. Also cited by Max Müller in *Chips From a German Workshop*, vol. 1, Introduction.

14. Thomas K. Penniman, *A Hundred Years of Anthropology* (New York: William Morrow and Co., 1974), 70. Cf. E. E. Evans-Pritchard, *Theories of Primitive Religion* (Oxford: Clarendon Press, 1965), 30.

15. David Livingstone, *Missionary Travels and Researches in South Africa* (1858; reprint, Freeport, NY: Books for Libraries Press, 1972), 26–27.

16. Marian S. Benham, *Henry Callaway: First Bishop of Kaffraria, His Life-History and Work* (London and New York: Macmillan, 1876), 228. See also, Henry Callaway, *Nursery Tales, Traditions and Histories of the Zulus, In Their Own Words, With a Translation into English, and Notes* (Westport, CT: Negro Universities Press, 1970), Preface. Originally published in Springvale, Natal: John A. Blair, and London: Trübner and Company, 1868.

17. The following biographical material is largely drawn from Peter B. Hinchliff, *The Anglican Church in South Africa* (London: Darton, Longman and Todd, 1963), and the article by Peter Hinchliff, "Henry Callaway" in *Dictionary of South Africa Biography*, edited by W. J. deKock, Cape Town: Human Services Research Council, 1968, vol. 1, 150–153.

18. Ibid., Hinchliff, "Henry Callaway," 151.

19. Callaway claims in the preface to his *Nursery Tales Traditions and History of the Zulus* to have researched the linguistic resources available in 1854 to study Zulu and found few except a valuable paper by J. D. Byrant "The Zulu Language," and Lewis Grout's "The Zulu and Other Dialects of Southern Africa" in the first volume of *The Journal of the American Oriental Society*. In the Xhosa dialect, there were the *Grammars* of Appleyard and Boyce, and the small *Vocabulary* of Ayliff, but they were of little use in the study of Zulu.

20. Henry Callaway, *Nursery Tales*, Preface, i.

21. Ibid.

22. Marian Benham, *Henry Callaway: First Bishop of Kaffraria, His Life-History and Work* (London and New York: Macmillan, 1876), 225.

23. Henry Callaway, Preface to *Nursery Tales, Traditions and Histories*, 1868, n. p.

24. Ibid. Callaway's publisher has collected reviews from the press in Great Britain, South Africa, and missionary periodicals and inserted them in an unnumbered page between the table of contents and Callaway's "Preface to the First Volume."

25. Henry Callaway, *The Religious System of the Amazulu: Izinyanga Zakubula; or Divination, As Existing Among the Amazulu, in Their Own Words, With a Translation Into English, and Notes*, (1870; reprint London: The Folk Lore Society, 1884).

26. Henry Callaway, Preface to *Nursery Tales* (1868) n. p.

27. Ibid., "Opinions of the Press," n. p.

28. E. B. Tylor, as quoted in Benham, 247.

29. Callaway, *Nursery Tales*, Preface, iv–v.

30. Benham, 227. The cover page of *Religion of the Amazulu* (1870) refers to Callaway as the local secretary of the ASL (Anthropological Society of London).

31. Max Müller, *Chips from a German Workshop*, vol. 2, *Essays on Mythology, Traditions, and Customs* (New York: Charles Scribner and Co., 1871), 206–216.

32. Henry Callaway as quoted in Benham, 237.

33. Max Müller, *Chips from a German Workshop*, xxi.

34. Henry Callaway as quoted in Benham, 222.

35. Henry Callaway, "On Divination and Analogous Phenomena Among the Natives of Natal," *Journal of the Anthropological Institute* 1 (1871–72): 163–185.

36. Peter Hinchliff, "Callaway," 151. See also, Benham, 251.

37. Several dimensions in the development of anthropology as a discipline are significant here. Ancestral to the Royal Anthropological Institute was the Ethnological Society, which itself was an offshoot of the Aborigines Protection Society which was the product of Wilberforce's campaign against slavery. The Ethnological Society became a strong partisan of philanthropists and abolitionists. The anthropologists in contrast to the ethnologists regarded the varieties of humans as species. Europeans were innately superior. European technology was a marker of that superiority. These two movements merged in 1871 to form The

Anthropological Institute. Quaker humanitarianism was a major factor in both the antislavery movement and English ethnology. It is not without significance that both E. B. Tylor and Henry Callaway, who were close to the center of the development of anthropology as a discipline, had strong roots in the Society of Friends. Tylor's mentor, Henry Christy, a middle aged Quaker banker, was active in the revival of the Ethnological Society of London, whose meetings Tylor attended in 1862. For further information on these developments, see: Edmund Leach, "Anthropology of Religion: British and French Schools" in *Nineteenth Century Religious Thought in the West*, vol. 3, edited by Ninian Smart (London: Cambridge University Press, 1985), 216. Alfred Haddon, *History of Anthropology* (New York, London: G. P. Putnam's Sons, 1910), 78–79. George W. Stocking, Jr., "Edward Burnett Tylor" in *International Encyclopedia of Social Sciences*, vol. 16, ed. David L. Sills (New York: Macmillan Co. and Free Press, 1968), 171.

38. Evans-Pritchard, 26.

39. James G. Frazer, "Questions on the Manners, Customs, Religion, Superstitions of Uncivilized or Semi-Civilized Peoples," *The Journal of the Royal Anthropological Institute* 18 (1881–89): 431–439.

40. James G. Frazer, *The Golden Bough*, "Preface to the First Edition, March, 1890," "Preface to the Second Edition, September 1900," "Preface to the 3d Edition, December 1910" in *Classical Approaches to the Study of Religion*, ed. Jacques Waardenburg (Mouton: The Hague, Paris, 1973), 245–256.

41. Evans-Pritchard, 27–28.

42. Frazer, 245–256.

43. G. F. Moore, "The History of Religions in the Nineteenth Century," *Congress of Arts and Science*, St. Louis, 1904, 440, as quoted in *History of Anthropology* by Alfred C. Haddon (New York and London: G. P. Putnam and Sons, 1910), 174.

44. E. E. Evans-Pritchard, *Theories of Primitive Religion* (Oxford: Clarendon Press, 1965), 29–30. Pritchard discusses Tylor and Frazer's theories at length in chapter II, "Psychological Theories."

45. James Frazer, "Preface to the Second Edition," 1900, reprinted in Jacques Waardenburg, 247.

46. Obituary, "Canon John Roscoe: Native Tribes of East Africa," *The Times*, December 5, 1932.

47. James G. Frazer, "Obituary: Canon John Roscoe," *Nature* 130, no. 3294 (December 17, 1930), 917–919.

48. R. R. Marett, "The Tabu-Mana Formula as a Minimum Definition of Religion" in *Archiv für Religionwissenschaft*, 12 (1909). Reprinted in *Classical Approaches to the Study of Religion* by Jacques Waardenburg (Mouton: The Hague, Paris, 1973), 259.

49. P. J. Baylis, "High Gods and the Study of Religion: The History of A New Idea," in *Essays in Religious Studies for Andrew Walls*, edited by James Thrower (Aberdeen: Department of Religious Studies, University of Aberdeen, 1986), 89–96.

50. E. B. Tylor, "On the Limits of Savage Religion," *Journal of the Anthropological Institute*, vol. 26 (1892), 283–299. Tylor suggests that the presence of high god concepts can be explained in terms of missionary influence and thus he feels it is not an indigenous feature of savage belief.

51. R. R. Marett, *The Threshold of Religion*, 2d ed. (1914) xxxi, as quoted in E. E. Evans-Pritchard, *Theories of Primitive Religion*, 33.

52. R. R. Marett, "The Tabu-Mana Formula as a Minimum Definition of Religion," in *Archiv für Religionswissenschaft*, xii (1909), reprinted in *Classical Approaches to the Study of Religion: Aim, Methods and Theories of Research*, vol. I, Introduction and Anthology by Jacques Waardenburg (Mouton: The Hague, Paris, 1973), 258–263. R. H. Codrington's book, *The Melanesians*, was published by Oxford in 1891, and E. Tregear's *The Maori-Polynesian Comparative Dictionary*, was published the same year by Wellington, New Zealand, 1891.

53. R. R. Marett, *The Threshold of Religion*, 2d ed. (London: Methuen, 1914). The first edition of this book was published in 1909 just prior to Edinburgh 1910.

54. George W. Stocking, Jr., "Codrington, R. H." in *The Encyclopedia of Religion*, ed. Mercea Eliade vol. 3 (New York: Macmillan, 1987), 558. A considerable body of Codrington's correspondence and relevant printed materials are preserved in Rhodes House, Oxford. A bibliography of his writings is collected in the obituary by Sidney Ray in *Man* 97 (1922), 169–171.

55. Charles E. Fox, *Lord of the Southern Isles: The Story of Anglican Mission in Melanesia, 1849–1949* (London: Mowbray, 1958).

56. R. H. Codrington, *The Melanesians: Studies in Their Anthropology and Folklore* (1891; reprint New Haven, CT: Human Relations Area Files, Inc., 1957), vii.

57. George W. Stocking, "R. H. Codrington" vol. 3 in *The Encyclopedia of Religion*, ed. Mercea Eliade (New York: Macmillan, 1987), 558.

58. R. H. Codrington, "Languages of Melanesia,"*Journal of the Anthropological Institute*, 14 (1885).

59. Codrington, *The Melanesians*, vi.

60. Stocking, 558.

61. Ibid., 119.

62. Ibid., 118.

63. Rudolf Otto, *The Idea of the Holy: An Inquiry into the Non-rational Factor in the Idea of the Divine and its Relation to the Rational*, (translated from the 1917 German edition by John W. Harvey), London: Oxford University Press, 1923. See pages 15, 20, 74. Otto recognizes that R. R. Marett in *The Threshold of Religion* (1909) and M. Soderblom in *Das Werden des Gottesglaubens* (1915) are moving in the same direction.

64. Ernest Beaglehole, "R. H. Codrington" in the *International Encyclopedia of Social Sciences*, vol. 2 ed. David L. Sills (New York: Macmillan Co. and Free Press, 1968), 534.

65. Junod still awaits a biographer and a scholarly analysis of his missiology and anthropology. There are several biographical sketches of his life. The fullest, but more from a family perspective, is the work by his son, Henri-Philippe Junod, *Henri A. Junod: Missionaire et Savant* 1863–1934 (Lausanne: Mission Suisse Dans L'Afrique Du Sud, 1934). See also: an article written by his daughter, Violaine Junod, "Junod, Henri Alexandre," in *The International Encyclopedia to the Social Sciences*, vol. 8 ed. David L. Sills (New York: The Macmillan Co. and The Free Press, 1968), 330–332. A. J. Lamont Smith, "Junod, Henri-Alexandre" in *Dictionary of South African Biography*, vol. 2 ed. W. J. de Kock (Capetown: Human Services Research Council, 1968), 349–351. Per Hassing, "Junod, Henri Alexandre" in *Concise Dictionary of the Christian World Mission*, eds., Stephen Neill, Gerald Anderson, John Goodwin (Nashville and New York: Abingdon Press, 1971), 315–316.

66. A. J. Lamont Smith, "Paul Berthoud,"*Dictionary of South African Biography*, vol. 1 ed. W. J. DeKock (Capetown: Human Services Research Council, 1968), 72.

67. G. Jan van Butselaar, "The Gospel and Culture in Nineteenth-Century Mozambique," *Missiology: An International Review*, 16, no. 1, (January 1988):

45. van Butselaar draws upon his own research published in *Africaines, Missionaires et Colonialistes: Les Origines de l' Eglise Presbyterienne du Mozambique (Mission Suisse), 1880–1896,* (Leiden: Brill, 1984).

68. Keith Irvine, "Foreword" in Henri A. Junod, *Life of an African Tribe,* rev. ed. (New York: University Books Inc., 1962), v.

69. Henri A. Junod, "La faune entomologique de Delagoa,"*Bulletin de la Societe' Neuchateloise des Sciences Naturellus*, No. 27, (1891–99), cited in A. J. Lamont Smith, "Junod, Henri-Alexandre,"*Dictionary of South African Biography*, vol. 2, 350.

70. Edwin Smith, "Book Review of *The Life of a South African Tribe,*" *Africa*, vol. 1 (1928): 391.

71. *The Life of a South African Tribe* was reissued by University Books, Inc. of New Hyde Park, New York in 1962. This edition adds to Henri A. Junod's final version of the book, thirteen full-page photographs taken by A. M. Duggan-Cronin, which were published in *The Bantu Tribes of South Africa*, edited by Junod's son, Henri Phillipe Junod, in 1935.

72. H. P. Junod, *Henri A. Junod,* 65.

73. Junod, *Life*, vol. 2, 159.

74. Ibid., 448–450; see also, 623–628.

75. Ibid., vol. 1, 2.

76. Ibid., 1.

77. Ibid., 7.

78. Ibid.

79. Ibid.

80. Ibid., 8.

81. *Missionary Message*, 271.

82. Ibid., 8–9.

83. Ibid., 10.

84. Ibid., 11.

85. Ibid., 10.

86. Henri A. Junod, "God's Way in the Bantu Soul," *International Review of Missions*, vol. 3 (1914), 96–106. Referred to hereafter in the notes as "Bantu Soul."

87. Henri A. Junod, "The Magic Conception of Nature Amongst Bantus," *South African Journal of Science* (Imprint: Marshalltown: South African Association for the Advancement of Science, November, 1920), 76–85. Referred to hereafter in the notes as "Magic Conception."

88. Henri A. Junod, "The Fate of the Widows Amongst the Ba-Ronga," Basutoland, South Africa: Africa Books, 1908. Excerpted from the Report of the South Africa Association for the Advancement of Science, 1908, 363–375.

89. "Bantu Soul," 96.

90. Ibid., 96.

91. Ibid., 97.

92. Junod, *Life*, vol. 2, 596.

93. Ibid., 595.

94. Ibid., 451.

95. Ibid., 445–450.

96. "Bantu Soul," 98.

97. Ibid., 100; see also, *Life*, vol. 2, 445–450.

98. "Bantu Soul," 101.

99. Ibid., 102.

100. Barrett suggests that seven out of ten Christian conversions in Africa happen in African Independent Churches. See also, Harold Turner, *African Independent Church*.

101. *Life*, 573; see also, "Bantu Soul," 103.

102. "Bantu Soul," 105–106.

103. Ibid.

104. Ibid.

105. *Life*, vol. 2, 451.

106. Ibid., 452.

107. Ibid., 369.

108. Ibid., vol. 1, 337–340, vol. 2, 451–572. Junod has elaborately described the "throwing of divinatory bones" (*blahluba*), as an example of magic that is based on the principle of similarity. Among the Thonga, the bones are mostly astragalus bones from the legs of different animals. The bones of domestic animals such as goats represent common folk, sheep—the royal family, lion—the chief, he goat—the father, etc. The patterns of these bones when thrown are then interpreted by the *wabula* (diviner) in foreseeing the future or understanding the present. Divination is discussed in *Life*, vol. 2, 536–572.

109. "Bantu Soul," 102.

110. Ibid.

111. "The Magic Conception," 84.

112. Ibid., 85.

113. Eric J. Sharpe, *Comparative Religion: A History* 2d ed. (La Salle, IL: Open Court, 2, 1986), 140f.

114. F. D. Maurice, *The Religions of the World* (6th ed., 1886), 244, as cited in Eric J. Sharpe, *Comparative Religion: A History* 2d. ed. (La Salle, IL: Open Court, 1986), 147.

115. Marian S. Benham, *Henry Callaway: First Bishop of Kaffraria, His Life, History and Work* (London/New York: Macmillan & Co., 1896), 55.

116. H. Callaway, *The Religious System of the Amazulu* (London: Trübner & Co., 1870), 1f.

117. Charles Hardwick, *Christ and Other Masters* (3rd ed., 1874) 28, cited in Eric Sharpe, *Comparative Religion*, 147.

118.   Benham, 218–219.

119.   Ibid., 219.

120.   Eric Sharpe, *Comparative Religion*, 148.

121.   Henry Callaway, Letter of February 8, 1972, to Mr. Hanbury, quoted in Marian S. Benham, *Henry Callaway*, 222.

122.   There are two basic texts by Max Müller that set out his Science of Religion: *Chips From a German Workshop*, vol. 1, *Essays on the Science of Religion* (New York: Charles Scribners Sons, 1871). See especially the Preface, vii–xxxiii; also *Introduction to the Science of Religion*, (1873; reprint London: Longmans, 1882).

123.   Müller, *Introduction to the Science of Religion*, 263.

124.   Ibid., 18.

125.   Max Müller, *Three Lectures on the Vedanta Philosophy* (1898) in Brian Morris, *Anthropological Studies of Religion* (Cambridge: Cambridge University Press, 1987), 94.

126.   Henry Callaway, "On the Religious Sentiment Amongst the Tribes of South Africa," Paper given at Kokstad, n. p., 1876.

127.   *Introduction to Science of Religion*, 148. See also *Chips*, vol. 1 (1867), xx.

128.   Max Müller, *Life and Letters*, vol. 2, 135 as quoted in Eric Sharpe, *Not to Destroy but to Fulfill* (Uppsala: Gleerup, 1965), 44.

129.   *Chips*, vol. 1, Preface, xxii.

130.   Ibid.

131.   Ibid., xxi.

132.   Henry Callaway, "On the Religious Sentiment Amongst the Tribes of South Africa," 4. This lecture was given in 1876. It is available as a pamphlet at the Library of the University of California at Los Angeles. The call number is BL 2480 K11C13.

133.   Ibid., 4.

134.   Ibid., 5

135.   Ibid.

136.   Ibid., 4.

137.   Callaway in Benham, 222.

138.   Ibid., Callaway says: "I have from time to time spoken out very strongly on the subject, as last year in a sermon on the 'Education of the World' . . . [but] I have been shy of being too forward with the teaching. It tells perhaps more widely than Max Müller is himself aware of; I think I see the bearings of it, and the necessary results, deep and practical, which must follow its acceptance; and yet it may be I do not see how widely its acceptance may affect current theological teaching."

139.   Callaway, *Nursery Tales*, preface to the first volume, 1868, n. p.

140.   Benham, 102.

141.   Callaway, *Nursery Tales*, preface, n. p.

142.   "Zulu Nursery Tales" in *Chips*, 209–210.

143.   Henry Callaway, "On Divination and Analogous Phenomena Among the Natives of Natal," *Journal of the Anthropological Institute of Great Britain and Ireland*, 1 (1871–72), 184.

144.   Ibid., 163–185.

145.   Henry Callaway, "On the Religious Sentiment. . .,"165

146.   Callaway, "On Divination . . ,"165.

147.   Ibid., 179.

148.   Ibid., 175.

149.   Ibid., 176.

150.   Ibid., 164.

151.   Ibid., 175–178.

152.   Ibid., 184. This remark is attributed to Mr. Dendy in the discussion following Callaway's presentation.

153. Ibid.

154. Ibid.

155. Callaway, "On Religious Sentiment. . ," 5.

156. Ibid., 7.

157. This term, *Unkulunkulu,* has been translated by missionaries as God. Callaway was unwilling to use this term for God.

158. Callaway, "On Religious Sentiment. . .," 7.

159. Ibid.

160. Ibid., 13.

161. Ibid.

162. Ibid., 12–13.

163. Ibid., 13–14.

164. E. B. Tylor, "On the Limits of Savage Religion," *Royal Anthropological Institute of Great Britain and Ireland* 21 (1891–92): 283–301.

165. John S. Mbiti, *African Religions and Philosophy* (London: Heinemann, 1969), 6–7.

IV. German Lutheran Missiology

1. World Missionary Conference, 1910, *Report of Commission IV: The Missionary Message in Relation to Non-Christian Religions* (Edinburgh and London: Oliphant, Anderson and Ferrier, and New York: Fleming H. Revell Co., 1910), ix–x. Hereafter, referred to as *Missionary Message.*

2. J. W. Gunning wrote a history of missions in the Dutch East Indies under the title, *Hedendaagsche Zending in Onze Oost* (Den Haag: Boekhandel Van Den Zendinststudie Raad, 1914).

3. *Missionary Message,* 39.

4. In print, W. P. Paterson seems only occasionally to have approached animistic religions. He has a chapter on "The Problem of Origins" in his Gifford Lectures at

the University of Glasgow in 1924–1925 published under the title, *The Nature of Religion* (London: Hodder and Stoughton, 1925), 427–256.

5. William R. Hogg, *Ecumenical Foundations: A History of the International Missionary Council and Its Nineteenth Century Background* (New York: Harper and Brothers), 116.

6. Warneck produced several important books just prior to and after Edinburgh 1910, *Die Christianisierung der Batakschen Sprache* (1904), *Die Religion der Batak* (1908), *Die Lebenskräfte des Evangeliums* (1908), *Paulus im Lichte der bentigen Heidenmission* (1913).

7. *The Living Christ and Dying Heathenism* (New York: Fleming H. Revell, 1909), and *The Living Forces of the Gospel* (Edinburgh and London: Oliphant, Anderson, and Ferrier, 1909). (This book was published in English with two different titles.)

8. This book has recently been reissued in English by Fleming H. Revell in 1986 and in German by Verlag der Liebenzeller Mission in 1986.

9. Olav G. Myklebust, *The Study of Missions in Theological Education*, vol. 2 (Oslo: Egede Institutet, 1958), 110.

10. David Cairns, "General Conclusions," *Missionary Message*, 271.

11. Although some replies from missionaries in India were over 100 pages, discussing Christianity in relation to various Indian religions, such as Hinduism, Warneck's is clearly the most comprehensive regarding animistic religions.

12. *Missionary Message*, chapter 2.

13. W. P. Paterson cites Warneck in his report on "Animistic Religions" in *Missionary Message*, 8, and Junod on pp 7, 13.

14. Warneck, *The Living Christ*, 97 f.

15. Ibid., 13.

16. W. P. Paterson, "Animistic Religions," *Missionary Message*, 23.

17. Warneck's Commission IV Questionnaire, 11.

18. Warneck, *Living Christ and Dying Heathenism*, 210.

19. In the responses to the questionnaires that informed Commission IV's report on animistic religions, there are several reports of people's or mass movements. Warneck reports on the people's movement among the Batak in Sumatra. His colleague, Kruyt, relates his experiences among the Toradjas in the Celebes. Sundermann tells about a similar occurrence on the Island of Nias, and Hahn reports on people's movements among the Kols of Chota Nagpur. Perhaps the most famous of these people's movements among tribal societies are found in the work of Christian Keysser in New Guinea and Bruno Guttmann in Tanzania. These, however, came into prominence in the 1920s and so are just outside the parameters of this present study.

20. Rev. Professor Carl Mirbt, "The Extent and Characteristics of German Missions," World Missionary Conference 1910, *History, Records and Addresses*, vol. 9 (New York: Fleming H. Revell, 1910), 214.

21. Peter Byerhaus and Harry Lefever, *The Responsible Church and Foreign Mission*, (Grand Rapids: Eerdmans, 1965), 45–46. If the English missiologist, Henry Venn, and the American missiologist, Rufus Anderson, stressed the autonomous nature of young churches, Gustav Warneck stressed their indigenous character as churches related to the soil, in which the national character and social relations were to be preserved.

22. Ibid., 47. See also: Gustav Warneck, *Evangelische Missionslehre* (Gotha: Perthes, 1897–1903), and J. Merle Davis, "The Batak Church," in the Tambaram Report, vol. 5 (New York: International Missionary Council, 1939).

23. W. Holsten, "Gustav Warneck," *Concise Dictionary of the Christian World Mission*, ed. Stephen Neill (Nashville: Abingdon Press, 1971), 643. Another work of Gustav Warneck, circulating in English, was: *Modern Missions and Culture: Their Mutual Relations*, 2d ed., trans. by Thomas Smith (Edinburgh: James Gemmeli, 1888).

24. Ibid., 644. See also, J. C. Hoekendijk, *Kirche und Volk in der deutschen Missionswissenschaft* (München: Chr. Kaiser Verlag, 1967).

25. Hendrik Kraemer, *From Mission Field to Independent Church* (London: SCM Press, 1958), 44. See also Walter Freytag, *Spiritual Revolution in the East* (London: Lutterworth Press, 1940), 77–80.

26. Johannes Warneck, "The Growth of the Church in the Mission Field," *International Review of Missions*, 1, no. 1, (1912): 20.

27. Paul Pedersen, *Batak Blood and Protestant Soul: The Development of National Batak Churches in North Sumatra* (Grand Rapids: Eerdmans, 1970), 33–35.

28. J. Merle Davis, *The Economic Basis of the Church* "The Madras Series," vol. 5 (Preparatory Studies for the International Missionary Council at Tambaram, India, 1938) (New York: International Missionary Council, 1939), 428.

29. Ibid., 394

30. Bengt Sundkler, *The World Of Mission* (Grand Rapids: Wm. B. Eerdmans, 1965), 189. Sundkler was a Lutheran Bishop in Bukoba, Tanzania and later a Professor of Church History and Missions at Uppsala University.

31. J. Merle Davis, *The Economic Basis of The Church*, 411.

32. Hendrik Kraemer, *From Mission Field To Independent Church* (London: SCM Press, 1958), 47.

33. Ibid.

34. Paul B. Pedersen, In 1904, Nommensen was granted an honorary doctorate of theology by the University of Bonn.

35. Ibid., Pedersen cites his source as Lehman, *Gottes Volk in vielen Ländern*, Berlin: Evangelische Verlagsanstalt, 1955.

36. J. Merle Davis, *New Buildings on Old Foundations: A Handbook on Stabilizing the Younger Churches in Their Environment* (New York and London: International Missionary Council, 1945), 43.

37. Warneck, *Living Christ*, 251–257.

38. Ibid., 201.

39. Ibid., 138.

40. Ibid., 80–81.

41. Christian Keysser went to New Guinea in 1899 with the Neuendettelsauer Mission. He is quoted in Hendrik Kraemer, *The Christian Message in a Non Christian World* (New York: Harper Brothers for International Missionary Council, 1938), 350.

42. Warneck, *The Living Christ*, 25.

43. Ibid., 23.

44. The opening chapter is a summary of Warneck's book, *Die Religion der Batak*, which came out in 1907 before *The Living Christ and Dying Heathen* (New York: Revel, 1909).

45. *Living Christ*, 25. Warneck draws heavily upon A. C. Kruyt and Adriani's work among the Toradja in the Celebes, and his fellow Rheinish missionaries, H. Sundermann's description of work in Indonesia, *Die Insel Nias*, Spieth's book, *Die Ewe-Stemme*, on the Ewe of West Africa, and Jellinghaus, *Die Kols*, on the tribal peoples of India.

46. Ibid., 266.

47. Martin Köhler, "Gustav Warneck's Sendung," *Allegemeine Missions-Zeitschrift* (1911): 124 f, cited in Olav G. Myklebust, *The Study of Missions in Theological Education*, vol. 1 (Oslo: Forlaget Land og Kirke, 1955), 281.

48. K. D. Garrison, "Preface," Johannes Warneck's *The Living Christ and Dying Heathenism* (Grand Rapids: Eerdmans, 1955), n. p.

49. Warneck, Questionnaire, 12.

50. Warneck, *The Living Christ*, 90.

51. Ibid., 22.

52. Warneck, *Living Forces of the Gospel*, 3d ed. trans. by Neil Buchanan, 10.

53. Nathan Soderblom, quoted in Warneck, *The Living Christ*, 98–99.

54. *The Living Christ*, 210.

55. Warneck, Questionnaire, 11.

56. L. Nottrott, *Die Gossnersche Mission unter den Kolhs* (1874; reprint, Halle: Richard Mühlmann, 1895), is a valuable source for the early years of the Lutheran Mission in Chota Nagpur. See also, H. W. Gensichen, "Gossner Mission Society" and Bernard H. Mather, "Gossner, Johannes Evangelista" in *Concise Dictionary of the Christian World Mission*, ed. Stephen Neill (Nashville: Abingdon Press, 1971), 232.

57. Bengt Sundkler, *The World of Mission* (Grand Rapids: Eerdmans Publishing Co., 1965), 202. This book originally appeared as *Missionens, Varld, Missionskunskap och Missionshistoria* (Stockholm, Sweden: Svenska Bokforlaget, 1963).

58. Ferdinand Hahn, Questionnaire, 3. See also, W. Holsten, *Johannes Evangelista Gossner Glaube und Gemeinde* (Göttingen, 1949), n. p.

59. Ibid., 3.

60. Fidelis de Sa, *Crisis in Chota Nagpur: The Judicial Conflict Between Jesuit Missionaries and the British Government Officials, November 1889-March 1890* (Bangalore, India: Redemptorist Publication, 1975), 81–82. See also, W. Holsten, *Johannes Evangelista Gossner Glaube und Gemeinde* (Göttingen, 1949). Holsten was the last person to see some of the original documents in the Berlin Archives of the Gossner Mission which were damaged during World War II. He, like Fidelis de Sa, stresses the social aspect of the mass or group movement in Chota Nagpur.

61. J. Wascom Pickett, *Christian Mass Movements in India* (New York: Abingdon Press, 1933), 46. Pickett, an American Methodist missionary, was the Director of the Mass Movement Study of the National Christian Council of India, Burma and Ceylon. He worked closely with Donald McGavran in India. McGavran's book, *The Bridges of God: A Study in the Strategy of Missions* (New York: Friendship Press, 1955), is an analysis of peoples movements and gives the early theoretical basis for the Church Growth Movement. There is additional material in Donald McGavran, *How Churches Grow: New Frontiers In Mission* (London: World Dominion Press, 1955).

62. Pickett, 46.

63. Ibid., 47. Sundkler, 204, writing in 1963 reports a population of 6,000,000 tribal peoples in Chota Nagpur of which 760,000 are Christians: Roman Catholics, 300,000; Lutherans, 200,000; Anglicans, 200,000. According to Sundkler, it is the Christians who set the tone of tribal life.

64. Pickett, 46.

65. Ferdinand Hahn, Questionnaire, 1.

66. Ferdinand Hahn's *Oroan Folk-Lore*, 1905, was reissued by the Catholic Mission of Chota Nagpur under the title, *Hahn's Oroan Folk-Lore in the Original*, with a critical text and translation notes by A. Grignard, S.J., (Patna: Government Printing, 1931).

67. See Hermann Dalton's introduction to Ferdinand Hahn's book, *Blicke in die Geisteswelt der heidenischen Kols; Sammlung von Sagen, Märhen und Liedern der Oroan in Chota Nagpur* (Gütersloh: Bertelsmann, 1906), iii–vii.

68. Ferdinand Hahn, "Some Notes on the Religion and Superstitions of the Oroans," *Journal of the Asiatic Society of Bengal*, 71, pt. 3, (Imprint: Calcutta Bishops College Press, 1903): 1–15.

69. Ferdinand Hahn, *Einführung in das Gebiet der Kols-Mission: Geschichte, Gebräuche, Religion und Christianisierung der Kols* (Gütersloh: Bertelsmann, 1907).

70. Hahn, Questionnaire, 4.

71. Ibid.

72. Ibid.

73. Ibid.

74. Kruyt, Questionnaire, 5.

75. Ibid.

76. Ibid., 7.

77. Ibid., 6.

78. Ibid., 7.

79. Kruyt, Questionnaire, 5.

80. Ibid., 2.

81. J. L. Swellengrebel, "Adriani, Nicolaus," in *Concise Dictionary of the Christian World Mission*, ed. Stephen Neill (Nashville: Abingdon Press, 1971), 5–6.

82. A. C. Kruyt, "The Presentation of Christianity to Primitive Peoples: The Toradja Tribes of Central Celebes,"*International Review of Missions*, vol. 4 (1915), 89. Adriani published these stories, which he transposed into the Toradja way of life and story-telling, in his Biblical Readers (NT, 1903, OT 1907). According to Swellengrebel, 6, the Bare'e New Testament started by Adriani was completed in 1933 by A. C. Kruyt and Mrs. Adriani.

83. A. C. Kruyt, *Het Animisme in den Indischen Archipel* ('S-Gravenhage: Martinus Nijhoff, 1906). A bibliography of Kruyt's major works is to be found in Jacques Waardenburg, *Classical Approaches to the Study of Religion: Aim, Methods and Theories of Research*, vol. 2, *Bibliography* (The Hague, Paris: Mouton, 1974),

140–141. The value of Kruyt's work was recognized by the University of Utrecht, which conferred upon him in 1915, the degree, Doctor of Theology, *honoris causa.* According to "Notes on Contributors," *International Review of Missions* 4 (1915): 137, this was the first time this degree had been given to a Dutch missionary.

84. Kruyt, "The Presentation of Christianity . . .,"86–91. See also Kruyt's Questionnaire, 4–5.

85. Bengt Sundkler, *The World of Mission*, 193–194.

86. Kruyt, "The Presentation of Christianity . . .," 90.

87. Kruyt, Questionnaire, 4.

88. Ibid.

89. Kruyt, "The Presentation of Christianity . . .," 91–92.

90. Kruyt, Questionnaire, 4.

91. Kruyt, "The Presentation of Christianity . . .," 85–86.

92. Ibid., 86.

93. Sundkler, 194. The Posso Church has been independent since 1947 and in 1963 had 50,000 baptized members.

94. A. C. Kruyt, "The Appropriation of Christianity by Primitive Heathen in Central Celebes," *International Review of Missions* 13 (1924): 271.

95. Ibid., 275.

96. *The Living Christ*, 210.

97. Kruyt, Questionnaire, 2.

98. Byerhaus & Lefever, 47f.

V. British and American Missiology

1. Donald Fraser, *The Future of Africa* (1911; reissued by Negro Universities Press, Westport, CT. 1970), 144.

2.   Donald Fraser, "The Evangelistic Approach to the African," *International Review of Missions* 15 (July, 1926): 445.

3.   Andrew F. Walls, "British Missions,"*Missionary Ideologies in the Imperialist Era: 1880–1920*, eds. Torben Cristensen and William R. Hutchison (Denmark: Aros, 1982), 159.

4.   Ibid., 159–160. Between 1880 and 1904 the Church Missionary Society produced 50 percent more missionaries than it had in the previous 80 years. In 80 years prior to 1880 the CMS sent out 991 missionaries; in the following 25 years it sent out 1478.

5.   W. Richey Hogg, "Student Volunteer Movement," *Concise Dictionary of the Christian World Mission*, ed. Stephen Neill (Nashville: Abingdon Press, 1971), 571–172.

6.   John Pollock, "Keswick Convention," *Concise Dictionary of the Christian World Mission*, ed. Stephen Neill (Nashville: Abingdon Press, 1971), 322.

7.   Andrew Walls, 164.

8.   For a careful treatment of the British colonial officer, Sir Harry Johnston, involved in the extension of Protectorate status to Nyasaland see Roland Oliver, *Sir Harry Johnston and the Scramble for Africa* (New York: St. Martin's Press, 1958), 124–172.

9.   Agnes R. Fraser, *Donald Fraser of Livingstonia* (London: Hodder and Stoughton, 1934), 12–13.

10.   Tissington Tatlow, *The Story of the Student Christian Movement of Great Britain and Ireland* (London: SCM Press, 1933), 23.

11.   Ibid., 16. See also Donald Fraser's "Questionnaire", 7. Fraser is one of the few missionaries responding in a positive manner to the question on the impact that higher criticism and modern Western thought exert on the mission field. Fraser states, "In so far as higher criticism and modern thought have enabled men to present a more balanced theology, and a sane reasonable interpretation of Scriptures, the people have benefitted, and have been saved at the start from assuming positions which afterwards would only be abandoned with pain and difficulty.":7.

12.   In 1889, the British made treaties with tribal chiefs on the western shore of Lake Nyasa. Two years later, Britain proclaimed the territory as the protectorate of Nyasaland. In July, 1964, the Protectorate became the independent nation of

Malawi. Given the time frame of this study this territory will be referred to as Nyasaland.

13. Donald Fraser, *The Story of Our Mission: Livingstonia* (Edinburgh: Foreign Missions Committee of United Free Church of Scotland, 1915), 4 f. Roland Oliver, *The Missionary Factor In East Africa* 2d ed. (London: Longman's Green & Co., 1965), 35.

14. Roland Oliver, *The Missionary Factor In East Africa* 2d ed. (London: Longman's Green & Co., 1965), 36.

15. Kenneth Scott Latourette, *History of the Expansion of Christianity* vol. 5 (Grand Rapids: Zondervan, CEP Edition, 1970), 393. Latourette cites Law's *Reminiscences of Livingstonia* and W. P. Livingstone, *Laws of Livingstonia* (London: Hodder and Stoughton, 1921).

16. Donald Fraser, "The Growth of the Church in the Mission Field," *International Review of Missions* 2 (1913): 236.

17. Donald Fraser, *Winning a Primitive People: Sixteen Years Work Among the Warlike Tribe of the Ngoni and the Senga and Tumbuka Peoples of Central Africa* (London: Seeley, Service, and Co., 1914), 7.

18. The chief known among Europeans as Mombera was really named Umbela (from *ukumbela*, to bury). "The tendency in most Nyasa tribes is to change the l sound to r; hence he was frequently called Umbera, and Europeans, not hearing accurately, called him Mombera, which name has been practically adopted by the natives out of courtesy and deference to Europeans." Donald Fraser, *Winning A Primitive People*, 312.

19. Roland Oliver, *The Missionary Factor*, 56–57.

20. Fraser, *Winning a Primitive People*, 118.

21. Donald Fraser, *Livingstonia*, 14.

22. Roland Oliver, *The Missionary Factor*, 59.

23. Fraser, *Livingstonia*, 25.

24. Roland Oliver, *The Missionary Factor*, 65.

25. Donald Fraser, *Livingstonia*, 19–22. See also, Roland Oliver, *Missionary Factor*, 122.

26.   Roland Oliver, 123.

27.   Roland Oliver, *The Missionary Factor*, quoting Harry Johnston, 127–128.   The four missionary societies he referred to were the Church of Scotland Mission, the Free Church Mission, the Universities Mission and the London Missionary Society.

28.   Andrew Walls, "British Missions,"164.

29.   Fraser, *The Future of Africa*, 253.

30.   Ibid., 253–254.

31.   Fraser once asked one of his elders, "How it was [that there was] not a greater increase of population considering that wars no longer claimed its annual tale of victims?" His answer was, "There is more deadly war today. It is the mines of South Africa." *Winning a Primitive People*, 308.

32.   Fraser, *The Future of Africa*, 253.

33.   Fraser, *Winning a Primitive People*, 112–115.

34.   Fraser, *Livingstonia*, 78–79.

35.   Donald Fraser, *Winning A Primitive People*, 196 f.

36.   Thomas J. Thompson, "Fraser and the Ngoni," (Ph.D. Diss., University of Edinburgh, 1980), 188.

37.   Fraser, *Winning A Primitive People*, 219.

38.   Patrick Millar, "Donald Fraser, Knight-errant of Christ," *Life and Work: The Record of the Church of Scotland* (October 1933): 394. See 392–395 for full text of details.

39.   Thomas Thompson, 214. See also chapter 3 in W. A. Elmslie, *Among the Wild Ngoni* (Edinburgh, 1899), and "Modifications," chapter 18 in Fraser's *The Winning of a Primitive People*, 182–195.

40.   Ibid., 214.

41.   Fraser, "The Evangelistic Approach to the Africans," *International Review of Missions* 15 (1926). Donald Fraser, *The Autobiography of an African: Retold in Biographical Form and in the Wild African Setting of the Life of Daniel Mtusu*

(1925; reprint, Westport, CT: Negro Universities Press, 1970), 115. See also, Thomas Thompson, 216. While older missionary colleagues opposed the *ingoma* dances, Fraser's younger colleague, Cullen Young, held dances in the cattle kraal at Loudon while Fraser was on furlough in 1912.

42. Thomas Thompson, 220, citing North Livingstonia Presbytery Minutes of October 20, 1911.

43. Ibid.

44. Fraser, *Primitive People*, 198–199.

45. Fraser, *Winning Primitive People*, 9. See also, *Livingstonia*, 85.

46. Fraser's *Livingstonia*, 86–88.

47. *Livingstonia*, 85.

48. Ibid., 85.

49. Thompson, "Fraser and the Ngoni,"187.

50. Fraser, *The Future of Africa*, 244–247.

51. Fraser, *Winning Primitive People*, 9.

52. Ibid.

53. Fraser, *The Future of Africa*, 244–247.

54. Fraser, *Future of Africa*, 232.

55. Robert E. Speer, *Missionary Principles and Practice* (New York: Fleming H. Revell, 1902), 121.

56. Robert E. Speer, quoting Macmurray in "What is the Value of the Religious Values of the Non-Christian Religions?" *The Christian Life and Message in Relation to the Non-Christian System of Life and Thought*, vol. 1, Proceedings of the International Missionary Council that met in Jerusalem in 1928, (London/New York: International Missionary Council, 1928), 366–367.

57. Ibid., 366.

58. Ibid., 366–367.

59. Robert E. Speer, *The Finality of Christ* (1933; reprint, Grand Rapids, MI: Zondervan Publishing House, 1968). This book is a compilation of the "L. P. Stone lectures given at Princeton, 1932–1933.

60. Fraser, Questionnaire, 1.

61. Fraser, *Winning A Primitive People*, 120.

62. Fraser, *Winning a Primitive People*, 120; also *Livingstonia*, 57.

63. Thompson, 214.

64. Donald Fraser, "The Evangelistic Approach to the African," *International Review of Missions* 15 (July 1926): 438–449.

65. Donald Fraser, *The New Africa* (1927; reprint, New York: Negro Universities Press, 1969).

66. Fraser, "Evangelistic Approach," 445.

67. Fraser, Questionnaire, 4–5.

68. Ibid.

69. Fraser, *The New Africa*, 43.

70. Ibid.

71. Fraser, *The New Africa*, 45.

72. Fraser, *Livingstonia*, 78.

73. Fraser, *Livingstonia*, 59.

74. Fraser, *Arican Idylls*, 188.

75. Fraser, *New Africa*, 37.

76. Ibid., 35.

77. Fraser, *Winning a Primitive People*, 140.

78. Fraser, *Future of Africa*, 124.

79. Fraser, *African Idylls*, 198.

80. Fraser, "Evangelistic Approach,"445.

81. Fraser, *The New Africa*, 45.

82. Fraser, *Future of Africa*, 104.

83. Ibid., 116.

84. Fraser, *African Idylls*, 149.

85. Fraser, *Winning a Primitive People*, 10.

86. Fraser, *African Idylls*, 187.

87. Ibid.

88. Harold Turner, *A Bibliography of Modern African Religious Movements* (Evanston, IL: Northwestern University Press, 1966).

89. Fraser, *Livingstonia*, 85.

90. Paul Bohannan, *Africa and Africans* (Garden City, NY: Natural History Press, 1964), 22–23.

91. Ibid., 22.

92. Ibid., 22–23.

93. Thomas Thompson, 216.

94. Nyasaland became a British protectorate in 1891. Malawi received its independence in 1964 and became a Republic in 1966.

95. Donald Fraser, "The Evangelistic Approach To The African," *International Review of Missions* 15 (July, 1926): 438–449.

96. *Missionary Message*, "Animistic Religions," 6, 24.

97. W. D. Armstrong, Questionnaire, 1.

98. Elizabeth Chadwick, Questionnaire, 1.

99.   W. D. Armstrong, Questionnaire, 2.

100. Ibid.

101. Elizabeth Chadwick, "Bantu Women of Equatorial Africa," *The Church Missionary Review* 59 (March 1908): 139–143. There are letters or mention of Ms. Chadwick in *The Uganda Mission* (May, 1898): 350–353, *The Mission-Field* (August, 1901): 624–627, and in *Reports of Workers in the Capital of Uganda* (May, 1900): 350.

102. W. D. Armstrong, "The Struggle of the Soul," *Regions Beyond* (February 1909): 28–29. "Letter," *Regions Beyond* (Aug-Sept, 1908): 172. "Revival at Bonginda," *Regions Beyond* (November 1908): 198–199.

103. John Roscoe, *The Baganda* (New York: Macmillan, 1911). *The Northern Bantu* (Cambridge: Cambridge University Press, 1915). *The Soul of Central Africa* (London: Cassell, 1922). After leaving the CMS in Uganda, Roscoe taught anthropology at Cambridge University.

104. Paterson, "Animistic Religions," *The Missionary Message*, 6.

105. Chadwick, Questionnaire, 3.

106. Ibid, 3.

107. John Pollock, "Regions Beyond Missionary Union," in *Concise Dictionary of Christian World Mission*, 514–515.

108. Harry Guinness, *"Not Unto Us"*: *A Record of Twenty One Years of Missionary Service* (London: Regions Beyond Missionary Union, 1908), 68.

109. C. P. Groves, *The Planting of Christianity in Africa*, vol. 3 (London: Lutterworth Press, 1955), 267, citing Harry H. Johnston, *George Granfell and the Congo,* vol. 1 (London: Hutchinson and Co. 1908), 414–415.

110. Ibid.

111. For a full discussion of the role missionaries played, see Ruth M. Slade, *English-Speaking Missions in the Congo Independent State (1878–1908)* (Brussels: Academie Royale des Sciences Coloniales, 1959).

112. Edmund D. Morel, *Red Rubber*: *The Story of the Rubber Slave Trade Flourishing on the Congo in the Year of Grace 1906* (1906; reprint, with an Introduction by Sir Harry H. Johnston, New York: Negro University Press, 1969).

113. Guinness, 77.

114. Robert Nassau, *Fetichism in West Africa* (New York: Charles Scribner's Sons 1904), vii–viii. Nassau's work had been for several years (1874–1880) at Lambarene at the head of the Ogwe River Delta where Dr. Albert Schweitzer later had his ministry from 1913–1965. The Presbyterian work on the Ogwe River was transferred to the Paris Evangelical Society in 1892.

115. Ibid., ix. See also, Raymond W. Teeuwissen, "Robert Hamill Nassau, 1835–1921, Presbyterian Pioneer Missionary to Equatorial West Africa,"(S.T.M. thesis, Louisville Presbyterian Theological Seminary, 1973), 88.

116. David Mandeng, "The Philosophy of Mission of Robert Hamill Nassau in the Contemporary World,"(Ph.D. diss., Temple University, 1970), 194.

117. Robert Nassau, *Fetichism in West Africa* (New York: Charles Scribner's Sons, 1904); *Where Animals Talk: West African Folk Lore Tales* (Boston: The Gorham Press, 1912). For a complete bibliography of Nassau's work, see Raymond Teeuwissen, 191–195.

118. Nassau, *Fetichism*, 27.

119. Ibid., 28.

120. Ibid.

121. Ibid., 32.

122. Nassau, *Fetichism.*, 30 f.

123. Ibid., 49.

124. Ibid., 33. See also Nassau's Questionnaire, 4.

125. Nassau, *Fetichism*, 32.

126. Ibid., 25.

127. Teeuwissen, 90.

128. Nassau, Questionnaire, p. 6.

129. Teeuwissen, 91 cites a review signed, M. M. in *Annee Sociologique 1904–1905*, ed. Emile Durkheim (Paris: Falcon, 1905): 191–194.

130.   Ibid.

131.   Mandeng, 118.

132.   Ibid., 30, citing Nassau's unpublished autobiography, 86.

133.   Nassau, Questionnaire, 3.

134.   Teeuwissen, 129.

135.   Nassau Questionnaire, 4.

136.   John V. Taylor, *The Primal Vision* (London: SCM Press, 1965).

137.   R. H. W. Shepherd, "Godfrey Callaway," in vol. 1 of *Dictionary of South African Biography*, ed. W. J. de Kock (Capetown: Human Services Research Council, 1968), 150.

138.   E. D. Sedding, ed., *Godfrey Callaway, Missionary in Kaffraria, 1892–1942: His Life and Writings* (London: Society for Promoting Christian Knowledge, 1945).

139.   Godfrey Callaway, "Sowers and Spoilers of the Veld" in E. D. Sedding, *Godfrey Callaway*, 5. Callaway described the Transkei in 1913, as a region which remained outside the sphere of actual hostility during the Boer War (1899–1902). It was a large native reserve of some 180,000 square miles. The Transkei is wedged between the Cape Colony on the south and Natal to the north and the Indian Ocean to the East. Ecclesiastically this region was referred to as the Diocese of St. John's Kaffraria. It had a population approaching a million, with a relatively small European population.

140.   R. H. W. Shepherd, "Godfrey Callaway," in vol. 1 of *Dictionary of South African Biography*, 149. See also E. D. Sedding, ed., *Godfrey Callaway*. See especially "Biographical Preface" by Father Ley, 9–22.

141.   Godfrey Callaway, *Sketches of Kafir Life* (Oxford: Mowbray, 1905), xi.

142.   Callaway, *Sketches of Kafir Life*, 34.

143.   Peter Hinchliff, *The Anglican Church in South Africa* (London: Darton, Longman, & Todd, 1963), 175, citing Godfrey Callaway, *Shepherd of the Veld* (London: Wells, Gardner & Darton, 1912), 58.

144.   Ibid., 176.

145. Ibid.

146. Ibid., 177.

147. Father Ley in E. D. Sedding, *Godfrey Callaway*, 11.

148. Hinchliff, 190.

149. Ibid., 191.

150. The founder of the Society of St. John the Evangelist was R. M. Benson (1824–1915). See M. V. Woodgate, *Father Benson: Founder of the Cowley Fathers*, London, 1953. According to Eric J. Sharpe, *Not to Destroy But To Fulfill* (Uppsala: Swedish Institute of Missionary Research, 1965), 88, the first phase of the Oxford movement was not particularly missionary oriented, but by the 1870s there was at Oxford a mission directed to the educated classes of the Indian Universities.

151. Father Ley, in E. D. Sedding, *Godfrey Callaway*, 18–19.

152. Callaway, Questionnaire, 1.

153. Ibid.

154. Ibid, 2.

155. Ibid., 2

156. Ibid., 2.

157. Callaway, *Sketches*, 33–34.

158. Ibid.

159. Godfrey Callaway, "Ubuntu (Humanity)," *The East and The West* 22 (1924): 213–220.

160. Godfrey Callaway, "Further Thoughts about 'Ubuntu'," *The East and The West*, 23 (1925): 232–241.

161. Callaway, "Ubuntu (Humanity)," 216.

162. Ibid.

163. Ibid., 217.

164. Ibid., 216

165. Ibid., 214.

166. Callaway, *Pioneers in Pondoland*, 109–113.

167. Ibid.

168. Callaway, *Fellowship of the Veld*, vi.

169. Ibid., 29.

VI. The Legacy of Edinburgh 1910

1. Gardiner, 137.

2. John S. Mbiti, *African Religions and Philosophy* (London: Heinemann, 1969), 6–7.

3. Kwame Bediako, *Theology and Identity*, 233.

4. Constance E. Padwick, *Temple Gairdner of Cairo* (London: 1929), 302.

5. David Bosch, *Transforming Mission: Paradigm Shifts in Theology of Mission*, American Society of Missiology Series no. 16. (Mary Knoll, NY: Orbis Books, 1990), 484.

6. Ibid.

7. John S. Mbiti, *African Religions and Philosophy* (London: Heinemann, 1969). Bolaji Idowu, *Towards an Indigenous Church* (London and Ibadan: Oxford University Press, 1965).

8. Hendrik Kraemer, *Religion and the Christian Faith.* London: Lutterworth, 1961 (first published in 1956), p. 76 f. Lesslie Newbigin, *The Finality of Christ* (London: SCM Press, 1969), 28, 43 f.

9. Marian S. Benham, *Henry Callaway: First Bishop of Kaffraria, His Life-History And Work* (London and New York: Macmillan, 1896), 220.

Appendix A

1. This is taken verbatim from *The Report Of Commission IV: The Missionary Message*, 2.

Appendix B

1. This list is taken verbatim from *The Report of Commission IV: The Missionary Message*, 1910, xi–xii.

2. Rev. W. Barbrooke Grubb contributed papers dealing in part with Animism.

3. Rev. Fred. Hahn contributed papers dealing in part with Animism.

4. Rev. Geo. Whitehead contributed papers dealing in part with Animism.

Bibliography

Ajayi, J. F. A. *Christian Missions in Nigeria 1841–1891: The Making of a New Elite.* London: Longmans, Green & Co., 1965.

Ariarajah, Wesley. *Hindus and Christians: A Century of Protestant Ecumenical Thought.* Grand Rapids: William B. Eerdmans Publishing Co., 1991.

_____. *The Bible and People of Other Faiths.* The Risk Book Series, 26, Geneva: World Council of Churches, 1987.

_____. "The Implications of Recent Ecumenical Thought for the Christian-Hindu Relationship." Ph.D. diss., n. p., 1987.

Armstrong, W. D. "The Struggle of the Soul." *Regions Beyond* (February 1909): 28–29, 172, 198–99.

Azariah, Bishop V. S. "The Problem of Co-operation Between Foreign and Native Workers." In *The History, and Records of the Conference, Together with Addresses Delivered at the Evening Meetings,* World Missionary Conference, 1910, vol. IX, 306–315. New York: Fleming H. Revell, 1910.

Ayandele, E. A. *The Missionary Impact on Modern Nigeria, 1842–1914: A Political and Social Analysis.* London: Longmans, Green and Co., 1966.

Baker, Samuel. "The Races of the Nile Basin." *Transactions of the Ethnological Society of London,* 5 (1867): 231.

Balfour, Lord Burleigh. "Opening Address." In World Missionary Conference 1910, vol. IX. *The History and Records of the Conference Together with the Addresses Delivered at the Evening Meetings.* New York: Fleming H. Revell, 1910.

Barrett, David B., ed. *Schism and Renewal in Africa: An Analysis of 6000 Contemporary Religious Movements. Nairobi: Oxford University Press, 1968.*

_____. *World Christian Encyclopedia: A Comprehensive Study of Churches and Religions in the Modern World, A.D. 1900–2000. Nairobi: Oxford University Press, 1982.*

Baylis, P. J. "High Gods and the Study of Religion: The History of a New Idea." In *Essays in Religious Studies for Andrew Walls*. James Thrower, Ed. University of Aberdeen: Department of Religious Studies, 1986, 81–96.

Beaglehole, Earnest. "R. H. Codrington" In *International Encyclopedia of Social Sciences* vol. 2. David L. Sills, ed. New York: Macmillan Co. and Free Press, 1968.

Bediako, Kwame. "The Roots of African Theology." *International Bulletin of Missionary Research* 13, no. 2 (April 1989): 58–59.

_____. *Theology And Identity: The Impact of Culture Upon Christian Thought in the Second Century and Modern Africa.* Oxford: Regnum Books, 1992.

Benham, Marian S. *Henry Callaway: First Bishop of Kaffraria, His Life-History and Work.* London and New York: Macmillan, 1896.

Beyerhaus, Peter and Henry Lefever. *The Responsible Church and the Foreign Mission*. Grand Rapids: W. B. Eerdmans Publishing Company, 1964.

"Bibliography on Edinburgh 1910." *Occasional Bulletin of the Missionary Research Library* 11, no. 5 (June 14, 1960): 1–12.

Blyden, Edward W. *Christianity, Islam and the Negro Race*, with an Introduction by Christopher Fyfe. Edinburgh: Edinburgh University Press, 1967.

Bohannon, Paul. *Africa and Africans*. Garden City, NY: The Natural History Press, 1964.

Bolaji, Idowu. *Towards An Indigenous Church*. London: Oxford University Press, 1965.

Bosch, David. *Transforming Mission: Paradigm Shifts in Theology of Mission*. Maryknoll, NY: Orbis Books, 1990.

Bowen, Thomas J. *Adventures and Missionary Labours*. 1857. Reprint, London: Frank Cass & Co., Ltd., 1968.

Brain, J. B. *Christian Indians In Natal 1869–1911*. Cape Town: Oxford University Press, 1983.

Burton, Richard F. *A Mission to Gelele, King of Dahome*. 2 vols., 2d ed. London: Trinsley Brothers, 1864.

Cairns, David S. *The Reasonableness of the Christian Faith*. London: Hodder & Stoughton Lmt., 1920.

Callaway, Godfrey. *The Fellowship of the Veld: Sketches of Native Life in South Africa*. 1926. Reprint. New York: Negro Universities Press, 1969.

_____. "Further Thoughts about 'Ubuntu'." *The East and The West* 23 (1925): 232–241.

_____. *Pioneers in Pondoland*. Lovedale, South Africa: Lovedale Press, n.d. [1939].

_____. *Shepherd of the Veld*. London: Wells, Gardner and Darton, 1912.

_____. *Sketches of Kafir Life*. Oxford: Mowbray, 1905.

_____. "Sowers and Spoilers of the Veld." *Godfrey Callaway, Missionary in Kaffraria, 1892–1942; His Life and Writings*. Edited by E. D. Sedding. London: Society for Promoting Christian Knowledge, 1945.

_____. "Ubuntu (Humanity)." *The East and The West* 22 (1924): 213–220.

Callaway, Henry. *Nursery Tales, Traditions and Histories of the Zulus*, 1868. Reprint, Westport, CT: Negro Universities Press, 1970.

_____. "On Divination and Analogous Phenomena Among the Natives of Natal." *Journal of the Anthropological Institute* 1 (1871–72): 163–185.

_____. "On the Religious Sentiment Amongst the Tribes of South Africa," A lecture delivered at Kokstad, 1876. n. p. 16 pp. Available at UCLA, and Northwestern University.

_____. *The Religious System of the Amazulu. Izinyanga Zakubula: Or Divination, as Existing Among the Amazulu, in Their Own Words, With a Translation into English, and Notes*. London: The Folk Lore Society, 1884.

Casalis, Eugene. *My Life In Basutoland*. Cape Town: C. Struik Ltd., 1871.

_____. *The Basutos: Or Twenty Three Years In South Africa*. London: James Nisbet, 1865.

Chadwick, Elizabeth. "Bantu Women of Equatorial Africa," *The Church Missionary Review* 59 (March 1908): 139–143.

Codrington, R. H. *The Melanesians: Studies in Their Anthropology and Folklore*. Oxford: The Clarendon Press, 1891.

Cracknell, Kenneth. "The Theology of Religion in the IMC and WCC 1910–1989." *Current Dialogue* 19 (January 1991): 3–17.

Dalton, Hermann. *Blicke in die Geisteswelt der Heidnischen Kols; Sammlung von Sagen, Märchen und Liedern der Oroan in Chota Nagpur*. Gütersloh: Bertelsmann, 1906.

Davis, J. Merle. "The Batak Church." In *The Economic Basis of the Church*. Tambarem Series, vol. 5. New York: International Missionary Council 1939.

_____. *New Buildings on Old Foundations: A Handbook on Stabilizing the Younger Churches in Their Environment*. New York and London: International Missionary Council, 1945.

de Sa, Fidelis. *Crisis in Chota Nagpur: The Judicial Conflict Between Jesuit Missionaries and the British Government Officials, November 1889–March 1890*. Bangalore, India: Redemptorist Publication, 1975.

de Vries, Jan. *Perspectives in the History of Religions*. Translated with an Introduction by Kees W. Bolle. Berkeley: University of California Press, 1967.

Du Plessis, J. *A History of Christian Missions In South Africa*. Cape Town: C. Struik, 1965.

Durkheim, Emile. Ed. Review of Nassau's *Fetichism in West Africa* Signed, M. M. In *Année Sociologique*. Paris: Falcon, 1905.

Evans-Pritchard, E. E. *Essays In Social Anthropology*. New York: The Free Press of Glencoe, Inc. 1962.

_____. *Theories of Primitive Religion*. London: Oxford, 1965.

_____. "Sources, with Particular Reference to the Southern Sudan." *Cahiers a'Etudes Africaines* 11, no. 41 (1971): 144–45.

Fox, Charles E. *Lord of the Southern Isles: The Story of the Anglican Mission in Melanesia, 1849–1949*. London: Mowbray, 1958.

Fraser, Agnes R. *Donald Fraser of Livingstonia*, London: Hodder and Stoughton, 1934.

Fraser, Donald. *The Autobiography of an African: Retold in Biographical Form and in the Wild African Setting of the Life of Daniel Mtusu*. 1925. Reprint, Westport, CT: Negro Universities Press, 1970.

_____. *The Future of Africa*. 1911. Reprint: Westport, CT: Negro Universities Press, 1970.

_____. "The Evangelistic Approach to the African." *International Review of Missions* 15 (July, 1926): 438–449.

_____. "The Growth of the Church in the Mission Field." *International Review of Missions* 2 (1913): 236–254.

_____. *The New Africa*. London: Edinburgh House Press, 1927.

_____. *The Story of Our Mission: Livingstonia*. Edinburgh: Foreign Missions Committee of United Free Church of Scotland, 1915.

_____. *Winning a Primitive People: Sixteen Years Work Among the Warlike Tribe of the Ngoni and the Senga and Tumbuka Peoples of Central Africa*. London: Seeley, Service, and Co., 1914.

Frazer, James G. "Questions on the Manners, Customs, Religion, Superstition of Uncivilized or Semi-Civilized Peoples." *The Journal of the Royal Anthropological Institute* 18 (1888–1889): 431–439.

_____. *The Golden Bough*, "Preface to the First Edition, March, 1890," "Preface to the Second Edition, September 1900," "Preface to the Third Edition, December 1910." In *Classical Approaches to the Study of Religion*. Ed. Jacques Waardenburg. Mouton: The Hague, Paris, 1973.

_____. "Obituary, Canon John Roscoe." *Nature* 130, no. 3294 (December 17, 1930): 917–919.

Freytag, Walter. *Spiritual Revolution in the East*, London: Lutterworth Press, 1940.

Gairdner, W. H. T. *"Edinburgh 1910"*: *An Account and Interpretation of the World Missionary Conference*. Edinburgh and London: Oliphant, Anderson, & Ferrier, 1910.

Gensichen, H. W. "Gossner Mission Society." In *Concise Dictionary of the Christian World Mission* Ed. Stephen Neill. Nashville: Abingdon Press, 1971.

Groves, C.P. *The Planting Of Christianity In Africa*, vol. III. London: Lutterworth Press, 1955.

Guinness, Harry. *"Not Unto Us"*: *A Record of Twenty-One Years of Missionary Service*. London: Regions Beyond Missionary Union, 1968.

Gunning, J. W. *Hedendaagsche Zending in Onze Oost*. Den Haag: Boekhandel Van Den Zendinstudie Raad, 1914.

Haddon, Alfred C. *History of Anthropology*. New York: G. P. Putnam, 1910.

Hahn, Ferdinand. "Some Notes on the Religion and Superstitions of the Oroans." *Journal of the Asiatic Society of Bengal* 71, pt. 3 (1903): 1–15.

_____. *Hahn's Oroan Folk-Lore in the Original*. A critical text with translation and notes by A. Grignard. Patna: Government Printing, 1931.

_____. *Einführung in das Gebiet der Kols-Mission. Gerbräuche, Religion und Christianisierung der Kols*. Gütersloh: Bertelsmann, 1907.

Hinchliff, Peter. *The Anglican Church in South Africa*. London: Darton, Longman & Todd, 1963.

_____. "Henry Callaway." In *Dictionary of South Africa Biography*. vol. 1. Ed. W. J. deKock. Cape Town: Human Services Research Council, 1968.

Hoekendijk, J. C. *Kirche und Volk in der deutschen Missionswissenschaft*, München: Chr. Kaiser Verlag, 1967.

Hogg, William Richey. *Ecumenical Foundations*, New York: Harper Brothers, 1952.

_____. "Student Volunteer Movement." In *Concise Dictionary of the Christian World Mission*. Ed. Stephen Neill. Nashville, New York: Abingdon Press, 1971.

Holsten, W. "Gustav Warneck." In *Concise Dictionary of the Christian World Mission*, Ed. Stephen Neill. Nashville, New York: Abingdon Press, 1971.

Irvine, Keith. "Foreword." In Henri A. Junod, *Life of an African Tribe.* Rev. ed. New York: University Books Inc., 1962.

Jensen, Adolf E. *Myth and Cult Among Primitive Peoples.* Translated by Marianna T. Choldin & Wolfgang Weissleder. Chicago: The University of Chicago Press, 1951.

Junod, Henri A. *The Fate of the Widows Amongst the Ba-Ronga.* Basutoland, South Africa: Africa Books, 1908. Excerpted from the Report of the South African Association for the Advancement of Science. 1908, 363–375.

_____. "God's Way in the Bantu Soul." *International Review of Missions* 3 (1914): 96–106.

_____. "La faune entomologique de Delagoa." *Bulletin de la Société Neuchateloise des Sciences Naturelles.* no. 27, 1891–1899.

_____. *The Life of a South Africa Tribe.* 2d. rev. ed., 2 vols. London: Macmillan, 1927.

_____. "The Magic Conception of Nature Amongst Bantus." *South African Journal of Science* (November 1920): 76–85. Marshalltown: South African Association for the Advancement of Science, 1920.

Junod, Henri-Philippe. *Henri-A. Junod: Missionnaire et Savant, 1863–1934.* Lusanne: Mission Suisse dans L'Afrique du Sud, 1934. ᔨᖯ·

Kraemer, H. *From Mission Field to Independent Church.* London: SCM Press, 1958.

_____. *The Christian Message in a Non-Christian World.* New York: Harper Brothers for International Missionary Council, 1938.

Kruyt, A. C. *Het Animisme in den Indischen Archipel*. 'S-Gravenhage: Martinus Nijhoff, 1906.

_____. "The Presentation of Christianity to Primitive Peoples: The Toradja Tribes of Central Celebes." *International Review of Missions* 4 (1915): 82–95.

_____. "The Appropriation of Christianity by Primitive Heathen In Central Celebes." *International Review of Missions* 13 (1924): 267–275.

Langmore, Diane. *Missionary Lives: Papua, 1874–1914*. Pacific Islands Monograph Series, no. 6. Honolulu: University of Hawaii Press, 1989.

Latourette, Kenneth Scott. *A History of the Expansion of Christianity*. New York: Harper and Row, 1941.

_____. Ecumenical Bearings of the Missionary Movement and the International Missionary Council. in S.C. Neill and Ruth Rouse, *A History of Ecumenical Movement 1517–1948*. London: SPCK, 1954, 353–401.

_____. "Developments in the 'younger churches' since Edinburgh 1910." *Religion in Life* 29, no. 3, (Spring 1960): 352–362.

Leach, Sir Edmund. "Anthropology of Religion: British and French Schools." In *Nineteenth Century Religious Thought in the West*, vol. 3, edited by Ninian Smart, John Clayton, Steven Katz, and Patrick Sherry. Cambridge: Cambridge University Press, 1985.

Lessa, William A. and Evon Z. Vogt. *Reader in Comparative Religion: An Anthropological Approach*. 3d ed. New York: Harper & Row, 1958.

Livingstone, David. *Missionary Travels and Researches in South Africa*. New York: Harper & Brothers, Publishers, 1858.

Livingstone, W. P. *Laws of Livingstonia*. London: Hodder and Stoughton, 1921.

Lugard, Sir Frederick J. Dealtry. *The Dual Mandate in British Tropical Africa*. Edinburgh: Blackwood, 1922.

Mandeng, David Jonathan. "The Philosophy of Mission of Robert Hamill Nassau in the Contemporary World." Ph.D. diss., Temple University, 1970.

Marett, Robert R. *Anthropology*. New York: Henry Holt & Co., 1912.

_____. "The Tabu-Mana Formula as a Minimum Definition of Religion." in *Archiv für Religionswissenschaft*, XII (1909). Chapter 3.

_____. *The Threshold of Religion*. 1909, 2d ed. London: Methuen, 1914.

Mather, Bernard H. "Johannes Evangelista Gossner." In *Concise Dictionary of the Christian World Mission*. Ed. Stephen Neill. Nashville: Abingdon Press, 1971, 232.

Maurice, F. D. *Kingdom of Christ*, London: 1842. New Edition edited by Alec R. Vilder, SCM Press, 1958.

Mbiti, John S. *African Religions and Philosophy*. London: Heinemann, 1969. Reprint, 1975.

McGavran, Donald. *How Churches Grow: New Frontiers in Mission*. London: World Dominion Press, 1955.

_____. *The Bridges of God*. New York: Friendship Press, 1955.

_____. *Understanding Church Growth*. Grand Rapids: Eerdmans Publishing Co., 1970.

Millar, Patrick. "Donald Fraser, Knight-errant of Christ." *Life and Work: The Record of the Church of Scotland* (October 1933): 392–395.

Moore, G. F. "The History of Religions in the Nineteenth Century." *Congress of Arts and Science* (St. Louis, 1904), Selected papers reprinted, New York: Arno Press, 1974, 440.

Morel, Edmund D. *Red Rubber: The Story of the Rubber Slave Trade Flourishing on the Congo in the Year of Grace 1906*. New York: The Nassau Print, 1906. Reprint. New York: Negro Universities Press, 1969.

Morris, Brian. *Anthropological Studies of Religion: An Introductory Text*. Cambridge: Cambridge University Press, 1987.

Müller, F. Max. *Chips from a German Workshop*. Vol. 2, *Essays on Mythology, Traditions, and Customs*. New York: Charles Scribner's Sons, 1871.

_____. *Essays on the Science of Religion*. New York: Charles Scribner's Sons, 1871.

_____. *Introduction to the Science of Religion* 1873. Reprint, London: Longmans, 1882).

Myklebust, Olav G. *The Study of Missions in Theological Education*. 2 vols. Oslo: Egede Institutet, 1955, 1958.

Nassau, Robert H. *Fetichism in West Africa: Forty Years' Observation of Native Customs and Superstitions*. New York: Charles Scribner's Sons, 1904.

_____. *Where Animals Talk: West African Folk Lore Tales.* Boston: The Gorham Press, 1912.

Neill, Stephen. Ed. *A History Of Christian Missions.* Harmondsworth: 1964. Penguin Books.

_____. *Concise Dictionary of the Christian World Mission.* Nashville and New York: Abingdon Press, 1971.

_____. "The Missionary Contribution to Ethnology." In *Wort und Religion: Kalima No Dini.* Edited by Ernst Dammann. Stuttgart: Evangelischer Missionsverlag, 1969.

Nottrott, L. *Die Gossnersche Mission unter den Kolhs.* Halle: Richard Mühlmann, 2 vols., 1887, 1888.

Obituary. "Canon John Roscoe: Native Tribes of East Africa." *The Times*, London, Monday, 5 December 1932.

Oliver, Roland. *Sir Harry Johnston and the Scramble for Africa.* New York: St. Martin's Press, 1958.

_____. *The Missionary Factor In East Africa.* 2d. ed. London: Longman's Green & Co., 1965.

Otto, Rudolf. *The Idea of the Holy: An Inquiry into the Non-Rational Factor in the Idea of the Divine and Its Relation to the Rational.* London: Oxford University Press, 1923.

P'bitek, Okot. *African Religions in Western Scholarship.* Kampala, Nairobi, Dar Es Salaam: East African Literature Bureau, n.d.

Pedersen, Paul. *Batak Blood and Protestant Soul: The Development of National Batak Churches in North Sumatra.* Grand Rapids: Eerdmans, 1970.

_____. *Gottes Volk im vielen Ländern.* Berlin: Evangelische Verlagsanstalt, 1955.

Penniman, Thomas K., Beatrice Blackwood, and J. S. Weiner. *A Hundred Years of Anthropology.* 1965. Reprint, New York: William Morrow, 1974.

Pickett, J. Wascom. *Christian Mass Movements in India.* New York: Abingdon Press, 1933.

Pollock, John. "Keswick Convention." In *Concise Dictionary of the Christian World Mission,* ed. by Stephen Neill. Nashville, New York: Abingdon Press, 1971, 322.

_____. "Regions Beyond Missionary Union." In *Concise Dictionary of Christian World Mission,* Nashville, New York: Abingdon Press, 1971, 514–515.

Potter, Phillip. "From Edinburgh to Melbourne." In *Your Kingdom Come: Mission Perspectives.* Geneva: World Council of Churches, Commission on World Mission and Evangelism, 1980. Report on the World Conference on Mission and Evangelism, Melbourne, Australia, (12–25 May, 1980), 6–21.

Ray, Benjamin C. *African Religions: Symbol, Ritual, and Community.* Englewood Cliffs: Prentice-Hall, 1976.

Roscoe, John. *The Baganda,* New York: Macmillan, 1911.

_____. *The Northern Bantu,* Cambridge: Cambridge University Press, 1915.

_____. *The Soul of Central Africa,* London: Cassell, 1922.

Sawyerr, Harry, "The First World Missionary Conference: Edinburgh 1910. *International Review of Mission* 67, no. 265 (July 1978): 271.

Sedding, E. D.   Ed. *Godfrey Callaway, Missionary in Kaffraria, 1892–1942; His Life and Writings.* London: Society for Promoting Christian Knowledge, 1945.

Shepherd, R. H. W. "Godfrey Callaway." In *Dictionary of South African Biography.* Vol. 1, ed. by W. J. de Kock. Capetown: Human Services Research Council, 1968.

Sharpe, Eric J. *Comparative Religion*: *A History.* 1975. 2d. ed. La Salle, IL: Open Court Publishing Co., 1986

_____. *Not to Destroy But to Fulfill*: *The Contribution of J.N. Farquhar to Protestant Missionary Thought in India Before 1914.* Uppsala: Gleerup, 1965.

_____. *John Nicol Farquhar*: *A Memoir.* Calcutta: Y.M.C.A. Publishing House, 1963.

_____. *John Nicol Farquhar and the Missionary Study of Hinduism.* Aberdeen: Department of Religious Studies, University of Aberdeen in Association with the Scottish Institute of Missionary Studies, 1971.

_____. "The Legacy of A.G. Hogg," *The International Bulletin of Missionary Research* 6 (April, 1982): 65–69.

Sills, David L., ed. "Tylor, Edward Burnett." *International Encyclopedia of Social Sciences.* New York: Macmillan Co. and Free Press, 1968.

Sitiloane, Gabriel M. *The Image of God Among the Sotho-Tswana.* Rotterdam: A. A. Balkerna, 1976.

Slade, Ruth M. *English-Speaking Missions in the Congo Independent State (1878–1908)*. Brussels: Academie Royale des sciences coloniales, 1959.

Smith, A. J. Lamont. "Paul Berthoud." In *Dictionary of South African Biography*, ed. by W. J. DeKock, Capetown: Human Services Research Council, 1968.

Smith, Edwin. "Review of *The Life of a South African Tribe*." *Africa* (1928), 391.

Speer, Robert E. *The Finality of Christ*. New York: Fleming H. Revell, 1933.

_____. *Missionary Principles and Practice*. New York: Fleming H. Revell, 1902.

_____. "What is the Value of the Religious Values of the Non-Christian Religions?" *The Christian Life and Message in Relation to the Non-Christian System of Life and Thought*. Vol. 1. London, New York: International Missionary Council, 1928.

Stocking Jr., George W. "Codrington, R. H." In *The Encyclopedia of Religion*. Vol. 3, ed. by Mercea Eliade. New York: Macmillan, 1987.

Sundkler, Bengt. *The World of Mission*. Grand Rapids: Eerdmans Publishing Co., 1965.

Swellengrebel, J. L. "Adriani, Nicolaus." In *Concise Dictionary of the Christian World Mission*, ed. by Stephen Neill. Nashville, New York: Abingdon Press, 1971.

Tatlow, Tissington. *The Story of the Student Christian Movement of Great Britain and Ireland*. London: SCM Press, 1933.

Taylor, John V. *The Primal Vision*. London: SCM Press, 1965.

Tippett, A. R. *Solomon Islands Christianity: A Study in Growth and Obstruction*. World Studies of Churches in Mission. London: Lutterworth Press, 1967.

Teeuwissen, Raymond W. "Robert Hamill Nassau 1835–1921, Presbyterian Pioneer Missionary to Equatorial West Africa." S.T.M. thesis, Louisville Presbyterian Theological Seminary, 1973.

Thompson, Thomas J. "Fraser and the Ngoni." Ph.D. diss., University of Edinburgh, 1980.

Tucker, Alfred R. *Eighteen Years in Uganda And East Africa*. 1911. Reprint, Westport, CT: Negro Universities Press, 1970.

Turner, Bryan S. "The Re-Appraisal of Tylor's Concept of Religion: The Interactionist Analogy," 138–149 In *International Yearbook for the Sociology of Religion*. Vol. 7, Religion and Social Change, ed. by Thomas Luckmann and Joachim Matthes. Opladen: Westdeutscher Verlag , 1971.

Turner, Harold W. *African Independent Church*. 2 vols. Oxford: Clarendon Press, 1967.

_____. *A Bibliography of Modern African Religious Movements*. Evanston: Northwestern University Press, 1966.

_____. *Living Tribal Religions*. London: Ward Lock Educational, 1971.

Tylor, Edward Burnett. "On the Limits of Savage Religion." *Journal of the Anthropological Institute of Great Britain and Ireland* no. 26, 21, (1891–1892): 283–299.

_____. *Religion in Primitive Culture*. New York: Harper & Brothers, 1958.

Tutu, Desmond. "Whither African Theology?" In E. W. Fashole-Luke et al., editors, *Christianity in Independent Africa*. London: Rex Collins, 1978.

van Butselaar, G. Jan. "The Gospel and Culture in Nineteenth-Century Mozambique." *Missiology: An International Review* 16, no. 1 (January 1988): 45–55.

Waardenburg, Jacques. *Classical Approaches to the Study of Religion*: *Aims, Methods and Theories of Research*. (The Hague: Mouton, 1974).

Walls, Andrew F. "British Missions" In *Missionary Ideologies in the Imperialist Era: 1880–1920*, ed. by Torben Christensen and William R. Hutchinson. Denmark: Aros, 1982.

Warneck, Gustav. *Evangelische Missionslehre*. Gotha: Perthes, (1897–1905).

_____. *Modern Missions and Culture: Their Mutual Relations*. 2d. ed. Translated by Thomas Smith. Edinburgh: James Gemmeli, 1888.

Warneck, Johannes. *The Living Christ and the Dying Heathenism*. New York: Fleming H. Revell, 1909.

_____. *The Living Forces of the Gospel*. Edinburgh and London: Oliphant, Anderson, and Ferrier, 1909.

_____. "The Growth of the the Church in the Mission Field." *International Review of Missions* 1, no. 1 (1912): 20–43.

Walshe, Peter. *Black Nationalism in South Africa: A Short History.* Johannesburg: Raven Press, 1963.

Webster, James B. *The African Churches Among the Yoruba 1888–1922.* Oxford: The Clarendon Press, 1964.

Westerbund, David. *African Religion in African Scholarship: A Preliminary Study of the Religious and Political Background.* Stockholm: University of Stockholm, 1985.

Williams, Walter L. *Black Americans and the Evangelization of Africa 1877–1900.* Madison: The University of Wisconsin Press, 1982.

Willoughby, William C. *The Soul of The Bantu:* A Sympathetic Study of the Magico-Religious Practices and Beliefs of the Bantu Tribes of Africa. Garden City, NY: Doubleday, Doran & Co, Inc., 1928.

Woodgate, Mildred V. *Father Benson: Founder of the Cowley Fathers.* London: Bles, 1953.

World Missionary Conference 1910. Report of Commission I, *Carrying the Gospel to All the Non-Christian World.* Edinburgh and London: Oliphant, Anderson & Ferrier, and New York, Chicago and Toronto: Fleming H. Revell, 1910.

_____. Report of Commission II, *The Church In the Mission Field.* Edinburgh and London: Oliphant, Anderson & Ferrier, and New York, Chicago and Toronto: Fleming H. Revell, 1910.

_____. Report of Commission III, *Education in Relation to the Christianization of National Life.* Edinburgh and London: Oliphant, Anderson & Ferrier, and New York, Chicago and Toronto: Fleming H. Revell, 1910.

_____. Report of Commission IV, *The Missionary Message In Relation To Non-Christian Religions.* Edinburgh and London: Oliphant, Anderson & Ferrier, and New York, Chicago and Toronto: Fleming H. Revell, 1910.

_____. Report of Commission V, *Preparation of Missionaries.* Edinburgh and London: Oliphant, Anderson & Ferrier, and New York, Chicago and Toronto: Fleming H. Revell, 1910.

_____. Report of Commission VI, *The Home Base of Missions.* Edinburgh and London: Oliphant, Anderson & Ferrier, and New York, Chicago and Toronto: Fleming H. Revell, 1910.

_____. Report of Commission VII, *Missions and Governments.* Edinburgh and London: Oliphant, Anderson & Ferrier, and New York, Chicago and Toronto: Fleming H. Revell, 1910.

_____. Report of Commission VII, *Co-operation and the Promotion of Unity.* Edinburgh and London: Oliphant, Anderson & Ferrier, and New York, Chicago and Toronto: Fleming H. Revell, 1910.

_____. *The History and Records of the Conference: Together With Addresses Delivered At The Evening Meetings.* This volume includes "General Account of the Conference." Edinburgh and London: Oliphant, Anderson & Ferrier, and New York, Chicago and Toronto: Fleming H. Revell, 1910.

World Missionary Conference, Commission IV Questionnaire Reponses on "Animstic Religions." Unpublished typed manuscripts of 25 missionaries located at Day Missions Library, Yale Divinity School, New Haven, CT.

Yates, T. E. "Christian Approaches to Other Religious Traditions: The International Review of Missions 1912–1939." *Mission Studies* 6, no. 1 (1989): 41–50.

_____. "Edinburgh Revisited: Edinburgh 1910 to Melbourne 1980." *Churchman* 94, no. 2 (1980): 145–155.

Index

Studies in Church History

General Editor: William L. Fox

This series in Church History offers a place for diverse scholarship that is sometimes too particularly calibrated for any other publishing category. Rather, the richness of the Church History series is in its scope, which variously mixes historical theology and historical hermeneutics, doctrine and practices of piety, religious or spiritual movements, and institutional configurations. Western Europe and the United States continue to provide grounds for exploration and discourse, but this series will also publish books on Christianity in Asia, Africa, and Latin America. Traditional periodization (Early Christian, Medieval, Reformation and Modern eras) grants maximum representation.

The particular focus of the series is the treatment of religious thought as being vital to the historical context and outcome of Christian experience. Fresh interpretations of classic and well-known Christian thinkers (e.g., Augustine, Luther, Calvin, Edwards, etc.) using multicultural perspectives, the critical approaches of feminist and men's studies form the foundation of the series. Meanwhile, new voices from Christian history need illumination and explication by church historians in this series. Authors who are versatile enough to "cross-over" disciplinary boundaries have enormous opportunity in this series to reach an international audience.